Mobilizing Piety

MOBILIZING PIETY

Islam and Feminism in Indonesia

Rachel Rinaldo

OXFORD
UNIVERSITY PRESS

Oxford University Press is a department of the University of Oxford.
It furthers the University's objective of excellence in research, scholarship,
and education by publishing worldwide.

Oxford   New York
Auckland   Cape Town   Dar es Salaam   Hong Kong   Karachi
Kuala Lumpur   Madrid   Melbourne   Mexico City   Nairobi
New Delhi   Shanghai   Taipei   Toronto

With offices in
Argentina   Austria   Brazil   Chile   Czech Republic   France   Greece
Guatemala   Hungary   Italy   Japan   Poland   Portugal   Singapore
South Korea   Switzerland   Thailand   Turkey   Ukraine   Vietnam

Oxford is a registered trademark of Oxford University Press
in the UK and certain other countries.

Published in the United States of America by
Oxford University Press
198 Madison Avenue, New York, NY 10016

Library of Congress Cataloging-in-Publication Data
Rinaldo, Rachel, author.
Mobilizing piety : Islam and feminism in Indonesia / Rachel Rinaldo.
pages cm.
Includes bibliographical references and index.
ISBN 978-0-19-994810-9 (hardcover : alk. paper) — ISBN 978-0-19-994812-3
(pbk. : alk. paper)   1. Muslim women—Political activity—Indonesia—Jakarta.
2. Muslim women—Indonesia—Jakarta—Societies and clubs.   3. Women in Islam—
Indonesia—Jakarta.   4. Feminism—Indonesia—Jakarta.   5. Feminism—Religious
aspects—Islam.   I. Title.
HQ1170.R58 2013
305.4209598'22–dc23
2013003238

9 7 5 3 1 2 4 6 8
Printed in the United States of America
on acid-free paper

CONTENTS

ACKNOWLEDGMENTS

This book would not have come to fruition without the assistance of many people and organizations. First and foremost, I appreciate the participation of Solidaritas Perempuan, Fatayat NU, Rahima, and Partai Keadilan Sejahtera in this research project. Their hospitality and willingness to work with a foreign researcher have been beyond compare. I would especially like to thank Ciciek Farha, Syafiq Hasyim, Maria Ulfah Ansor, Dwi Rubiyanti Kholifah, Salma Safitri, Titi Soentoro, Risma Umar, Nursanita Nasution, Ledia Hanifa, and Sri Utami for their time and assistance during my fieldwork in Jakarta. I am indebted to Eva Amrullah for her excellent work as a research assistant in 2005 and 2008, and for her continued willingness to comment on chapter drafts.

This book is based on dissertation research and writing that was made possible by grants from the U.S.–Indonesia Society, a Fulbright-Hays Dissertation Research Fellowship, a National Science Foundation Dissertation Improvement Grant, and writing fellowships from the Committee on Southern Asian Studies at the University of Chicago. I conducted additional fieldwork and began working on the book during post-doctoral fellowships at the Asia Research Institute (National University of Singapore) and the Center for the Pacific Rim at the University of San Francisco. The final stages of writing were supported by a University of Virginia Sesquicentennial Fellowship.

Colleagues at all of these academic institutions helped me to develop this project. My committee members at the University of Chicago were especially influential. Leslie Salzinger has known me from my first days as a graduate student in the sociology department. It was in her Ethnography Practicum that I learned the joys and frustrations of conducting ethnography. Over the years she has given me both intellectual guidance and crucial career advice. Andreas Glaeser encouraged me to make structural changes that greatly improved the dissertation and has continued to be a strong supporter of this project. Danilyn Rutherford supervised the dissertation from its inception, which was not long after I took her extraordinary class on the ethnography and history of Indonesia. And Saskia Sassen has been unfailingly encouraging and supportive of a project that crosses disciplinary boundaries. I depended on the support of my dissertation writing group, which included Phaedra Daipha, who helped me work through the structure of my arguments and whose friendship has long been a source of sustenance.

At NUS, Bryan S. Turner and colleagues at the Asia Research Institute provided critical feedback and much intellectual stimulation as I began the process of revising my dissertation. My postdoctoral year at USF provided precious time and space and a supportive environment to develop my ideas, as well as the assistance of Danicar Mariano, who is now working on her own PhD. At the University of Virginia, my writing group colleagues Simone Polillo and Rina Williams helped me to weld an overly detailed dissertation into a book manuscript. Their conceptual insights have been very significant for me and I learned much from working with them.

As the manuscript approached completion, Ann Tickamyer and Orit Avishai offered incredibly perceptive and crucial suggestions that helped to shape its final form. Rachel Mann provided excellent editing on a short timeline. And I am also indebted to the anonymous reviewers for Oxford University Press.

I have presented parts of this book at too many conferences, workshops, and seminars to count. I am grateful for all the comments and advice I have received at such events, but a few stand out: the Religion and Utopia panel organized by Orit Avishai at the American Sociological Association meeting (2012); the Sawyer Seminar on Globalization and the New Politics of Women's Rights at the Center for Research on Gender and Women at the University of Wisconsin–Madison (2011); the Theorizing through Religion panel organized by Michal Pagis at the Association for the Sociology of Religion (2010); the Religion in Politics: Resistance, Negotiation and Transcendence conference at the Institute for Southeast Asian Studies in Singapore (2008); and an invited presentation at Kapal Perempuan in Jakarta (2008), at which Indonesian women's rights activists encouraged me to think more critically.

Friends and family are crucial for such a long project as this. I am especially thankful for the support of the Rinaldo family, especially my parents, who always encouraged me to pursue my dream of writing a book. The Wyrod family has also given me tremendous support. I am also grateful to the family of Djanalis Djanaid in Malang, Indonesia. I spent a year with them as an American Field Service high school exchange student, and they introduced me to the beauty of their country. Their daughter Mely Noviryani has kindly hosted me on return visits to Indonesia, and I've enjoyed seeing her children grow and her career develop.

Finally, I am forever in debt to the University of Chicago for bringing me together with Robert Wyrod. He has been my companion in every way possible and he has made my life meaningful even through the difficult years of dissertation and book writing.

Mobilizing Piety

CHAPTER 1
Islam and Feminism in Jakarta

INTRODUCTION

The Nahdlatul Ulama building, headquarters of Indonesia's largest Muslim organization, rises up from a hectic Jakarta thoroughfare. Its calm sandstone color and vaguely Arabic design are distinctive in this enormous city of glittering skyscrapers and packed residential neighborhoods.

I stood at the entrance to this building on a muggy morning in 2002 because I had come to Jakarta to study women's activism in this Muslim majority country. The eclectic cityscape around me mirrored the interesting and creative ways in which women participated in the tumultuous process of democratization. This process began in 1998 after a massive economic crisis and a burgeoning grassroots opposition movement led Indonesia's longtime dictator Suharto to resign. In a country where women are often encouraged to fulfill traditional expectations as daughters, wives, and mothers, these same women were proving to be impassioned agents for reform. Women swelled the ranks of rallies calling for change, mobilized food deliveries for the poor, organized commemorations of one of the country's female heroines, and demanded an end to violence against women after dozens of Chinese-Indonesian women were raped during the riots that accompanied the regime's demise. Some of these activists worked for nongovernmental organizations (NGOs) advocating gender equality, human rights, and social justice. In addition, many younger women were becoming committed to Islam as they joined activist alliances. In this new atmosphere of unparalleled political freedom, I wanted to know how these women activists were adapting ideas about women's rights for the Indonesian context.

This book is inspired by my own background as a feminist sociologist and a middle-class American who spent a formative year as a high school exchange student in East Java. Trying to grasp the new contours of the post-9/11 world, I returned to Indonesia to delve into the lives of women activists at a crucial historical conjuncture. In 2002 it was not an easy time to be an American researcher in Jakarta. After 9/11 and the American invasion of Afghanistan, Indonesians were increasingly angered by US foreign policy. Many considered the war on terror to be a war against Muslims. Just after I arrived in Jakarta, a terrorist bombing in Bali killed 202 people, and the US embassy urged Americans to leave the country. Although daily life felt fairly normal in the metropolis, there were frequent warnings of terrorist threats to public places, and many Indonesians voiced heated critiques of the deepening American and British involvement in the Middle East. Despite the risks, I stayed to pursue my research. But these events formed the backdrop to the activism I was studying.

Aside from democratization, Indonesia was changing in other interesting ways. Since the 1980s, many Indonesians had become increasingly attracted to Islam. They were taking Quranic study classes, attending Muslim schools, and discussing religious matters more publicly. Especially noticeable were the many young women adopting the Muslim headscarf. In the 1990s, the Indonesian women's movement consisted mostly of small NGOs run by energetic activists with a secular outlook. These organizations, working on issues like domestic violence, feminist education, and legal aid for women, are still the heart of the women's movement.

But as I began to map out the landscape of women's activism in post-Suharto Indonesia, I encountered new religiously informed actors. There were newly politicized Muslim women's organizations, as well as women in Muslim political parties, some of whom expressed more conservative ideas about gender. Some insisted, for example, that the home should be women's primary focus. This dynamic and shifting terrain raised intriguing questions. What were the differences among these women activists? How were Muslim women activists informed by their religion? And what were the implications for women's rights in religious contexts?

Some scholars have argued that the global resurgence of politicized and socially conservative religion in recent decades is in part a backlash against modernizing reforms such as women's rights (Moghadam 1994; Almond, Appleby, and Sivan 2003). Yet the landscape I encountered in 2002 seemed to challenge this view. I focused, therefore, on understanding how Indonesian women activists, both Muslim and secular, thought about Islam and feminism at a time when they were often viewed as incompatible.

What emerged from my fieldwork was the importance of what social scientists call *agency*—people's capacity to make choices and take action. Central to feminism is the idea that women have, or should have, agency to empower themselves and challenge subordination. The rights to vote, work, and control one's body are important to feminists because they promote women's agency. Islam is sometimes considered to be at odds with feminism because some interpretations of Islamic texts provide lesser rights to women or give men power over women. Given these concerns, I wanted to examine what the case of Indonesia might tell us about women's agency and activism in an increasingly Muslim context. More specifically, I wanted to know how exactly Islam was influencing the agency of women activists.

This book uses a framework that considers religion as a heterogeneous cultural schema to investigate the kinds of agency that have emerged in the Indonesian public sphere in the wake of democratization. This means that religion is not confined to the temple, mosque, or church, but that it also intersects with many areas of society. Piety—meaning an emphasis on practicing religion in daily life—is integrated into and expressed in multiple social and political arenas. In the wake of democratization in Indonesia, there is increasing overlap of Islamic politics and gender politics, and this has fostered new forms of agency for women activists. This includes forms of agency that incorporate both Islam and feminism. My fieldwork in Jakarta also revealed that the diverse ways in which women activists engage with religion and feminism are deeply shaped by their own life trajectories and experiences in different social milieus (Rinaldo 2008, 2011).

THE ISLAMIC REVIVAL AND WOMEN'S RIGHTS

It is now widely recognized that Islam has experienced a global revival in recent decades, and this has fostered widespread concerns about women's rights in Indonesia and elsewhere. Scholars have used the term *Islamic revival* since the 1980s to track a transnational revitalization of Muslim religious practice (Salvatore and LeVine 2005; Roy 2006). In the decade after 9/11, the Afghan *burqa* and the headscarf became global emblems of an Islam that is believed by many to be intensely patriarchal. Some scholars even argue that women's rights are a dividing line between Western and Muslim societies. For example, Inglehart and Norris (2003, 68) state: "the real fault line between the West and Islam … concerns gender equality and sexual liberalization. As younger generations in the West have gradually become more liberal on these issues, Muslim nations have remained the most traditional societies in the world." Going further, Moghissi (1999, 141) proposes that Islam is not an appropriate framework for women's rights because Islamic law is not compatible with modern principles of individual rights and equality. Such claims mirror the ideas of radical

Muslim thinkers, such as Sayyid Qutb, an inspiration for many contemporary Islamists, who argued that sexual liberalism and female freedom in the West were signs of a corrupt secular society, and that Islamic governance was necessary to counter such trends (Kepel 2002).[1]

In this polarized atmosphere, the Western media often celebrates political figures critical of Islam, such as the Somali-Dutch Ayaan Hirsi Ali, who draws on her harrowing life experiences to argue that Muslim women cannot be truly free until they escape the constraints of Islam (2010). Similarly, in a climate of anxiety about Muslim migrants, some European feminists support legislation to ban the wearing of face veils or headscarves in public places, on the grounds that such garments are oppressive to women (Winter 2008). Some American pundits also argue that violations of women's rights justify continued intervention in the Middle East (Goldberg 2011).

Not surprisingly, such arguments have led some scholars to criticize the way Muslim women have been portrayed. Mohanty (1988) points out that American and British feminism has tended to depict "third world women" as victims, reproducing the unequal power relations between the West and the rest. More recently, other scholars suggest that feminism has become part of the justification for renewed Western imperialism, an echo of the way colonial powers seized on practices like veiling as evidence of native people's backwardness (Abu-Lughod 2002). Others propose that scholars need to be more aware of how Muslim women's agency may be very different from conventional Western notions of agency (Mahmood 2005). As a result of such controversies, women's agency, feminism, and rights have become significant themes in studies of Muslim societies, and in discussions of global politics more generally (Deeb 2006; Charrad 2011).

It is important to note that those who identify Islam with the disempowerment of women have some compelling evidence. Increased regulation of women's bodies has been a leitmotif of late twentieth-century Islamist movements from Morocco to Iran to Malaysia. Influential organizations like the Egyptian Muslim Brotherhood argue that women's place is primarily in the domestic sphere, and they have sought stronger gender segregation in public spaces. Emphasizing women's domestic role is characteristic of many revivalist religious movements, including evangelical Christianity and ultra-Orthodox Judaism.[2] However, anxieties about Muslim women's rights have sharpened in the wake of the uprisings that have shaken the Middle East since 2011. Women featured prominently in the protests in Egypt, Tunisia, and Yemen, and they continue to agitate for reforms in Bahrain and elsewhere. Although most Middle Eastern dictatorships have not had strong records on women's rights, there is concern that women's and minority rights will be under attack as strongmen are replaced by popularly elected Islamist parties.

Such controversies have also surfaced in Indonesia since democratization. With a population of more than 240 million people, Indonesia has more Muslims than any other country in the world. While the country has a history of women's mobilization and a vibrant and politically diverse tradition of Muslim intellectual discourse, in the wake of the transition to democracy Indonesian Islam seemed to take a conservative turn (Sidel 2006; Bruinessen 2011). The years after 9/11 were marred by terrorist bombings linked to Muslim extremists, as well as religious and ethnic violence. Some Muslim organizations called for Indonesians to embrace "traditional" gender roles and for stronger state regulation of morality. There was increasing social pressure for women to comply with Muslim clothing guidelines, and some municipalities enacted laws requiring Muslim women to wear the headscarf or forbidding them from going out at night without a suitable male escort.[3] It was such changes that drew me back to Indonesia. With democratization *and* an ongoing Islamic revival, I wanted to know what Indonesian women activists thought about women's rights and Islam, and what broader lessons might Indonesia offer for thinking about agency in religious contexts.

IN THE FIELD: AN INTRODUCTION TO WOMEN'S ACTIVISM IN JAKARTA

To explore these issues, I undertook an ethnographic study of Muslim and secular women activists in Jakarta, the Indonesian capitol. I use the term *woman activist* as a general label for women who mobilize politically as women. I was particularly interested in women activists who sought political, economic, and social changes they believed would benefit women.

Nahdlatul Ulama, founded in 1926, is one of Indonesia's most established Muslim organizations, and it has an estimated 45 million members. I was visiting its Jakarta headquarters to meet with Fatayat, its organization for women ages twenty-five to forty-five. But given the tense political climate, I wasn't sure if they would consider participating in the study.

Relieved to enter the air-conditioned lobby, I took the elevator to a quiet reception area outside Fatayat's small offices. There I was greeted by Farida, then head of Fatayat. At the time, few researchers had studied Fatayat, and I knew little about what they did.

Farida was in her late thirties. She wore an elegant, embroidered headscarf with a long, slim skirt. I was genuinely surprised when she began discussing the organization's programs to empower women and its recent focus on reproductive health. In a calm, authoritative voice she explained about Fatayat's campaign for reproductive rights, which included centers where women could access information about reproductive health matters, including family planning and sexuality. Given its history as part of a venerable Muslim organization, I assumed that Fatayat would be doing uncontroversial charity work. In fact, I expected Fatayat to represent the politically quietist end of women's activism in my study. Talking about "women's reproductive rights" didn't sound uncontroversial, and it certainly didn't fit with stereotypes of traditional Muslim women. I was eager to know more about Fatayat and their ideas about Islam and women.

A few days later, I visited Rahima, a new Muslim NGO. Their office occupied a modest house in a middle-class neighborhood. I knew that Rahima focused on women's rights in Islam, but I wasn't sure what that meant. And once again, I was startled when a petite young woman with a silk headscarf began to recount Rahima's "gender sensitivity trainings" in Muslim boarding schools. Santhi said that Rahima tries to train religious leaders, teachers, and students to understand that the notion that men and women have different essential natures is a social construction. She explained that Rahima's mission is to disseminate an "alternative perspective on Islam," one that is egalitarian. She was quick to tell me that she rarely uses the word *feminist*, because in Indonesia it is associated with both the West and Communism. But she also said that Rahima's perspective is feminist, and she felt that feminist ideas have gained acceptance in many of the communities where Rahima works, especially if they are translated into Islamic terms. What Santhi was telling me was that the word *feminism* has negative connotations but that ideas about women's rights and equality are not anathema to Muslims, especially if they are explained in a framework that people respect.

The third organization I studied was Solidaritas Perempuan, one of Indonesia's best-known women's rights NGOs. The name means Women's Solidarity, and it was one of the first NGOs to advocate for the rights of the thousands of Indonesian women who migrate overseas to work as domestics. When I first visited their office, a two-story house in a tranquil neighborhood, I was intrigued by the mixture of staff. Some wore t-shirts and tight jeans, while others were in headscarves and modest outfits. The mood was youthful and energetic. Ninik, then head of Solidaritas Perempuan, was in her midforties and was a veteran of social movement activism. She wore a short-sleeved blouse and skirt without a headscarf. Ninik readily described her organization as feminist, which I found surprising given my earlier conversation about feminism with Santhi from Rahima.

It was beginning to be clear to me that Islam and feminism were not necessarily incompatible for some Indonesian activists. I was keen to grasp how activists connected these ideas. These interactions also underscored a key question for me during my fieldwork: What new kinds of agency might arise from intersections between Islam and feminism?

Six months later, eager to meet more conservative women activists, I talked with Kadira, head of the women's division of the Prosperous Justice Party (PKS). PKS is a Muslim political party that advocates Islam as a source of values for national law and policy. Their offices were in a commercial building on a busy, lackluster boulevard (by 2010 the party had moved into a more substantial five-story building on the southern edge of the city). The party had a reputation for promoting a more "Middle Eastern" style of Islam, including more stringent segregation of men and women than is typical in Indonesia. I was treated respectfully, but warily, as I sat in the visitors' waiting room. Once I was ushered into a small room to talk with Kadira, however, she proved quite friendly. In her forties, Kadira wore a bulky white headscarf that covered her shoulders and torso. She told me that she thought feminism was "excessive" because it concentrated too much on women's problems, and she argued that men experience oppression as well. While Farida and Santhi were concerned that Islam was being misused to justify discrimination against women, Kadira said that discrimination was due to society not being Islamic enough.

Nevertheless, Kadira took pride in the history of women's mobilization in Indonesia, telling me, "Women's movements have been around since the time of Indonesia's independence. They struggled for the independence of the archipelago, struggled in order to develop the people. Now there are many active women in Indonesia and we must support them.... Indonesia makes women's leadership possible, compared to the Muslim countries in the Middle East. Even more possible compared to Western countries."

Farida and Santhi are devout, well-educated Muslim women who advocate for women's rights from a feminist perspective. In contrast, Kadira does not prioritize women's rights or gender equality in her political agenda, and she disagrees with some aspects of these ideas. Yet it is possible to see the influence of women's rights in some of her comments. In retrospect, I was ignorant, but certainly not alone, in my assumption that pious Muslims are inherently uncomfortable with women's rights.

What I had expected was that Indonesian Muslim women activists might advocate for more women's political participation (i.e., voting), tempered by arguments about men and women's essential differences. Indeed, this does describe much of what Kadira said to me, although I wasn't expecting her to be such an advocate for women's involvement in public life. But

Farida and Santhi seemed to be articulating a vision of more than just formal political equality. Fatayat lists as one of its objectives "*Terwujudnya masyarakat yang berkeadilan gender*," which translates as "To create a society with gender justice."[4] As Santhi said, feminism is indeed looked upon by many Indonesians as foreign and secular. But as she pointed out, that doesn't necessarily mean they disagree with the substance of feminism, especially the core idea that women should have the same political, social, and economic rights as men.

Santhi's words contradict more conservative Islamist rhetoric about feminism and women's rights being aspects of Western immorality, as well as Western media representations of oppressed Muslim women and a clash of civilizations. Santhi's statements also sit uneasily with Western progressives' concerns about what they see as a global resurgence of conservative religion, particularly Islam, which many believe seeks to turn back the clock on women's rights. In essence, Muslim women are often presented as having limited agency—a view that is at odds with what I was hearing from Farida, Santhi, and Kadira.

The cultural baggage feminism has assumed is part of the problem. In places like Indonesia, at a time when many are critical of American power, feminism is identified as culturally inauthentic or, worse, a form of Western imperialism. Throughout this book, I use feminism to refer to a set of ideas and institutions that seek to challenge women's subordination to men (Ferree and Tripp 2006). Feminism defined as such can be used by individuals and organizations in many different ways. Although feminism began as an organized social movement in the United States and Europe and has since spread around the globe, I do not think feminist ideas are limited to the West. In this book, I refer to people or organizations as feminist if they themselves do so. However, I think it is important to distinguish between those who challenge women's subordination to men and those who do not. To capture this difference, I use the terms *women's rights activists* for those who challenge women's subordination and *women activists* as a more general term for politically active women who may or may not challenge gender inequality.[5]

Given the supposed clash between Islam and feminism, what are we to make of veiled women like Farida and Santhi advocating for women's rights and gender equality? And of a Muslim political party activist like Kadira promoting her country's history of female mobilization? This puzzle animates the central questions of this book: How do Indonesian women activists connect their piety and their politics? More specifically, how do they understand and make use of global discourses of Islam and feminism, especially at a time when these ideas are viewed as incommensurable?

And given the widespread concerns about religion and women's rights, how exactly does Islam constrain or enable particular forms of agency for women activists?

Through my fieldwork in Indonesia, I have come to see that answering these questions requires a more precise understanding of how people interpret religious ideas. As sociologist John Levi Martin (2011) proposes, we can better understand people's actions by paying attention to the particulars of their own experiences, including how they grasp the norms and values of their social contexts. This perspective is valuable in understanding how the Indonesian women activists I met adapt Islam and feminism in different ways. My examination of how these activists put ideas into practice is in keeping with a sociological perspective that sees culture not simply as a matter of beliefs but rather as the available habits, skills, and styles that people utilize to construct their own strategies of action (Swidler 1986). In addition, as Sewell (2005) reminds us, cultural schemas are in fact key components of social structures, and these schemas can guide action and be used differently in various contexts. In this sense, I see religion as a particular cultural schema that the women activists in this study use differently depending on their experiences and social locations.

However, as this book reveals, the ways women activists engage with feminism and Islam are neither random nor exactly freely chosen. Women's educational backgrounds and previous activist experiences lead them to organizations that teach them particular ways of interpreting Islam and adapting ideas of women's rights. This is because these organizations are linked to different Islamic milieus which have diverse approaches to interpreting foundational religious texts. As I discuss later in this chapter, women in Fatayat and Rahima tend to come from religious and educational backgrounds in which they learned an approach to Islamic texts that facilitates contextual interpretation. Fatayat, with its connections to international NGOs, capitalizes on this background, teaching its members this perspective in order to emphasize Islam's compatibility with gender equality. In contrast, PKS women were part of a wave of Islamic campus activism in the 1980s and 1990s that was inspired by Middle Eastern Islamists such as the Muslim Brotherhood. From this network, they learned a more textualist approach to interpreting Islam. The party also promotes this textualist approach, which is not necessarily hostile to women's rights but emphasizes that men and women have different "natural" roles.

Islam therefore provides resources for different kinds of agency. I identify three distinct but overlapping types of agency among Indonesian women activists, two of which are deeply informed by Islam. I define pious agency as an agency that is influenced by religion and for which being a religious subject is central. Among the activists of Fatayat and Rahima, we see the emergence of *pious critical agency*. This agency involves a critical, public engagement with interpretations of religious texts, generally based on a contextual interpretive method. This agency facilitates activism for women's rights and equality. The women activists of PKS demonstrate *pious activating agency*. PKS women cadres activate the party's interpretations of religious texts to advocate for women's greater political participation, but they also use them to support policies that are opposed by many feminists. Finally, Solidaritas Perempuan activists demonstrate an inclusive *feminist agency*. Their feminist agency aims at gender equality and the empowerment of women. These activists do so through building a feminist movement that is critical of neoliberal globalization but can also incorporate Islamic piety. What this demonstrates is that the rise of religious agency in Indonesia has not undermined feminist agency. Pious agency and feminist agency are not dichotomous; they can and do intersect.

WHY INDONESIA? ACTIVISM IN A DEMOCRATIZING MUSLIM SETTING

The events of the Arab Spring and the extensive participation of women in democratic upheavals across the Middle East and North Africa demand attention to how gender is shifting in Muslim settings. For example, in post-revolutionary Egypt, where women played a substantial role in the democracy movement, incidents of sexual harassment and assault seem to be on the rise (Sheikh and Kirkpatrick 2013). Activists have demanded a stronger response from the Morsi government, which has so far been reluctant to pursue the issue. The ongoing transformations suggest that the appeal of Islamic piety for many women coexists with desires for social change and rights, perhaps including gender equality. Moreover, the uprisings demonstrate the power of global flows of information, with social media and television helping to disseminate the civic ideals of Tahrir Square to Bahrain, Yemen, and beyond. Indonesia's 1998 upheaval, which resulted in the fall of a military dictatorship, no longer seems anomalous. For the social scientist in an era of upheaval, Indonesia provides a fascinating, but no longer unusual, combination of women's participation, a religious revival, and democratization that is now evident in other countries and regions.

My approach to ethnographic fieldwork was to find a diverse selection of women working for activist organizations in the fast-growing megalopolis of Jakarta (see Figure 1.1).[6] Solidaritas Perempuan is a feminist NGO that advocates for the rights of women who migrate overseas to work as

Figure 1.1: Central Jakarta at dusk.

domestics, and it also aims to build a broader women's rights movement. Rahima is an NGO that educates Muslims about women's rights in Islam, especially by providing alternative interpretations of Islamic texts. Fatayat NU is the women's division of Nahdlatul Ulama and it works on various issues ranging from empowering low-income women, to providing information about reproductive health, to teaching women about their rights in Islam. Finally, I also studied women in PKS, a Muslim political party that promotes a greater role for Islam in the state. I chose these organizations because they represent different positions within the mainstream spectrum of women's activism in Indonesia.[7] By mainstream, I mean organizations that are generally accepted actors in social movements, civil society, and formal politics.

I conducted twelve months of ethnographic fieldwork in 2002–2003, three additional months in 2005, and another three months in 2008 and 2010. The ethnography included participant observation, forty-seven in-depth interviews and eighteen follow-up interviews with members of these groups.[8] The book is structured around my core questions of how women activists understand Islam and feminism, how they use these frameworks in their activism, and the modes of agency these activists embody.

Activism in Indonesia looks rather different than in the United States. During the authoritarian Suharto regime, political expression outside state-controlled organizations was restricted. In the 1980s, however,

NGOs and religious organizations became a loophole for political activism. Quite a few of the activists in the 1990s democracy movement came out of feminist and religious NGOs. These organizations have professionalized since the 1990s, yet many continue to have an activist component. Staff and volunteers still attend demonstrations and protests and see themselves as part of movements for social justice and human rights.

As an ethnographer, I worked as a volunteer for the organizations in my study, which usually meant spending time in their offices assisting with translation of documents (as I discuss in Appendix A, I was not able to do this with PKS). I attended staff meetings; conferences, trainings, and workshops with "stakeholders" and the public; and even the occasional meeting with government officials. My days at the office were not always exciting, but they gave me a chance to get to know people over time. More stimulating were the opportunities to attend demonstrations, including a million-person protest against the US war in Iraq and a spirited "dance-in" to support a pop star under fire for allegedly licentious performances.

A methodological limitation, but also a virtue, of this book is that it is a study of activists. My definition of an activist is a person who seeks to bring about social and political change, through various means. Activists are unique in some ways. They are obviously agentive, in that they are working for change. They are ideological, or at least have given considerable thought to political and religious ideas. They are often more educated than average. If they are religious, as are most of my informants, then religion probably plays a larger role in their worldviews. Activists in Jakarta, Indonesia's most global city, are more cosmopolitan and educated than most Indonesians. Although they do not represent the entire social and economic range of Indonesia's population, there are good reasons to study activists. Certainly, they are often at the vanguard of change. More importantly, if we recognize that in the course of their struggles activists develop and express moral visions for social change (Jasper 1999), examining such visions can provide insights into how society is transforming. That said, this is not a typical social movement study. Social movement scholars are usually interested in questions of mobilization and organization, success and failure. The questions that interest me are the social contexts that shape activist visions and the forms of agency emerging in Muslim societies.

The vast changes in Indonesia over the past few decades, especially those related to women, make this setting ripe for a sociological analysis. With 240 million citizens, almost 90% of whom are Muslim, Indonesia has the world's largest Muslim population, but it is not Arab. Indonesian Islam has always been in dialogue with both global currents and local cultural practices. The country's gender relations have also long fascinated social scientists. Some have argued that Indonesian women have more mobility in public spaces and control over financial matters than women in other parts of the world, and others highlight older traditions of fluidity in gender roles (C. Geertz 1973; Stoler 1977; Peletz 2009). Recent studies stress that such characteristics are not synonymous with gender equality, and that Indonesian women's access to power is limited by a state-reinforced patriarchal ideology (Tickamyer and Kusujiarti 2012).

Even more importantly, Indonesia in the 2000s was a country in the midst of democratization. When I began this project, my interest was the women's movement that blossomed during the reform effort that compelled Suharto to resign the presidency in 1998 after more than thirty years of authoritarian rule. Since then, Indonesia has become an electoral democracy and democratization has coincided with other transformations.

Since the 1980s, many Indonesians have embraced what they believe to be more orthodox Islamic practices, the most visible of which is veiling for women. When I first lived in East Java as a high school exchange student in 1990, few women wore Muslim dress other than on religious holidays. But by the early 2000s, it seemed to me that a majority of young women in Jakarta were wearing the *jilbab*, the new form of headscarf inspired by Arab styles that completely covers the hair, and often the upper chest. Magazines showed women in luxurious Muslim fashions, while pamphlets passed out by Muslim groups on university campuses instructed women about the right and wrong ways to wear "Muslim clothing."[9] Although a few groups encourage men to wear Arabic clothing, most pious men wear Western styles. Thus, the very appearance of the Islamic revival in Indonesia is gendered.

Pious appearances have also been politicized by some Indonesian Muslims. Since the decentralization of political power that accompanied democratization in the early 2000s, some provincial parliaments have passed morality laws, a number of which require women and girls to wear the *jilbab* or place restrictions on women's mobility and clothing (ostensibly to control the sex trade). These phenomena, along with legislation such as the 2008 pornography bill, have generated anxiety about the rights of women and religious minorities in the new Indonesia.

The question of why Indonesian women are attracted to new and seemingly constraining forms of religious discipline is one that has been studied extensively. Social scientists studying other Muslim societies have found complex reasons for women's embrace of revivalist Islam. Some argue that becoming pious and wearing the veil give women a way to pursue higher education and careers while still fulfilling some aspects of tradition

(Macleod 1992). Others argue that women are asserting their own way of being modern and Muslim by rejecting, selectively appropriating, or even reworking Western conceptions of modernity (Göle 1996; Deeb 2006). More recently, Saba Mahmood (2005) has proposed that women derive pleasure from the process of becoming pious. Similarly, scholars of Indonesia maintain that young women see piety as a way to balance being modern and Muslim (Brenner 1996; Smith-Hefner 2007). What remains to be understood are the consequences of increasing Islamic piety for women's activism and agency. These consequences are the core concerns of this book—namely, how Indonesian women activists connect Islam and feminism and the forms of agency such connections produce.

A newly public Islam is not the only outcome of democratization and social change in Indonesia. Transnational feminism has flourished as well. Since the late 1980s, NGOs and social movements dedicated to women's rights have been increasingly active globally, and in Indonesia they have benefited from the opening up of political space. NGOs have trained a generation of Indonesian activists to become interested in gender. I was amazed at how familiar activists were with feminist concepts, such as the idea that gender is socially constructed. While Santhi was correct that *feminism* is a controversial word in Indonesia, Indonesia has many outspoken activists who mobilize women explicitly for rights and equality. Additionally, Indonesian women are entering higher education in large numbers and moving into professional careers. Some are becoming Islamic teachers and scholars. Indeed, I encountered women activists who had training in Islamic theology. Thus, not only are ideas about women's rights and empowerment influential, but also this is happening as women are entering new social arenas. All of these developments coincide with the Islamic revival, which makes Indonesia an especially exciting setting in which to examine Islam and women's agency (Rinaldo 2010a).

ISLAM AND WOMEN'S ACTIVISM: BREAKING DOWN BINARIES

Religion and Modernity

To understand the intersections of Islam and feminism in Indonesia requires first questioning the common assumption that religion, especially Islam, is inherently antimodern. For much of the twentieth century, social scientists claimed that as societies modernized, religion would be relegated to the private sphere. The surge of Christian evangelicalism in the United States in the 1980s and the rise of other politicized religious movements caused scholars to rethink this thesis. Indeed, some scholars now say that religion has played a crucial role in the development of robust, modern public spheres in many countries (Casanova 1994; Gorski 2003).

Yet when it comes to Islam there is still debate about whether it is modern. This is partly due to the perception that Islam, and by extension Muslim societies, are uniquely backward in their treatment of women. Scholars like Samuel Huntington (1993) and Bernard Lewis (2001) see a fundamental clash between Islam and modernity, with the emancipation of women as a critical aspect of this clash. For Lewis, the treatment of women has been a key difference between Christian and Muslim societies. Lewis acknowledges that postcolonial Muslim societies made significant reforms in the twentieth century. However, he argues that such reforms are now a target of the Islamic revival: "From a traditional point of view, the emancipation of women . . . is an incitement to immorality and promiscuity, and a deadly blow to the heart of Islamic society, the Muslim family and home. The battle continues" (p. 70). While Lewis's generalization that Islam is antimodern is problematic, he is right to note the significance of the Islamic revival.

One of the defining characteristics of the Islamic revival is its emphasis on the public aspects of piety. There is no doubt that in places like Indonesia, Islam has indeed become more prominent in public life. Over the past several decades, scholars of Muslim societies have chronicled an upsurge in the building of mosques, increased modesty in women's clothing, greater observance of prayer and taboos on alcohol, the proliferation of Muslim schools, the rise of Muslim media and fashion, and of course, the influence of Islam in political parties (Eickelman and Piscatori 1996; Mahmood 2005; Deeb 2006). In sharp contrast to Lewis, these scholars emphasize that those attracted to revivalist Islam are usually urbanites who embrace modernity on their own terms.

The processes described as part of the Islamic revival are paralleled in other religions. Evangelicalism, Pentecostalism, and ultra-orthodox Judaism contest the secularization of everyday life by calling on believers to practice faith publicly and inculcate religious values throughout society (D. L. Martin 2003; Avishai 2008; Smilde 2009).[10] Religious renewal movements often advocate a return to more "traditional" gender roles. And as Lewis's writing indicates, revivalist Islam is often depicted as especially patriarchal. Yet, as I discuss in the next section, studies of such movements often find that their consequences for gender are complex and unpredictable. If we understand religious renewal movements as very much part of modernity and an increasingly globalized world, we should not assume that equality or emancipation appeal to all women. However, we should also not assume that such movements will necessarily sustain "traditional" gender practices, that religious women always adopt such practices whole-sale, or that pious religiosity is inherently inhospitable to gender equality. With this perspective, we can then ask, given that religion is increasingly entrenched in the public sphere in Indonesia and other countries, what consequences does a newly public Islam have for women's activism and agency?

Religion and Feminism

As I began my fieldwork, I was fascinated by the myriad styles of Muslim clothing in Jakarta. This was a conspicuous change from my first stay in Indonesia as a high school exchange student. I soon realized that women had varied reasons for wearing the veil, and I saw that many combined it with fashionable clothing. I noticed a few women who were adopting much more severe forms of covering, including the black face-veil (niqab).[11] Though I was taken aback by the niqab, the imaginative fusion of Muslim and Western styles that I saw in Jakarta streets and malls made me want to learn more about women's involvement in pious Islam.

Early accounts of religious revival movements such as Islamism or evangelical Christianity tended to depict women as victims of patriarchal backlash.[12] However, it soon became clear to scholars that women were important participants in religious revival movements. Social scientists soon began to examine why such movements appealed to women. They pro-posed that women may reinterpret religious teachings in feminist ways or make strategic use of religious traditions to gain certain kinds of power and opportunities, express identities, or alleviate personal difficulties (Macleod 1992; Davidman 1993; Bartkowski and Read 2003; Gallagher 2003, 2004; Chong 2008; Rinaldo 2010b). Many studies conclude that religious revival movements empower women in certain ways even while also reaffirming the gendered status quo. However, such studies generally view religion as a tool that women use, and rarely as a commitment in itself. Moreover, they often presuppose that revivalist religious movements are uniformly patriarchal.

Muslim revivalist movements do often emphasize rules about gender as part of a move toward more pious lifestyles. These lifestyles are expressed through the Islamization of women's clothing and greater segregation of men and women in public spaces (Ong 1995; Göle 1996). While many observers argue that such shifts imperil women's rights, others suggest that their impact is complex and not necessarily disempowering for women. For example, Macleod (1992) argued that adopting the headscarf gives urban Egyptian women greater public mobility, which they use to pursue careers while still presenting themselves as virtuous women.

Through such discussions, scholars of Muslim societies began to delve into the question of women's agency. Mohanty (1998) and other postcolonial scholars helped to spark an interest in understanding Muslim women's lives in their particular contexts, without depicting women as a monolithic category. In an influential article, Kandiyoti (1988) argued that women in patriarchal societies of the Middle East and Asia strategize within constraints of kinship, leading them to give up independence in return for power within the family, what Kandiyoti calls the patriarchal bargain. Examining 1980s Malaysia, Ong (1995) argued that women in revivalist Islamic movements exhibit a "paradoxical agency," as their choice to veil represents an acceptance of docility, as well as a demarcation of Muslim from non-Muslim. Göle (1996) maintains that Islamist women in Turkey demonstrate agency in their aim to be modern in an Islamic, rather than Western, manner. Göle was also one of the first to notice that more politicized Islamist movements presented a more active "missionary" role for women. For these scholars, a central theme is women choosing to submit to unequal gender norms.[13]

Building on such arguments, Mahmood (2005) used her study of women in the Egyptian mosque movement to both critique Western notions of agency and put forward a new conception of the "docile agent." For Mahmood, agency is a capacity for action that is historically and culturally contingent, located within structures of power rather than outside them (p. 34). Mahmood argues that feminism is founded on liberal ideas about human freedom and agency, which assume that women want autonomy and liberation (p. 13). However, for Mahmood, such goals are incompatible with pious Islam and its aim of total submission to religious discipline. Mahmood proposes that agency must be understood beyond the conventional binary of resistance versus submission. Instead, scholars need to understand the pleasure and sense of empowerment that women get from living up to pious ideals and actively creating themselves as religious subjects. For Mahmood, this "pious agency" of the mosque movement poses a challenge to the secular liberal imaginary on which feminist agency is predicated (pp. 5, 192).

Mahmood's work has generated a productive discussion on how people transform themselves through religious discipline, and it has become very influential for scholarship on religion and gender. Most crucially, it has opened the way for a new consideration of how agency can be conveyed through religious piety (Braidotti 2008). For example, Avishai (2008) argues in her study of orthodox Jewish women that their agency consists of "doing religion," that is, a mode of observant conduct and self-making that is done in the pursuit of religious goals.

Yet as Schielke (2010) and others have pointed out, in a complex, globalizing world, people's subjectivities are likely to combine pious and secular influences, and class and ethnicity may be as important in people's lives as religion.[14] I am uncomfortable with the tendency in some literature to present feminist agency and pious agency as opposites. Moreover, I am concerned that nonliberal or "docile" pious agency is sometimes presented as the primary agency manifested by pious women. For example, Göle and Billaud (2011, 129) propose that "Muslims who express their 'Muslimness' in the European public domain through their clothing, lifestyle, and certain demands for rights...present an image of non-liberal agency that challenges some of the fundamental values of Western democracies." This argument is echoed by European critics of Muslim immigrants who emphasize a clash between Muslim and Western subjectivities. But does demanding the right to wear religious clothing necessarily conflict with liberalism? And is nonliberal agency the *only* agency pious women manifest? In fact, Mahmood herself stresses that "the meaning of agency must be explored within the grammar of concepts within which it resides" (p. 34), and she acknowledges that the Egyptian mosque movement may be distinctive in its close relationship between the subject's desires and external religious authority (p. 31).

A related but differently nuanced view of agency emerges from scholars of women's movements and feminism in Muslim societies. Mir-Hosseini (2006) argues that an unintended consequence of Islamist rule in Iran is that it has catalyzed the emergence of new reformist and feminist voices in Islam. With Islam as the only legitimate frame of reference in that country, feminists have increasingly found support for their arguments from within the Islamic tradition. Mir-Hosseini observes that this development is helping to overcome the antinomy between Islam and feminism in Iran and is empowering women to make their own choices. Similarly, Badran (2009) argues that Islamic feminism (i.e., activists who couch arguments for women's equality in Islamic terms) is becoming mainstream and converging with secular feminism in many countries. In her essential recent study of Morocco, Salime (2011) shows that contemporary events, especially the US war on terror and transnational discourses about Islam as oppressive to women, have pushed the Islamist movement to adopt aspects of the women's rights agenda. Simultaneously, Salime notes that feminists have become more accepting of claims for women's empowerment that are situated within Islam. Salime finds that these two movements interact with and influence each other. Finally, Abu-Lughod (2010), Charrad (2011) and Hafez (2011) observe that Muslim women commonly use multiple frames, both secular and religious, to talk about rights and gender. This view is similar to the emphasis of recent scholars on intersectional identities, who emphasize that people's identities are shaped by multiple and intersecting social structures (Collins 2008). Scholars like Salime and Hafez agree that agency is produced in a dynamic relationship with social norms and structures. More crucially, they also suggest that pious agency can converge with feminism and that religious and secular frameworks may be combined.

I build on Mahmood's contributions, especially her insights that agency is not necessarily connected to liberation, that living up to pious norms can be a form of agency, and that agency must be understood as having multiple manifestations. However, in my view, docile or nonliberal agency does not exhaust the possibilities for agency among pious women. This mode of agency, with its focus on self-fashioning, also strikes me as more individual than collective. In this book, I suggest two additional modes of pious agency that I see among Indonesian women activists—*pious critical agency* and *pious activating agency*. Pious critical agency is the capacity to engage critically and publicly with interpretations of religious texts, while pious activating agency is the capacity to use interpretations of religious texts to mobilize in the public sphere.

In Indonesia, Islam and feminism sometimes contradict each other but often they are in dialogue. In fact, when I asked women in Fatayat and Rahima about how Islam influenced their views of women's rights, some told me they felt inspired by Islam because they saw at its heart a mission of social justice and equality. Pious agency and feminist agency are distinct, but not opposite, and they can intersect, overlap, and become entangled. New modes of pious agency in Indonesia are helping to create new activist repertoires, including those in which ideas from Islam and feminism are intertwined.

Religion and Agency

To grasp how Indonesian women activists engage with Islam and feminism, and the new modes of agency emerging in Muslim contexts, we must consider how religion influences agency from a broader sociological perspective. Journalistic and some scholarly accounts of women and Islam tend to assume that religious texts or discourses directly influence what people do. But does Islam completely dictate how women act and think, especially in diverse settings like Indonesia? And if so, what accounts for the unexpected mixtures we so often encounter in places like Indonesia, like women in skinny jeans with high heels and headscarves or pious women who vote for secular political parties?

We can better understand these issues related to religion and agency if we think of religion as part of culture. I refer here to culture in the broadest sense as a web of meaningful significance that humans have created and within which we exist (Weber 1949; C. Geertz 1973). The question of agency, then, is a question of how to account for innovative human action while recognizing the ways that action is embedded in rules, expectations, practices, and meanings (Goldstone 2010).

While there is a long history of cultural analysis in sociology, sociologists are conventionally more interested in social structures than in culture and agency. For instance, sociologists tend to look at how patterns of relationships produce action. My perspective is influenced by theorists who emphasize the mutual constitution of structure, culture, and agency, rather than seeing one as wholly determinative of the other. One of the most constructive contributions to social scientific understandings of agency comes from Sewell (1992, 2005). In his view, social structures consist of both symbolic and material aspects, and agency is embedded within such structures. Of particular significance is Sewell's insight that symbolic aspects of social structure can be understood as cultural schemas, or the meanings, rules, motivations, and recipes for action. In this perspective, structures shape what people do, but people's actions also constitute and reproduce structures (p. 4).

Agency for Sewell consists of the transposition of existing cultural schemas to new situations, or as he writes: "Agency arises from the actor's knowledge of schemas, which means the ability to apply them to new contexts" (p. 20). For Sewell, structures enable and constrain action but do not necessarily determine its outcome. Most significant is Sewell's recognition that just as structures are multiple and differentiated, so are the possibilities for agency (Sewell 2005).

Sewell's perspective has been crucial for renewing sociological attention to culture and agency. In Sewell's terms, the women activists I study exist within cultural schemas but also adapt schemas of Islam and feminism to the newly democratized context of Indonesia. Yet it is also important to recognize how agency and the use of cultural schemas are patterned. To address this issue, I use field theory, which builds on the work of Pierre Bourdieu. Bourdieu uses the concept of *field* to describe a social arena in which people maneuver and struggle in pursuit of resources. Society contains multiple fields, which are constituted according to underlying norms or values, and each field has its own forms of capital that agents can use to obtain advantage within it (Bourdieu and Wacquant 1992). People's actions within a field are coordinated by their *habitus*, which includes learned life-styles, preferences, and ways of acting that have been shaped by their social location (Bourdieu 1987).

Fligstein and McAdam (2012) extend field theory to propose that any given social arena consists of overlapping fields in which actors interact based on a common set of understandings about the fields. Fields are constantly changing and are constructed on a situational basis as actors define new issues as salient. In addition, Fligstein and McAdam empha-size the importance of interplay *between* fields and the broader environ-ments in which fields are embedded. Fligstein and McAdam's extension of field theory has implications for how we understand agency. They propose that the structure of a field and the positions actors occupy within it influ-ences how those actors enact agency (p. 180). Similarly, J. L. Martin (2011) emphasizes that people interact with the rules and expectations of a field, and they do so differently depending on their locations within those fields. From these contributions, it is evident that different fields give rise to dif-ferent capacities for action, or agency, and that different locations within a field can generate different types of agency.[15] In addition, we should be mindful of how actors may be positioned within multiple fields and the implications such locations have for types of agency.[16]

I bring these insights from Sewell, Bourdieu, Fligstein and McAdam, and Martin together to conceptualize the activists in this study as participat-ing in the two overlapping national fields of *Islamic politics* and *gender poli-tics*. As I discuss in chapter 2, these fields are part of the larger tapestry of the national public sphere in Indonesia (an arena that includes civil soci-ety organizations, political parties, NGOs, religious institutions, and the media). *Islamic politics* is the field of actors who strive to bring about a more Islamic society, via electoral politics or cultural change. It is constituted by the history of Indonesian Islam, with its diverse interpretive traditions and practices, as well as global influences. *Gender politics* is the field of political contestation around gender relations and includes women's rights activists influenced by feminist thought and those who seek a return to more tradi-tional gender arrangements. It is constituted by national and local gender norms, as well as global influences such as feminism. Since the democratic transition, both these fields have become more dynamic and intertwined.

With respect to the women activists who are the focus of this book, I see different forms of agency arising within different fields. Agency is therefore highly variable. Women activists' actions are in dialogue with established norms, meanings, hierarchies, and material constraints. Nevertheless, these activists also demonstrate imaginative and creative responses to their social contexts. The field perspective helps to highlight how social locations and life experiences shape women activists' agencies in different ways. Importantly, I found that religion may indeed enable agency, but not in a simple or monolithic manner. In this book, I attend closely to women's understandings of Islam and feminism, especially the way they use religious interpretations in their activism. However, I maintain that these interpretations come from the way activists are embedded in particular fields. The agency of Indonesian women activists is shaped by personal trajectories, but more significantly, by experiences within the specific fields of *Islamic politics* and *gender politics*. From this perspective, religion is a diverse cultural schema that can enable different modes of agency. Religion may therefore be a source of the norms that constitute a field, but it is also subject to interpretation by differently positioned actors.

The organizations discussed in this book are positioned in different ways in these two fields. Women's rights activists like Solidaritas Perempuan are located in the field of gender politics, while the Prosperous Justice Party is in the field of Islamic politics. These are not the only fields these activists may be involved in but they are the most relevant. Since the 1990s, these fields have begun to overlap and influence each other. This is partly a result of mutual exchange during the democracy movement, as I discuss in chapter 2. However, it also arises because Islamic politics and gender politics affect each other. Religion and feminism are both prescriptive, offering proposals for how people should live and how society should be organized. It is only Fatayat NU and Rahima who are truly operating within the overlap between these fields. Importantly, each of these positions in relation to the two fields corresponds to a different mode of agency (Figure 1.2).

Within the intersecting fields of Islamic politics and gender politics, Indonesian Muslim women activists demonstrate two distinct modes of pious agency: *critical* and *activating*. *Pious critical agency* is based on a critical

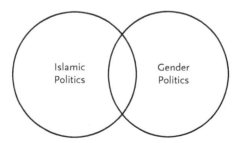

Figure 1.2: Fields of Islamic politics and gender politics.

engagement with religious texts and emphasizes the *interpretation* of texts to make claims for political and social change. This mode of agency is characteristic of the activists in Fatayat and Rahima, who argue for women's rights from an Islamic perspective. Their unique and quite recent position in the overlap between Islamic politics and gender politics helps foster this embrace of both women's rights and religious piety. For example, they use revisionist and contextual interpretations of Islamic texts to argue against polygamy and for women's control over their reproductive lives.

Pious activating agency is based on the *deployment* of religious texts to make claims for political and social change. Women make use of religious texts (and often in a selective way) but they tend not to be directly involved in the interpretation or discussion of such texts. Such activating or mobilizing agency is visible among all the organizations in this study, as it is very much a part of religious social activism. But it is most characteristic of women in the Prosperous Justice Party, who argue for a nation-state guided by Islamic values. This is an agency that emerges from women's recent entry into the field of Islamic politics, but it is still in dialogue with women's rights because of the influence of the field of gender politics. PKS women use the party's textualist interpretations to argue for policies such as stronger laws against pornography and for ideas such as the domestic sphere as women's priority. Their moderately conservative views on gender reflect the party's pragmatism, as well as an acceptance of some ideas of women's empowerment and rights.

These two modes of agency are different but not dichotomous. Increased overlap between the fields of Islamic politics and gender politics has promoted new modes of women's agency and activism. Pious critical and activating agency should not be understood as mutually exclusive, nor are they the only forms of agency available to Indonesian Muslim women. Nonetheless, both are forms of pious agency in the sense that they draw centrally on religious norms and aim at producing pious subjects.

Importantly, the rise of pious agency for women activists has not disabled the *feminist agency* of Solidaritas Perempuan (SP). SP's feminist agency emerges out of the organization's more exclusive involvement in the field of gender politics since the early 1990s and is shaped by transnational feminist and human rights discourses. SP activists use these frameworks to advocate for female migrant workers, promote environmental justice, and pursue other reforms. Interestingly, their feminist agency in this Indonesian context is inclusive and increasingly incorporates religious identities and more pious activists. In this sense, women activists in SP have also been influenced by the field of Islamic politics (Figure 1.3).

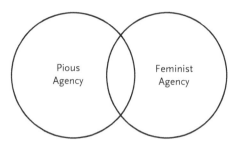

Figure 1.3: Modes of agency for Indonesian women activists.

Taken together, these three modes of agency are producing innovative and diverse forms of collective action. This includes a creative synthesis of Islam and feminism, an Islamism that expands women's conventional roles, and a feminism that accommodates religious piety. Yet, a vital question remains to be addressed: How exactly does Islam contribute to these modes of agency?

Islam and Women Activists' Agency

Anthropologist Talal Asad's theorization of Islam is helpful in understanding how exactly Islam contributes to these three modes of agency. For Asad, Islam is not simply a collection of beliefs, artifacts, customs, and morals, but instead it is a "discursive tradition." The Islamic discursive tradition is a historically evolving set of discourses embodied in the practices and institutions of Islamic societies, which are connected by a conception of the Islamic past and future, with reference to particular Islamic practice in the present (Asad 1986, 20). Asad maintains that being part of the Islamic tradition "does not preclude involvement in vigorous debates over the meaning of its formative texts (and even over which texts are formative) and over the need for radical reform of the tradition" (2003, 195). Scholars have long observed that Islam, like other religious traditions, comprises a variety of methods of interpretation. Some maintain that with its diverse traditions of interpretation and jurisprudence, Islam is deeply pluralist and that its texts are polysemic (Barlas 2002; Esposito 2004; Moustafa and Quraishi-Landes 2012). Historically, however, the authority to interpret Islamic texts has been limited to those with particular kinds of formal training, usually men.

In order to describe the two major interpretive approaches to Islam in Indonesia, I draw on Abdullah Saeed's (2005, 3) classification of Quranic interpretation. Contexualists take into account the sociohistorical context of the Quran and/or the context of the contemporary world. Textualists argue for a strict following of the text because they regard the meaning of the Quran as fixed and universal.[17]

Indonesia, therefore, encompasses diverse ways of interpreting and practicing Islam. This history is significant for Muslim women's activism. These different streams of Indonesian Islamic interpretation and practice are tied to specific social and organizational *milieus*. These various milieus structure the field of Islamic politics, which intersects with the field of gender politics. As I show in chapters 2 and 3, Fatayat and Rahima are embedded in the Nahdlatul Ulama milieu, which facilitates a more contextualist approach to interpreting religious texts, while PKS is rooted in a more textualist milieu.

We can therefore see how activist organizations rooted in different Islamic milieus and interacting in the overlapping fields of Islamic politics and gender politics teach women particular approaches to religious texts and practices. Influenced by a more contextualist milieu and an emphasis on interpretation, Fatayat and Rahima women activists develop *pious critical agency*. Their approach allows them to connect their religious beliefs with a women's rights agenda. The assumption that texts can be interpreted differently, and that Islam should be understood in ways that are relevant to contemporary needs, helps to promote a project of reinterpreting and contexualizing texts. In Indonesia and elsewhere, it is historically new that women are becoming so much more involved in the process of doing and discussing interpretation (Gade 2004; Van Doorn-Harder 2006). By interpretation, I mean not just the formal work of interpreting actual texts (although women are involved in such efforts), but a process of public discussion and debate about religious meanings.

In contrast, women in the more textualist milieu of PKS display *pious activating agency*, in which they activate their party's understandings of Islam to work toward a society with stronger public moral regulation. Importantly, I did not encounter much discussion or debate about religious meanings among these women. Pious activating agency can be seen among other activists, but it is the primary mode of agency for PKS women. The assumption that the text's meaning is fixed therefore promotes an agency that involves less debate about meaning. Textualism makes it harder to argue for changes in gender norms, as women are less able to reject conventional interpretations. Nevertheless, it is new to have women so involved in mobilizing the Muslim community and taking on very public roles as Muslim activists.

Pious critical and pious activating agency emerge from Islamic milieus that promote different interpretive approaches. These milieus shape the field of Islamic politics, which has been rejuvenated due to the Islamic revival and democratization. I suggest that pious critical and pious activating agency are prevalent wherever educated Muslims are able to engage actively with scriptures and traditions. This is especially the case today due to the global revival of Islam, the rise of new media, and the spread of Islamic education, all of which have helped to destabilize older forms of religious authority (Turner 2007). Moreover, variations of critical and activating agency are likely to be found in other religious traditions, especially those experiencing changes similar to those in Islam. Taken together, this demonstrates the importance of recognizing religion as a diverse cultural schema that can contribute to different kinds of agency.

ISLAM, FEMINISM, AND AGENCY

Indonesia is a vital place for the study of gender and social change. It is one of the world's largest and most heterogeneous countries, with a history of dynamic political activism, both peaceful and violent. Until recently, Indonesia and Turkey were the only majority Muslim electoral democracies. But they are no longer alone in this endeavor as waves of protest and democratization sweep the Middle East and North Africa. In Indonesia, feminist agency coexists with pious agency. This has facilitated new kinds of women's activism that at times intertwine Islam and feminism despite continuing rhetoric about their incommensurability.

The implications of the Indonesian case are significant for the study of religion and feminism. As this book illustrates, we should not assume that the relationship between religion and feminism is static or dichotomous. Religion and feminism can intersect in unexpected ways depending on the context. Around the world, women in Islam and other religious traditions are using revisionist interpretations of scriptures to make claims for rights and equality. The fact that some religious women reject feminism and some feminists reject religion does not mean that this is the only possible relationship between them. It may in fact be unsurprising that in places where religion is an important aspect of public life, women's rights activism can be infused with religious piety.

Pious critical, pious activating, and feminist agency are three modes of agency that can coexist and overlap. Influenced by different Islamic milieus, they facilitate different kinds of women's activism. These include an activism that combines ideas from Islam and feminism to promote women's rights and egalitarian democracy; an activism that aims at building a more moral society and a greater role for Islam in the state; and an activism that

Figure 1.4: Political poster by Taring Padi, 2005. Translation: "Independent women. Women of the world move forward and unite."

seeks women's rights and economic and social justice (Figure 1.4). The fields of Islamic politics and gender politics increasingly influence each other and this has helped to produce these modes of agency. It is in the overlap between fields, I argue, that the possibilities for agency are especially rich. Certainly, some of the most exciting women activists I came to know—those who creatively intermingle Islam and feminism—are situated squarely in this fertile social terrain.

My fieldwork demonstrates that religion in the public sphere is compatible with various forms of women's mobilization. However, its consequences for gender equality are more complicated and historically contingent. This book shows that activism for women's rights and equality is not necessarily threatened by a more public role for religion. Yet the new modes of women's agency emerging from the Islamic discursive tradition do not always map on to conventional feminist goals. As the example of PKS shows, women do not necessarily use their agency to promote equality or liberation. Transformations of social structures are not always emancipatory (Jeffery and Basu 1997; Mahmood 2005; Sewell 2005). But just as agency is not necessarily progressive, religious agency is not necessarily regressive.

It is also important to note the class dimensions of pious critical and pious activating agency. Sociologists since Weber have noted the "elective affinity" between the middle classes and (primarily Christian) religious piety. Weber's argument was that Protestant piety instilled discipline and a methodical approach to living that allowed people to feel ethical while pursuing material success (Weber 2001). In Indonesia, piety has also become especially prevalent among the urban middle class. The women in this study are in fact mostly middle class. This reflects the fact that the women's movement in Indonesia, as in many countries, has been mostly composed of middle-class women (Blackburn 2008). Just as the emerging European middle class began to define itself by its pious Protestant work ethic, so too Islamic piety seems to become a way for many middle-class women activists in Indonesia to define themselves and to become credible political actors. The women in this book embody different ways of being pious and middle class which are learned and practiced at least partly through their activism.

The Indonesian women activists I came to know inventively adapt Islam and feminism to advocate changes and to participate in their country's process of democratization. Religion was a crucial aspect of the activism of many of these women. Religion is a cultural schema that these women are embedded in and use differently depending on their social context and milieu. The case of Indonesia helps to illuminate how the Islamic revival interacts with and even fuels some women's aims for social transformation. In Indonesia, new kinds of agency are producing activism that cuts across the boundaries of religious and secular and expands women's involvement in national debates about religion, gender, and the future of the nation.

INDONESIAN WOMEN ACTIVISTS: TRAJECTORIES, MEANINGS, AND PUBLIC INTERVENTIONS

In a context where the Islamic revival and women's equality can seem to be at odds, the themes that drive this book are how Indonesian women connect Islam and feminism, and what their engagements with these frameworks tell us about emerging modes of agency in Muslim contexts. The empirical chapters are case studies of different connections between Islam and feminism. In each chapter, I explore how women became involved with an organization, their individual and collective understandings of Islam and feminism, their activism and ideals for Indonesia's future, and the modes of agency they embody.

Chapter 2 provides historical background for women's activism and Islam in Indonesia. I first sketch out the landscape of Islamic politics and gender politics in twentieth-century Indonesia. I show how Islam has intersected with women's movements and chart the rise of feminism and women's involvement in Muslim activism. The second part of this chapter situates the four organizations in this study within the Indonesian political and religious context.

Chapter 3 examines Rahima, a Muslim women's rights NGO, and Fatayat NU, the women's wing of Indonesia's largest Muslim organization. These groups are involved in efforts to bring ideas of women's rights into Muslim communities. In this chapter, I examine how the activists of Rahima and Fatayat demonstrate *pious critical agency* as they seek out Islamic justifications for gender equality. The chapter examines how they draw on discourses of transnational feminism and Islamic reformism, as well as Indonesia's Islamic heritage, to argue for women's rights and religious reform. Their contextual approach to religious texts allows for flexibility in interpretation, and their egalitarian understandings of Islam sustain group members' beliefs about women's rights.

The example of Fatayat and Rahima demonstrates that Islamic piety can be compatible with ideas of women's rights and equality. In synthesizing Islam and feminism, they represent a global trend for women to become more directly involved in interpreting religious texts. In the process, they are constructing a new middle-class Muslim womanhood based on more egalitarian gender relations.

Chapter 4 looks at women in the Prosperous Justice Party. PKS maintains that Islamic ideals should be the source for law and government policy. The party advocates cultural change to conform to Islamic norms, a process I and others call Islamization.

The women in PKS demonstrate *pious activating agency* and the complexities of political Islam. The party emphasizes women's domestic roles and attracts many female supporters. Women in PKS largely reject feminism as Western and secular and agree that women have greater responsibility in the domestic sphere. The party's textualist but pragmatic approach to Islam permits women to have careers and be involved in politics. Women's mobilization of the party's interpretations of Islam allows them to work toward a society with stronger public moral regulation, but the policies they advocate sometimes conflict with feminist goals of rights and empowerment for women.

Pious activating agency helps to create a fresh role for women in Islamist politics. Through their involvement in the party, PKS women construct modern middle-class selves and help to forge a collective identity based on particular kinds of pious practices and religious interpretations. The textualist approach leaves PKS women with a limited toolkit. But women feel empowered by their activism and they have helped to open up public space for devout women. Nevertheless, the party's goal of Islamizing Indonesia has the potential to marginalize others.

Chapter 5 examines women in a feminist NGO, Solidaritas Perempuan. Solidaritas Perempuan advocates for the rights of women who migrate overseas to work as domestics and also aims to build a broader women's rights movement in Indonesia. SP activists come from diverse backgrounds but once they join SP they are inculcated with a globally oriented feminism. This occurs via trainings and work experiences where they learn about human rights and equality and come to see themselves as part of a transnational movement for women's rights.

SP is the only group in this study that does not make religious arguments in its activism, though some of its staff members are pious Muslims. Influenced by diverse feminist and socialist thinkers, the organization adapts transnational discourses, especially human rights, to press its claims for social reforms and gender equality. Yet SP's *feminist agency* is inclusive of Islamic piety. Staff mobilize their Islamic identities and appeal to local histories and cultures to legitimize their call for equality. Conforming to the increasingly Muslim norms of the Indonesian public sphere sometimes requires SP staff to downplay their feminist identities. Nevertheless, the example of SP demonstrates that feminist activism can coexist with Islam.

Chapter 6 concludes by discussing the implications the Indonesian case has for understanding religion and politics in the contemporary world, especially the consequences of a more public Islam for women's activism and agency. Through their educations, social networks, and activist organizations, women develop distinct modes of agency that incorporate Islam and feminism in different ways. Feminist agency, pious critical agency, and pious activating agency facilitate women activists' diverse political visions. The first two are oriented toward a more egalitarian democracy, while the third is oriented toward building a society with stronger moral regulation.

The consequences of the Islamic revival for women's agency and equality are complex and certainly not yet resolved. While middle-class pious women feel empowered by their political activism, lower-class Indonesian women's lives do not seem to have changed much, although many of them are also pious. They remain poor and lack political power. Just as important, few women activists have addressed the increasing dominance of Islam in the Indonesian public sphere, a development that threatens to marginalize nonreligious and non-Muslim citizens. In addition, as this study of Indonesia makes clear, women's involvement in the public sphere does not necessarily translate to women having equality. Empowered women activists don't necessarily work for progressive social change or equality.

Public visibility should not be mistaken for the power to bring about social change, though the women in this study are indeed making changes, both personal and collective.

In Indonesia, Islam underpins very different moral visions for Indonesia's future. Democratization has helped to provide a more public role for Islam. Islam enables new modes of agency that are compatible with a wide range of women's mobilization, including challenges to gender hierarchies. Such a perspective is especially important for understanding social change in Muslim settings because it reveals how the multiplicity of the Islamic revival has catalyzed diverse forms of women activists' agency.

The framework I present here can be used to study many kinds of religious activism. The increasing influence of religion in the public sphere in many countries has generated profound concerns about the rights of women. Yet if we understand religion as a cultural schema that encompasses multiple meanings that people interpret and practice in different ways, then it is possible to see how religion and feminism can conflict, coexist, and even intersect.

CHAPTER 2

Islamic Politics and Gender Politics in Indonesia

A Nation in Waiting (1999) or *Land of Contrasts* (2011):[1] The vague titles of books and documentaries testify to how difficult it is to generalize about the vast Indonesian archipelago, the world's fourth-largest country. Nearly 90% of its 240 million people are Muslim, yet it is not an Islamic state. Christian minorities dominate some areas of the country, and there are significant numbers of Hindus, Buddhists, Confucians, and animists. The country has some of the world's wealthiest tycoons, but as of 2010 approximately 46% of its people lived on less than two dollars a day (World Bank).[2]

Indonesia's turbulent twentieth century was distinguished by an anticolonial revolution, struggles between Islam and nationalism, an economic boom and the rise of a middle class, and an expanding public role for women. Given the recent concerns about Islam and women's rights, the influence of Islam in the Indonesian public sphere calls for a historicized examination. In this chapter, I trace the rise of the discrete fields of Islamic and gender politics to understand how their relationship is significant for contemporary women's activism. As discussed in chapter 1, Islamic politics is the field of actors striving to bring about a more Islamic society, through a variety of means. Gender politics is the field of political negotiations about gender and can include actors who challenge gender inequality, attempt to help women in a variety of ways, and who may or may not seek to maintain conventional gender norms. Historical analysis shows that although there have always been connections between these fields, particularly because of the existence of Muslim women's organizations, by the end of the century they developed more extensive intersections. Finally, in this chapter I also discuss the background of the organizations in this study—Solidaritas Perempuan, Rahima, Fatayat NU, and the Prosperous Justice Party—situating them in their political and cultural context.

I consider Islamic and gender politics in four eras: the Nationalist Awakening (1911–1928), the Sukarno regime (1945–1965), the Suharto regime (1965–1998), and the post-Suharto period (1998–present). My analysis focuses most closely on the transformations of the Suharto era and the years following.

What is evident from this discussion is that during much of the twentieth century Islam played a modernizing role in Indonesia. Intersecting fields of Islamic and gender politics first emerged in the nationalist era and continue to be influential in public life. The nationalist movement fostered women's groups, as did early Muslim organizations. Later, the postcolonial state promoted limited rights for women while also mobilizing them in support of national development, but Islamic politics stagnated. In recent decades, Islamic politics and gender politics became more dynamic and intertwined. Muslim civil society groups, as well as the rise of state-supported Islamic institutions in the 1980s and 1990s, helped advance middle-class Muslim women's activism, while global processes boosted the influence of transnational feminism. Democratization since 1998 has meant that women have newfound freedom to organize, and this era has seen increasing interchange between Islamic politics and gender politics.

ISLAM AND GENDER IN INDONESIA

First, a brief introduction to Islam and gender in Indonesia is essential. Beginning in the 1400s, Sunni Muslim merchants from the Middle East and the Indian subcontinent brought Islam to port towns throughout the Malay archipelago. By the time agents of the Dutch East India Company arrived to colonize the archipelago in the early 1600s, much of Java and Sumatra had converted from Hinduism to Islam.

Indonesian Islam has often been portrayed by Western observers as "syncretic," mixed with mystical pre-Islamic beliefs and practices (Fuller 2002). It is probably better characterized by multiplicity. While parts of Sumatra and Sulawesi have long had extensive contacts with the Middle East, Java has been known for fusing Islam and Javanese rituals, and many Javanese Muslim thinkers have been inspired by Sufism. While the Quran and the Hadiths[3] are central to all Islamic traditions, Indonesian and Southeast Asian Islam have also emphasized *fikh*—or Islamic jurisprudence, in which the rulings of Islamic jurists are interpreted by trained scholars. More recently, this older emphasis has combined with a concern for *itjihad*, the application of reason to understanding Islamic texts.[4] Of the four traditional Sunni schools of Islamic jurisprudence (*madzhab*), mainstream Indonesian Muslim scholars tend to adhere to the *Syafi'i* school. In Indonesia, Islam requires education for true access. Because classical Arabic is the language of the Quran, few Indonesians are able to read the texts themselves.[5]

Anthropologist Clifford Geertz (1960) famously divided Javanese Muslim practice into three categories: *priyayi* (the upper class influenced by Hinduism and Buddhism), *santri* (the merchant class who practiced what they considered to be a more orthodox version of Islam), and *abangan* (nonstandard Islamic practitioners).[6] These categories are now challenged by some scholars but they continue to be used in Indonesia. Later scholars further categorized pious Indonesian Muslims as traditionalists and modernists, though these labels are also contested (Barton and Fealy 1996). Traditionalists, best represented by the organization Nahdlatul Ulama, are considered to be those who most emphasize the "interpretive" aspects of Islam, especially *fikh*; draw on texts and narratives other than the Quran to use as guides for practice; and tolerate or promote Javanese rituals. Indonesian modernists are influenced by the early twentieth-century reformist movement that arose in Egypt, which sought to reconcile Islam with contemporary science and technology. Modernists also de-emphasize traditional Islamic authorities in favor of a more individual, but also stricter interpretive approach to religious texts.

If Islam has been differentiated by region in Indonesia, sex/gender systems have as well. Indonesia's diverse ethnic and linguistic groups comprise a variety of kinship structures and gender practices. It was once common for scholars to argue that, relative to women in other parts of the world, women in Indonesian societies have enjoyed somewhat more economic independence and freedom of movement (H. Geertz 1961). More recent scholarship suggests that while gender differences may be somewhat less significant in Indonesia than class and status, spatial mobility should not be equated with power (Errington 1990). Though Southeast Asian gender systems seem to have been historically characterized by fluidity, the changes brought by modernity have shaped a more binary system of sex and gender (Peletz 2009). Contemporary Javanese gender ideology, which is influential throughout the country, idealizes submissive, self-sacrificing women, even though such notions coexist uneasily with a daily reality in which many women are educated and work outside the home (Brenner 1998, 1999). Tickamyer and Kusujiarti (2012) characterize this situation as a "gender paradox," in which potential sources of women's power are undermined by a state-reinforced, patriarchal gender ideology that limits women's autonomy.

Indonesian Islam has often emphasized women's domestic roles and exalted motherhood, but it has rarely prohibited women from taking on public roles (Blackburn 2004). In the past few decades, a growing number of Indonesian women have become avid public practitioners of Islam, with some specializing in Quranic recitation and thousands acting as Muslim preachers, interpreters, and proselytizers. Van Doorn-Harder (2006) argues that the presence of so many female specialists of Islam distinguishes Indonesia from most other Muslim majority countries.

Islam has provided an important source of discourse regarding women's roles in Indonesia, but it is not the only one. Islamic interpretations and influences coexist in people's lives with other allegiances and identities, such as class and ethnicity, the state, and other religions. Although Islam and nationalism have sometimes been at odds in Indonesia, both have produced opportunities for women's mobilization.

THE NATIONAL AWAKENING (1911–1928)

The era known as the National Awakening was a time of intellectual ferment. The National Awakening saw the rise of nationalism, communism, and Islamic politics. The emergence of women's activism in the Dutch colony also marked the beginning of the field of gender politics.

As in many colonies, nationalism in Indonesia developed among elites, especially the Javanese upper class, who were permitted to attend Dutch schools. This background shaped the intersections between nationalism and Islam, as Islam came to be used as a discourse of anticolonialism and as rhetoric against elites. The struggles between nationalism and Islam during this period were a precursor for the rest of the century (Shiraishi 1990).

The first native political organization, Budi Utomo, was formed in 1908 by upper-class Javanese, including doctors and government officials. Its sister organization, Putri Mardika, was the first native women's organization. Thus, the emerging women's movement was tied to nationalist mobilization, and it was also clearly a movement of elite women.

It soon became evident that Islam would have a role in the nationalist movement. The first nationalist organization to win mass support was Sarekat Islam, which began in 1912 as an association of Javanese Muslim batik traders. By 1919, Sarekat Islam claimed a membership of nearly 2.5 million, though these numbers have been disputed (Kahin

1952). Nevertheless, by 1921, the organization split due to strife between Marxists and Muslims (Hefner 2000).

A Sarekat Islam protégé named Sukarno helped to establish the Partai National Indonesia in 1927. The party's aim was complete independence for Indonesia, which it argued could only come about through noncooperation with the Dutch. Kahin (1952) describes Sukarno, who became Indonesia's first president, as having a unique ability to synthesize Islamic discourses with Western ideologies such as Marxism and intellectual influences from contemporaneous nationalist movements. According to Hefner (2000), most Muslims at the time supported the nationalists. However, many also hoped that Islam would become the basis of the new nation.

In the early twentieth century, a wave of Muslim reformism swept the country. Ahmad Dahlan, inspired by Egyptian modernizers like Mohammad Abduh, established Indonesia's first mass Muslim organization, Muhammadiyah, in 1912. Dahlan viewed the modernization of Islam as the best means for struggling against colonial rule. Early Muhammadiyah members were batik producers and traders in Central Javanese cities like Yogyakarta.

In 1917, Muhammadiyah established Aisyiyah, the first Indonesian Muslim women's organization. Aisyiyah promoted literacy and religious education for girls and women, at a time when few Indonesians were sent to school. Aisyiyah women wore the veil, uncommon at the time in Indonesia. The group's first major project was the construction of a Muslim preschool.[7] Unlike similar schools in the Middle East, this school was coeducational, though children were taught to behave in ways considered appropriate to their gender (Van Doorn-Harder 2006, 95).

Aisyiyah was named after the Prophet Muhammad's favorite wife, a woman who was economically independent and a religious authority in her own right but also obedient to her husband. Likewise, Aisyiyah as an organization was subservient to Muhammadiyah. Though some Aisyiyah activists privately opposed polygamy, in public they stressed that women must comply with the wishes of their husbands. Van Doorn-Harder (2006) proposes that the rigid gender roles imposed on Aisyiyah limited its leaders' influence in Muhammadiyah.

In reaction to reformist trends, a group of Javanese Muslim leaders formed the Nahdlatul Ulama (NU) in 1926 to safeguard Javanese Islamic traditions. NU's base was the rural areas of central and eastern Java. NU leaders supported the nationalists, though they also hoped for an Islamic state. Women were excluded from the socially conservative NU until 1946, when the organization established Muslimat, a group for women over forty. In 1950, Fatayat was created for women in their twenties and thirties.[8] Over the course of the twentieth century, Muhammadiyah and NU became the leading representatives of Indonesian Islam and competed for political influence. Both organizations continue to be mainstays of religious life in Indonesia.

By the mid-1920s many nationalist parties had also established women's branches. Nationalist men supported women's suffrage and the expansion of women's education because, like other nationalists in the developing world, they associated the advancement of women with modernity and progress (Jayawardena 1986). Women did not have leadership roles in the nationalist movement, but as Martyn (2005) argues, they had their own legitimate public spaces where they were able to develop their own ideas and activities.

Secular and Muslim women's groups made up the new field of gender politics. Secular women's groups were small and composed of elite women. Religious groups like Aisyiyah were larger, but their leaders were still elite compared to most of the population (Locher-Scholten 2000). However, the field of gender politics was divided. Women's groups were fragmented along ideological lines, with the most important split falling between Muslims and secular nationalists. Polygamy was one of the most divisive issues. Nevertheless, women's groups had many similarities: nearly all conceptualized women primarily as mothers; they supported girls' education and women's suffrage but believed the vote should be restricted to the educated; and they shared a commitment to *kemajuan* (progress) (Locher-Scholten 2000; Martyn 2005). Women now had the choice to mobilize around Islam and/or nationalism, although these options were generally limited to the educated.

The emergence of reformist Islam provided new space for women because of its emphasis on education and modernization. As Martyn writes, "In Aisjijah (*sic*) for example, women were not just the educators and reproducers of the nation but also had to teach women about Islam so they would produce good Muslims" (Martyn 2005, 37). By 1939, Aisyiyah was estimated to have twelve thousand members, dwarfing secular women's groups (Blackburn 2004). Because education was so limited at this time, one can imagine that the group's members were probably among the most prosperous and educated Muslims. Yet Aisyiyah marked the first time that Muslim women were mobilized as women. Thus, this period saw the emergence of linked fields of Islamic politics and gender politics, though there were significant divisions within both. The rise of reformist Islam and an inclusive nationalism made it possible for women of the nascent middle class to become educated and involved in public life.

After Indonesia declared independence from the Netherlands in 1945 and through the end of the revolution in 1949, tensions between Muslims and secular nationalists continued. Communism also emerged as a major challenge to Muslim visions for the country. In the 1945 constitution, nationalism took priority over Islam. By the 1960s, the fields of Islamic politics and gender politics diverged.

The Jakarta Charter, which both Muhammadiyah and NU supported, was a preamble to the constitution that would have required all Muslims to abide by Islamic *Shariah* law. After intense protests from Christian regions, the new leadership of President Sukarno and Vice President Mohammad Hatta replaced the Jakarta Charter with Pancasila as the governing moral philosophy of the country. The first of Pancasila's five tenets, "Belief in the one and only God," was felt to include adherents of the major religions in Indonesia, yet still satisfy Islamic monotheism.[9] NU's leader, Wahid Hasyim, supported the compromise, yet still hoped that the state would eventually be based on Islam (Feillard 1997).

During the Sukarno regime (1945–1965), it became clear that the Indonesian political class was divided into nationalist/secular/Christian, modernist Muslim (typified by Muhammadiyah), and traditionalist Muslim (typified by NU) strands, which Indonesians referred to as *aliran*. *Aliran* denotes ideological streams organized around religion, as well as class and education. Sidel (2001, 2006) argues that *aliran* were rooted in different networks of education. Traditionalist Muslims who attended *pesantren* (Muslim boarding schools) were largely shut out of political life, while modernist Muslims who attended *madrassah* (Islamic day schools) were funneled into the growing modernist Muslim political party Masyumi. Meanwhile, graduates of secular state schools or prestigious Christian missionary schools were channeled into the university system, the military, and the state bureaucracy.

The 1955 elections are considered a watershed moment in Indonesian political history because they mark the high point of Muslim political parties. They were also the country's last free election until 1999. The result was a standoff between the two main Muslim parties and their nationalist and Communist rivals. The Nationalist Party won 22.3% of the vote, Masyumi 20.9%, NU 18.4%, and the Communist Party (PKI) 16.4% (Hefner 2000).

The elections were soon overshadowed by a major rebellion within the military ranks, which grew to encompass Muslim separatists in Sulawesi and West Java. Once the rebellion was put down, Muslim leaders who had supported it were marginalized from national politics.

In 1959, Sukarno declared that Indonesia would operate under the rubric of Guided Democracy, signaling an end to the relatively free political atmosphere. NU supported the initiative, but Masyumi opposed it, and soon Indonesia's largest Muslim political party was banned. Muslim influence in politics entered into a period of decline. Rivalries between Muslims and Communists intensified, with Muslim student groups engaging in daily street fights with Communist youth.

How did this polarization affect the field of gender politics? After independence, women's groups were optimistic, as women had achieved constitutional equality. Activists across the spectrum worked to educate women about their political rights and responsibilities. Nevertheless, important issues, especially polygamy, remained unresolved (Martyn 2005).

Secular women's groups hoped for a ban on polygamy and to bring more women into politics. Meanwhile, Muslim women's groups worked on religious education and supported their respective organizations' campaigns for an Islamic state. Muslim women's groups felt bound to defend what they considered to be Islamic practices like polygamy from state interference (Locher-Scholten 2000; Blackburn 2004; Martyn 2005).

Secular organizations dominated gender politics during the Sukarno era, though they were disappointed by the president's marriage to a second wife (Martyn 2005) and the state's failure to revamp the marriage laws. A growing number of lower-class women were also involved in the Communist PKI's women's group Gerwani, which attempted to reconcile conventional notions of motherhood with the expansion of space for women in politics (Blackburn 2004).

Indonesian nation building provided women, especially those in secular groups with links to nationalist parties, with new opportunities to participate in formal politics. Maria Ullfah Santoso became the first female cabinet minister in 1945 and rose to head of the cabinet in 1956. Kongres Wanita Indonesia (KOWANI) was established in 1950 as a national umbrella organization for the women's movement.

Nevertheless, Martyn (2005) maintains that nation building took resources from women's groups. Women's groups spent time and money on nationalist efforts rather than initiatives to benefit women (Blackburn 2004). For example, even Muslim women's groups such as Fatayat participated in Sukarno's mass mobilizations in the early 1960s when Indonesia was asserting its right to control over the province of West Papua and during Indonesia's confrontation with Malaysia. These mobilizations provided military training for thousands of youth, male and female, to prepare them to defend the unity of the nation. A photograph included in Fatayat's history booklet depicts members of the group in military training during this time. Clasping rifles, they wear traditional *batik* skirts and the traditional veil, *kerudung*.

The political climate of the Sukarno regime did not advance Muslim politics. Van Doorn-Harder (2006) describes Muhammadiyah as increasingly hostile to new ideas in the decades following independence, while NU occupied the confrontational fringes. Secular nationalism was hegemonic, but communism was a rising force. As the field of Islamic politics stagnated, gender politics was increasingly defined by secular actors. Yet women's empowerment was limited. Women made up a tiny percentage of members of parliament, and they were sidelined to the realms of education and health. The image of a woman activist during the Sukarno years was that of an unveiled and elite woman such as Mariah Ullfah Santoso.

THE SUHARTO ERA: 1965–1998

The long regime of Suharto was one of both repression and transformation. It modernized Indonesia's economy, but at great cost to civil freedom and democratic participation. Initially, religion was marginalized from the public sphere, but eventually the state supported an Islamic revival. Islamic practices and interpretations were diverse, though by the end of the period, conservative interpretations seemed to be on the rise. Yet *aliran* determined one's position in the public sphere, and many Muslims felt excluded from mainstream politics. Women were mobilized into state-controlled organizations that de-emphasized religious identities. Pious Muslim women were marginal in the early years of the regime, but they became more empowered with the return of religion to the public sphere from the 1980s onward. By fostering an Islamic revival, the Suharto regime unwittingly helped create a Muslim civil society that produced a new generation of activists interested in ideas such as democracy, gender equality, and human rights. After years of quiescence, Islamic politics and gender politics began to intersect once again.

Islam and the Public Sphere under Suharto

Suharto's New Order regime was born out of mass killings and the violent eradication of communism. The Communist PKI claimed a membership of three million, with another fifteen million indirectly affiliated to it through labor unions, peasant associations, and other affiliates (Hefner 2000).

The murder of six senior army generals in September 1965 by junior army officers was blamed on a coup attempt by the PKI. Under the control of General Suharto, the army, militia groups, and ordinary citizens purged suspected communists, killing an estimated half-million people and destroying the PKI. Sukarno was forced to transfer political and military power to Suharto. In March 1967, the parliament named Suharto acting president. The events of 1965–1967 ended popular mobilization and returned control to the nationalist elite (Ricklefs 2008).

Muslim organizations supported the purge—NU's youth organization Ansor participated in rounding up and killing suspected communists. But NU's high hopes for the Suharto regime were soon thwarted by the lack of a formal role for Islam in the state.

The New Order state immediately attempted to manage religion, requiring all Indonesians to declare adherence to one of five official religions. In the wake of the turmoil, millions rushed to declare a religion to avoid being charged with atheism, which was associated with communism (Sidel 2006). Some Javanese converted to Christianity, which was viewed as more sympathetic to ex-Communists (Hefner 2000). These events, along with the marginalization of Muslims from politics, fostered competition for converts. New organizations emerged such as Dewan Dakwah Islamiyah Indonesia (DDII), created in 1967. DDII focused on religious education, proselytizing, and building religious schools and mosques, while also promulgating a more conservative way of practicing Islam. DDII found its greatest success in converting the waves of Muslim migrants to large cities in the 1970s (Sidel 2006).

State policies helped lay the groundwork for religious revival: "...New government regulations requiring all citizens to declare their faith, expanding religious classes in state schools, and impeding interfaith marriages strengthened the public markers and boundaries of religious identities" (Sidel 2006, 51). As Sidel contends, in the years following 1965, millions of lower-class Indonesians came to understand themselves as Muslims (p. 53).

Nevertheless, the government also repressed a small but growing Islamist movement in the 1970s and 1980s. After years of tensions with the government, NU decided in 1984 to withdraw from electoral politics. Gradually, the effect of NU's decision was that the organization became more integrated into mainstream society, dropped the call for an Islamic state, built public legitimacy, and improved its relations with the government (Feillard 1997).

Fascinatingly, this move away from party politics occurred at a time of revitalization of Islamic politics. In the 1970s and 1980s, Muslim intellectuals like Abdurrahman Wahid and Nurcholish Majid were developing new interpretations of religious teachings, as well as ideas about integrating

Islam with democratic institutions. Madjid's call, "Islam yes, Islamic parties no!" was taken up both by a generation of Muslim activists and by the government to advocate "cultural Islam," an alternative to political Islam. Van Doorn-Harder (2006) also suggests that the surge of progressive thought within NU was due to the organization's grounding in traditionalist Islam, which permitted scholars to seek out a broad swath of Islamic heritage rather than referring only to select texts, as was the case for the modernists of Muhammadiyah.

In the 1980s, the Suharto regime embarked on a program to promote "cultural Islam." The government encouraged Muslim content on state radio and television, banned lotteries, supported the creation of an Islamic bank, and funded Quranic recitation competitions. Some of these new policies were responses to mobilizations by Muslim groups demanding such reforms. Suharto himself gradually adopted a more pious personal style, culminating in a *haj* pilgrimage in 1991. Additionally, the state funded the building of mosques and prayer houses and created a system of Muslim day schools (*madrassah*, modeled on Muhammadiyah's modernist schools) to compete with traditional Muslim boarding schools. The government also established a system of state Islamic universities (Meuleman 2003).

As in other majority Muslim countries, the combination of state promotion of religion and the increased opening to global flows of culture resulted in a decentralization of religious authority (Turner 2007). While religious knowledge was once concentrated among traditional scholars, now anyone could send his or her child to Muslim educational institutions or to afterschool Arabic classes. Nevertheless, Islam continued to be perceived by many, especially the lower and middle classes, as a discourse of opposition to elites and the state (Sidel 2006).

Transnational flows of Islam were also becoming increasingly important in the 1980s. The *Tarbiyah* (Islamic education) movement arose on university campuses in the 1970s and 1980s, a result of students returning from scholarships to study in the Middle East. While a long-standing program with the Egyptian government has sent Indonesian students to Egypt since the 1950s, DDII and other groups began to send students to Saudi Arabia and Pakistan in the 1970s. Influenced by the Egyptian Muslim Brotherhood, the students came to reject any separation between religion and politics and aimed to Islamize every area of society. Returnees formed campus groups to spread *dakwah* (religious call) among their fellow students, encouraging them to adopt what they considered to be proper Islamic practice, especially prayer and veiling. The *Tarbiyah* movement also promoted a textual approach to the Quran that emphasized fixed and universal meanings (Machmudi 2008). The movement spread across the country and came to constitute a crucial network of student activism.

By the late 1980s, the New Order state's efforts to promote Islam, coupled with an economic boom, resulted in the ascendance of pious Muslims to the urban lower middle and middle classes (Sidel 2006). As revivalist Islam saturated the public sphere and spread via educational institutions and the media, it came to be equated with modernity by many believers. Islam was not a tradition they had left behind in their villages but rather constituted part of their new urban, modern lives. Nevertheless, the Muslim middle class felt blocked by secular and Christian elites who held political and economic power (Sidel 2006). An important change, however, was a series of shifts in education policy, so that by the 1990s graduates of Muslim schools could attend state universities (Azra, Afrianty, and Hefner 2007).

Also in the early 1990s, the government began to sponsor the Association of Indonesian Muslim Intellectuals (ICMI). ICMI marked the return of Islamic politics. With Suharto himself opening ICMI's annual conference and with leading government ministers participating, it was now legitimate for Muslim organizations to be politically active. Over the next few years, Muslim groups of all kinds, especially student organizations, began discussing democracy, gender equality, human rights, and pluralism, inspired by the ideas of intellectuals such as Abdurrahman Wahid of NU. By the mid-1990s, national Muslim student groups like Himpunan Mahasiswa Indonesia (HMI, associated with modernists) and Pergerakan Mahasiswa Islam Indonesia (PMII, associated with NU) were working in coalitions with women's groups and other social justice activists (Madrid 1999; Hefner 2000).

By the mid-1990s, a growing democratic reform movement included many young Muslims. Hefner maintains that the New Order government, in an effort to split the opposition, attempted to co-opt religious forces. According to Hefner, the state and elements of the military covertly funded and promoted extremist Muslim groups. Moreover, the state ignored the financial assistance some of these organizations received from Saudi Arabia and other foreign sources. These developments may have helped to lay the groundwork for the violence that plagued Indonesia in the early 2000s (Hefner 2000; Sidel 2006).

As Indonesia became integrated into the global economy, there were increasing influences from transnational Islam. Books, tracts, and cassettes by Middle Eastern Muslim figures flowed into stores and markets, conveying new ideas about what constitutes proper Muslim practice and how Islam should be integrated into society. While some Indonesians were drawn to ideas of human rights and democracy, others were enticed by visions of jihad or an Islamic state. Even within mainstream circles, the works of Sayyid Qutb, the inspiration of the contemporary jihadist movement, were widely read (Van Doorn-Harder 2006).

At the onset of the New Order regime, the field of Islamic politics was stagnant. Pious Muslims were economically weak and politically marginalized. But by the end of the Suharto regime, Islamic politics was revitalized. The revival of Islamic intellectual discourse brought new conservative and progressive Muslim voices into the public sphere.

Women and the Public Sphere in the New Order

Women's activism was one of the most significant casualties of the Suharto regime. Nevertheless, by the 1990s, middle-class women were moving into educational institutions and the formal workforce. The field of gender politics became more dynamic as an independent women's movement emerged, and intersections with Islamic politics expanded as young women were drawn to Islamic activism.

From the beginning, the New Order regime's plans for modernization were predicated on Western models,[10] and initiatives to reshape family life were a centerpiece of its programs. The regime sought to forge a restricted and masculinized public sphere, while women were identified with the private sphere. As Brenner asserts in *The Domestication of Desire* (1998), her account of social and economic change in a Central Javanese city in the 1990s:

> The insistence on the separation of workplace and home is accompanied by gender ideologies that associate women primarily with the domestic work of caring for the family, and men with the task of going out of the home to the workplace to earn a living for their families. Although it is recognized that women may also work outside the home to "supplement their husbands' incomes," their foremost duty is to tend to their husbands' needs, nurture the family, and socialize their children to become loyal and obedient citizens of the nation-state—as well as good consumers, one of the keys to promoting capitalist development...In short, the domestic sphere is being recast ideologically to fit an image that more closely resembles the stereotypes of American middle-class family life in the 1950s than any social reality in Java's (or Indonesia's history). (pp. 238–240)

Beginning in the 1970s, millions of Indonesian women were mobilized into state-controlled organizations, the most significant of which were

Dharma Wanita and the Family Welfare Initiative (PKK).[11] Dharma Wanita was a mandatory organization for the wives of government employees. Members were ranked according to their husbands' grades, and the activities of the group focused especially on teaching domestic skills to lower-class women. Dharma Wanita's Five Duties for Women included being companions for their husbands, producing future generations, being mothers and educators of children, being managers of the household and contributors to the household income, and being good citizens (Van Doorn-Harder 2006, 44).

PKK operated in a similar fashion but was primarily located in villages and concerned more with supporting government health initiatives, including family planning. Though the label "secular" was taboo after 1965 because of its association with communism, religion was not on the agenda of Dharma Wanita or PKK.

Indonesian feminist Julia Suryakusuma characterized the Suharto regime's gender ideology as "State Ibuism" (Ibu is the Indonesian word for married woman or mother). Suryakusuma (1996) argued that State Ibuism sought to define women first and foremost as wives in order to exert control over women and reproduction. Other scholars like Brenner (1998) suggest that the New Order's gender policies reflected its aim to maintain control over a massive archipelago. Nevertheless, the regime's policies toward women were contradictory. While middle-class women were domesticated, lower-class women were marshaled to work in the expanding export manufacturing sector or recruited for domestic service jobs overseas.

Attempts at activism from within the state women's organizations culminated in the 1974 Marriage Law. Secular women's groups had been campaigning for a ban on polygamy since the 1930s. Such reforms now suited the Suharto regime's emphasis on modernization. Moreover, Suharto wanted to ensure women's organizations' support for his development agenda, especially family planning, which aimed to reduce the number of children to two or three per family. The new law declared monogamy to be the norm for marriage and limited the conditions under which men whose religion permitted polygamy would be allowed to marry another wife. It raised the minimum age at marriage to sixteen for women and nineteen for men. Civil service employees were required to seek permission from their superiors if they wanted a divorce or a polygamous marriage, making it quite difficult. The law also stipulated that the husband was the head of the family and the breadwinner, while the wife was in charge of the household. While women activists at the time were apparently satisfied with the legislation, later generations grew more critical of the gendered implications of the law (Suryakusuma 1996; Blackburn 2004). Despite the domesticating aspects of state-controlled women's groups, they helped to create a precedent for middle-class women's activism (Rinaldo 2002; Anwar 2004).

The government was also compelled by international developments to pay lip service to women's rights. It created the Ministry for Women's Role in 1978 and ratified the Convention on the Elimination of All Forms of Discrimination against Women in 1984. By the 1990s, some leaders of Dharma Wanita and staff of the ministry began to adopt the languages of women's empowerment and gender equality (Blackburn 2004; Robinson 2009).

In the meantime, middle-class women were increasingly drawn to Islam. Many of these women were beneficiaries of the expansion of education, especially the increase in government scholarships. They also experienced Indonesia's economic development firsthand. Growing up in lower-class families, they took advantage of new opportunities to attend state or Muslim universities, and many sought professional jobs upon graduation.

By the late 1980s, a growing number of Indonesian women were adopting the Arabic-style headscarf, known as the *jilbab*. Headscarves had never been common in most of Indonesia, even among pious Muslims. The traditional form of veiling on Java did not fully cover the hair and was worn only for religious holidays in most parts of the archipelago. The new *jilbab* completely covered the hair, neck, and shoulders. It was considered by many to be a symbol of political Islam, and it was banned from public schools and government offices. Young women began to organize demonstrations against the prohibition, and in 1991, the government repealed it. It was one of the first instances of women's antistate mobilization during the New Order.

Although there was pressure from Muslim groups for women to adopt modest clothing and maintain conventional gender roles, Brenner (1996) argues that many young women saw in Islam a more modern form of womanhood. They rejected the state's definitions of modernity, as well as their own cultural traditions, which they regarded as provincial. They considered Islam a more cosmopolitan discourse. The *jilbab* was a symbol of a resurgent Islam that emphasized a global community of Muslims, but also a marker of opposition to the state.

At the same time, a new women's rights movement was emerging. In the 1980s, a few activists took advantage of government loopholes to form NGOs. They were inspired by the United Nations International Women's Conferences and by visits to Australia and India, where they came into contact with social movement activists. The new organizations obtained funding from international sources such as UNICEF, Oxfam, and the Ford Foundation, all of which were starting to prioritize women's rights in their donor agendas. A generation of activists arose through these NGOs, and some established new initiatives in the 1990s. Many of the new women's NGOs took a critical stance toward the government (Blackburn 2004; Brenner 2005).[12]

The discourse of women's rights and gender equality spread to Muslim women's groups. Some of my Fatayat informants recall attending gender trainings funded by the Ford Foundation as early as 1992 or 1993. While Fatayat traditionally focused on community service and education, by the mid-1990s it was emphasizing women's empowerment and rights, and it was also obtaining funding for its programs from international sources.

These activists were also part of a global trend for Muslim women to seek a greater role in the interpretation of religion. Groups like Sisters in Islam in Malaysia and the Iranian journal *Zanan* helped to initiate what has become known as Muslim feminism (Badran 2009). In the early 1990s, writings about Islam and gender equality by Middle Eastern feminists like Fatima Mernissi, Nawal el Saadawi, and Riffat Hassan were translated into Indonesian by NGO activists and widely circulated. Over the next decade, Indonesian women activists also became aware of efforts by Muslim feminist intellectuals in the West, especially Asma Barlas and Amina Wadud, to produce alternative, egalitarian interpretations of the Quran.[13]

NU and Muhammadiyah took notice of women activists by allowing women to join the bodies that produce *fatwas* and religious interpretations for the organizations. Nevertheless, women's participation in these bodies was and continues to be limited to a few individuals (Van Doorn-Harder 2006).

The women's movement grew alongside the student movement. Student activism was never completely suppressed under the New Order, but it wasn't until the late 1980s that it again became more popular. An event that galvanized many students was a 1989 government initiative to build a massive dam that would have flooded the land of thousands of rural villages in Central Java. Students flocked to the area to help defend the communities and protest the development.

Women's groups, environmental organizations, and Muslim student groups participated in the mobilization, and these events seem to have sparked significant cross-fertilization (Hefner 2000). Many of my informants spoke of the dynamic atmosphere of the democracy movement in the university city of Yogyakarta in the early 1990s. They were nostalgic for the risky but electrifying early demonstrations, as well as their study circles, whose eclectic readings ranged from Karl Marx and Erich Fromm, to modernist Muslim thinkers such as Nurcholish Madjid and Fazlur Rahman, to Middle Eastern feminists like Fatima Mernissi and Nawal el Sadaawi.[14]

Many human rights and women's NGOs, including Solidaritas Perempuan, were founded in the late 1980s and early 1990s, and leaders of such groups were often part of these early mobilizations.

Thus, secular women's groups were under state control in the early years of the New Order, and religious women's groups were marginalized. But the field of gender politics soon became animated as an independent women's movement emerged. The rise of Muslim women's activism was an unanticipated consequence of the religious revival and helped to produce an overlap between Islamic and gender politics. Muslim groups, student activists, and women's organizations developed a common discourse of human rights and democracy. These three constituencies became the backbone of the reformist movement that erupted in 1997 and culminated in Suharto's resignation in May 1998.

Summing Up: Women, Religion, and the Public Sphere in New Order Indonesia

The Suharto regime initially banished Islam from politics. Middle-class women were mobilized into state-controlled groups that promoted domesticity. New Order ideology constituted the public sphere as a controlled, masculine realm. The state managed religion to create a depoliticized and orderly society. With the lack of freedom of expression or independent mobilization, the fields of Islamic politics and gender politics were in steep decline.

Through a combination of state promotion and global influences, Islam claimed an increasing role in the public sphere in the 1980s and 1990s. The revitalization of Islamic thought sparked interest among women in issues of gender, democracy, and religious pluralism. These activists were empowered by changes in the educational system, which made it possible for many women to enter universities, obtain professional jobs, and join the urban middle classes.

Finally, the intermingling of the student movement and women's groups in the 1990s brought about a new interest in gender politics among students. Many of my informants recall being first exposed to feminist ideas while involved in student activism. Many student activists went on to work for women's NGOs like Solidaritas Perempuan and/or Muslim organizations, such as Fatayat and Rahima (founded in 2000). The influx of 1990s activists to such organizations produced a further blending of women's and Muslim activism.

Gender discourses in the 1990s weren't always progressive or egalitarian. Some Muslim groups questioned women's work outside the household, urged women to cover their entire bodies, and promoted polygamous marriage (Brenner 1999).

The 1990s were characterized by a diversity of Muslim interpretations and practices, ranging from a new interest in Islam and feminism to sharply conservative views on marriage and family life. These reflected the expanding intersections between the rejuvenated fields of Islamic politics and gender politics. If in the earlier period both secular and religious women were marginalized from the public sphere, by the 1990s Islam was becoming a resource for women's mobilization.

ISLAM, WOMEN, AND THE PUBLIC SPHERE SINCE 1998

Since the fall of Suharto's New Order regime, Islamic politics has taken on a greater role in Indonesian public life. Islamic practices and interpretations continue to be diverse, with Muslim leaders becoming politically influential. Nevertheless, older ways of being Muslim, such as Javanism, seem to be in decline, while organizations representing more conservative understandings of Islam, such as the Prosperous Justice Party, enjoy popularity. Additionally, the country endured a wave of ethnic and religious violence after the fall of the New Order. Though stability has returned, the new context has varied implications for contemporary women's activism. Islamic politics and gender politics are vibrant and interconnected, as new forms of activism that combine Islam and women's rights emerge in the overlap between these fields. Islamic politics and gender politics have also become mutually influencing. Yet while Muslim women activists are indeed empowered by the new public emphasis on Islam, not all Muslim women activists share the goal of gender equality.

The Asian economic crisis of 1997 sent the Indonesian economy into shock. With prices soaring, the IMF mandating austerity, and their savings wiped out, many middle-class Indonesians lost faith in the Suharto regime. Protests over subsidies for goods soon turned into demonstrations for *reformasi*. After Suharto resigned the presidency in May 1998, he appointed his vice president, B. J. Habibie, as his successor. This transitional period saw the founding of many new political parties, including the Prosperous Justice Party.

The 1999 election brought the opposition led by Sukarno's daughter Megawati to power. Because of Muslim opposition to her candidacy, the president of NU, Abdurrahman Wahid, who had also been a presidential candidate, was appointed as president, with Megawati as vice president. Wahid's unorthodox leadership style, liberal understanding of Islam, and attempts to reign in the military alienated many Indonesians. In 2001, Wahid was forced to resign amidst allegations of corruption and was replaced as president by Megawati. This time, most Muslim organizations did not oppose Megawati.

Instability plagued Indonesia between 1999 and 2004. Bombings by extremist Muslim groups affiliated with Al-Qaeda struck churches, a Bali nightclub, and upscale Jakarta hotels. At the same time, ethnic and religious conflict in Eastern Indonesia killed thousands. Some observers believed Indonesia was on the verge of breaking apart. Militant groups demanded Islamic law and promoted understandings of Islam that insisted on gender segregation. Sidel (2006) argues that ambiguity about Islam's place in the nation-state was at the heart of the violence. Nevertheless, he argues that the jihadist movement was a sign of the failure of political Islam in Indonesia. Indeed, the parliament's rejection (in 2002) of the Jakarta Charter, the document that would have instituted *Shariah* law, was a blow to Islamists.

In the country's first direct elections in 2004, Susilo Bambang Yudhoyono, a retired general, was elected president, and he was re-elected in 2009. Despite concerns about corruption, the days of disappearances of activists and media censorship seem to be gone. With the state actively pursuing terrorist suspects, and with the resolution of the regional conflicts in Maluku and Sulawesi, the violence has subsided, although small jihadist circles continue to be active.

Islam has also become more firmly entrenched in public life. For example, the parliament in 2003 mandated that the government increase faith and piety in education. The new education law requires private elementary and secondary schools to provide each student with religious instruction in his or her own faith.[15] Though this provision of the law is not always enforced, it sends a message about the public importance of religious identity, and it also attempts to enforce the boundaries of religious identities. The parliament also passed a restrictive antipornography law in 2008, which has already resulted in the imprisonment of a celebrity because of explicit sex videos that were circulated on YouTube.

Some forms of religious extremism seem to be increasing in Indonesia. Christians in many regions have become dismayed about the impossibility of building churches in their neighborhoods. Muslim groups often oppose the construction of churches and city governments appease them by holding back construction permits. More ominously, violent attacks on religious minorities such as the Ahmadiyah sect and Shiite Muslims have increased since 2008, with little government intervention. Of great concern to women's rights activists, in the early 2000s numerous provinces instituted legislation requiring Muslim women to wear headscarves or

Figure 2.1: Muslim fashion designer Jenny Cahyawati at work.

forbidding them from being out alone after dark. Such laws are often part of a campaign to assert a province's Islamic identity (Komnas Perempuan 2010). These bylaws have been challenged in court, but so far activists have had little success overturning them.

Muslim intellectuals and authorities abound in the new Indonesian public sphere. Schools offering Quranic studies classes have proliferated, while Muslim fashion has become big business, with shows held at elite hotels and upscale malls (Figure 2.1). Islamic-themed romance novels and films are fashionable as well.

Brenner (2005) proposes that Islamic networks and institutions now provide many women with careers. Women who graduate from Muslim universities and might otherwise be shut out of the formal job market, or whose families might be concerned about them taking jobs in an office setting, can find employment as teachers in Muslim schools or program officers in Muslim organizations. This trajectory was followed by some of the women I studied. Such careers barely existed twenty years ago. Similarly, Van Doorn-Harder connects the expansion of Muslim women's activism to the groundwork provided by Muhammadiyah and NU: "Not all women of Muhammadiyah and N.U. become activists or feminists, but the activities of their organizations helped create the foundation for contemporary women who advocate for women's rights from an Islamic frame of reference" (2006, 34).

Islamic politics has diversified. While the NU seems to be divided between reformers and an old guard, newer organizations such as the Prosperous Justice Party, the Liberal Islam Network, and NGOs like Rahima have appeared since the late 1990s. The divisions between Muslim political parties mean that they rarely form united coalitions in parliament. Nevertheless, new ways of being Muslim are still emerging, including a revived interest in Sufism among middle-class urbanites (Howell 2005).

Secular women's groups are still vigorous, but they have a lower public profile than was the case in the 1990s, when they were at the forefront of the democracy movement. This is partly because such groups are no longer directly opposed to the state and, in many cases, are oriented toward policy and legal reforms. Solidaritas Perempuan, for example, emphasizes transnational issues, especially the effects of economic globalization. While this strategy draws its legitimacy from international political discourses and institutions, it can sideline secular groups from discussions about religion and national politics.

Muslim and secular women activists are now more unified by concerns over the political uses of Islam. The tumult of the past decade has brought together many women activists around concerns about democracy, equality, and pluralism.

Not all women activists oppose efforts to implement Islamic regulations at the provincial level. Many of the women of the Prosperous Justice Party (PKS) endorse such developments as part of Indonesia's journey toward becoming a more Islamic society. While they share pious orientations with other women activists, the women of PKS envision different reforms than those advocated by many women's rights groups. Importantly, they prioritize greater regulation of moral life over equality. The divides among women activists are not merely about gender but also revolve around differing visions for the relationship between religion and the state.

There is no doubt that after 1998, Islamic politics has become a very significant aspect of the Indonesian public sphere, and that it has significant overlap with gender politics. Women activists seeking reform employ religious discourse to make their cases for change, and women from Muslim organizations are interested in gender politics. The post-1998 political and religious context has benefited Muslim women activists, and it has drawn together Muslim and secular women activists who share concerns about religious extremism and intolerance. Islamic politics and gender politics continue to be dynamic and mutually influential fields of action.

ISLAM, WOMEN, AND THE PUBLIC SPHERE IN
POSTCOLONIAL INDONESIA

Through the twentieth century, the fields of Islamic politics and gender politics developed, stagnated, and revived. They have broadened to include new actors and have developed important linkages. Muslim women's rights activists can now be said to exist in the overlap between these fields.

The institutionalization of Islam, along with Indonesia's diverse Islamic heritage, continues to facilitate middle-class Muslim women's activism. Muslim institutions have been a means for upward mobility, but more for women of the lower middle class than for those from poor backgrounds. Indeed, it remains to be seen whether new norms of religious discipline add to the constraints on poor women's lives. Nevertheless, the pluralism of Indonesian Islam gives Muslim women activists a means to circulate ideas for change and reform.

As I show in the next few chapters, the use of Islamic discourse and practices provides women activists with the legitimacy to advocate reforms that might otherwise be more contentious. Women activists use different but widely accepted interpretive approaches to Islam—contextual and textual—to mobilize and make claims for a range of political changes. While contextual approaches lend themselves to claims for women's rights and equality, textual approaches facilitate arguments for stronger public moral regulation. Islam's influence on women's activism is thus neither monolithic nor deterministic.

To explore how contemporary Indonesian women activists engage with global and local discourses of Islam and feminism, I examine women in four organizations. My analysis is based on seventeen months of ethnographic research and interviews, which I conducted from 2002 to 2003, with return visits in 2005, 2008, and 2010.[16] These groups exemplify the spectrum of mainstream Indonesian women's activism, ranging from the feminist NGO Solidaritas Perempuan to the Muslim women's rights organizations Fatayat NU and Rahima to the Prosperous Justice Party. I now turn to a more detailed introduction to each of these organizations.

SOLIDARITAS PEREMPUAN

Solidaritas Perempuan (SP), or Women's Solidarity, is one of Indonesia's most established NGOs and a well-known actor in the field of gender politics. My research was at SP's Jakarta headquarters, which at the time had twenty paid staff, nearly all women. Established in 1990, the group advocates for women who migrate overseas to work as domestics. SP also is active in the areas of environmental justice and HIV/AIDS. These are all considered contributions to their overarching goal of building a movement for women's rights and equality.

SP was founded by a group of educated, middle-class women who had connections with student and labor activists. They were influenced by their experiences with some of the early feminist NGOs in Indonesia, especially Kalyanamitra, a feminist information center that opened in Jakarta in 1985 to provide information about domestic violence. SP founders were also influenced by visits to India for activist conferences in the early 1990s.

SP leaders also had links to the land rights movement that emerged on Java in the late 1980s. A focal point of this movement was the proposed Kedung Ombo dam in Central Java. Students and others moved into rural communities to mobilize resistance against the dam. Although it began with the demand of fair compensation for villagers, the movement began to talk about democratization and social justice. It did not prevent construction of the dam, but Aspinall (2005) argues that these events helped crystallize a more radical current in the emerging student movement, influenced by similar movements in South Korea and the Philippines.

Over the years, SP has evolved from being a small group of outspoken activists facing government repression to an NGO that focuses on advocacy while working to build a broader women's movement in Indonesia. Its leaders remain outspoken about feminism, human rights, the environment, neoliberal economic policies, and state repression.

Solidaritas Perempuan is part of the subset of Indonesian women's rights organizations that are not specifically oriented toward religious reform[17] and that generally do not employ religious arguments in their activism. This is typical of the generation of Indonesian women activists who came to prominence in the 1980s and early 1990s.

Yet SP seems to be more accommodating of religious sensibilities than some other feminist groups. For example, I noticed during my visits to the offices of various feminist NGOs that Muslim clothing (including the *jilbab*) was much more common at SP. In 2002 and 2003, out of twenty full- and part-time staff members in the Jakarta headquarters, all were Muslim except for one Catholic and one person who chose not to specify her religion.[18] When I returned to SP in subsequent years, there seemed to be a few more non-Muslim staff members.

The SP staff I met were from families who might be described as lower middle class by Indonesian standards. These women were nearly all in their twenties and thirties (older staff often move on to other organizations). Nearly all attended state-run secondary schools and many were graduates of elite state universities such as Universitas Indonesia and Gadjah Mada University. Few had studied overseas, one of the hallmarks of the Jakarta upper middle class. Instead, the SP women I met had parents who were high school graduates who became civil servants or ran small businesses in Jakarta or other cities. Unmarried staff often lived with their families in Jakarta. A few stayed in *kos*, a dormitory-style accommodation for students and others lacking relatives in the area. Married staff lived in the sprawling exurbs.

SP has about a dozen "communities" around the country, as well as about two hundred individual members. The communities and individual members are volunteers but have substantial autonomy. Communities receive small amounts of funding from Jakarta for equipment or special programs but otherwise raise money for their activities. Major decisions are made by the whole organization at a congress held every three years.

During my fieldwork, much of SP's work on migrant workers was centered in West Java, a region with high rates of rural poverty and large numbers of female migrants. SP conducts educational trainings and seminars to help inform workers and families of their legal rights. They work with local groups to organize demonstrations or other public informational events.

One of SP's most important functions is to provide services such as legal aid for migrant workers. Staff members visit government offices to lobby for new or proposed policies, as well as to resolve individual cases of exploitation. SP also advocates for female workers who were abused or killed by employers overseas. They publicize cases and often push government officials to conduct medical examinations to find the cause of death or injury.

SP participates in coalitions of Indonesian NGOs working on migrant worker and environmental justice issues and is in frequent contact with Muslim progressive groups. After the 2004 tsunami, SP became very active in Aceh. SP Aceh supports activists struggling to reform the implementation of Islamic law in the province, as well as to assist women in areas affected by the tsunami.

RAHIMA

Rahima is a small NGO that was established in 2001. Its founders were male and female Muslim women's rights activists from the *Fiqh an-Nisa* division of the community development organization P3M.[19] As part of *Fiqh an-Nisa*, they studied women and Islamic law to promote gender equality in the traditional *pesantren* communities of Java. When the head of P3M took on a second wife, these activists decided to form a new organization, one that would continue working within the *pesantrens* but also, more widely, on issues of Islam and gender, including a much more critical stance on polygamy. They invited Nahdlatul Ulama scholars to serve on Rahima's board and as a result, the communities and schools in which Rahima works are usually NU affiliated and mostly on Java.

Rahima's name comes from the word *rahim,* which means womb or uterus in Indonesian (derives from Arabic). Located in a middle-class residential area, Rahima claims to promote women's rights within an Islamic framework. In 2002–2003, the organization had about ten paid staff in its Jakarta office, as well as interns, and it has stayed about the same size.

Many of the Rahima staff came from pious Javanese families loosely associated with NU. However, there were a few staff from mixed ethnic backgrounds or from poorer families. Most attended *pesantren* and continued on to state Islamic universities or elite public universities, and many had master's degrees. Some staff had connections to feminist and human rights activism, as well as the *reformasi* movement. Most staff members lived with their families in the suburbs, though a few younger staff lived with families or in shared housing in the city. Of all the activists I met, those of Rahima seemed to be the most highly educated, fluent in a variety of national and global social issues.

Rahima's education program includes trainings, discussions, and workshops for teachers and students of *pesantrens* and other groups on issues like gender and Islamic law, violence against women, and reproductive rights. They introduce Islamic scholars to ideas of gender equality and help them to disseminate these teachings in their communities. They also encourage *pesantrens* to engage female students and teachers more fully and are working to develop more female Islamic teachers and scholars. Rahima's public campaign programs include publishing a journal on gender and Islam called *Swara Rahima* (*Voice of Rahima*), as well as publishing books and holding seminars and workshops. The organization also functions as an information center and library for students or members of the public interested in researching issues related to Islam and gender.

Like SP and Fatayat, Rahima is an accepted member of Jakarta's progressive activist milieu. Rahima organizes activities with both those organizations, as well as with other women's rights groups, liberal Christian and other religious groups, the Liberal Islam Network, and the International Center for Islam and Pluralism (ICIP).

FATAYAT NU

Fatayat, the younger women's division of Nahdlatul Ulama, is one of Indonesia's largest and oldest women's organizations. As mentioned previously, NU was founded in 1926 by traditionalist Muslim scholars and is thought to have about 45 million members.[20] Fatayat was established in 1950 and is for women between the ages of twenty and forty-five.[21] As I discuss in chapter 4, Fatayat's recent orientation toward women's rights is surprising, given its history as a women's auxiliary. For decades, NU was quite conservative when it came to gender. But the revitalization of Islamic political thought in NU circles in the 1980s and 1990s helped to drive attention to issues of women's rights. While NU is a diverse organization whose members span the political spectrum and its leadership is entirely male, some figures within the organization have became supportive of women's rights. In the early 1990s, leaders of Fatayat began to attend some of the first "gender trainings" held by Western NGOs in Indonesia. Since then, the goal of gender equality has become much more prominent within Fatayat. As I argue in chapter 4, NU's interpretive approach, which allows for more contextual readings of Islamic texts and emphasizes *fikh* (Islamic jurisprudence), has been a significant tool for promoting women's rights.

Leaders estimate that Fatayat has about three million members around the country. Much like Indonesia's government-controlled organizations, it has a branch and subbranch structure that reaches down to the village level. During my fieldwork at Fatayat's national headquarters (near the NU building in Central Jakarta), there were three paid employees and thirty to forty part-time volunteers. The director of the organization is chosen every four years at a national conference, usually from among the volunteer program coordinators at the Jakarta office.

In its mission booklet, Fatayat's objectives are "to create and shape devoted young women to almighty Allah, to be moral, skillful, responsible, and beneficial to religion and nation; to create a society with gender equality; to create devotion toward the principles, beliefs, and objectives of N.U. in building Islamic *Shariah*." Fatayat's work is currently structured into seven major areas: organization and education; law, policy, and advocacy; health and environment; social, art, and culture; economy; *dakwah* (propagation of Islam) and building membership; and research and development. At their 2005 and 2008 conferences, they also emphasized reproductive health efforts.

Fatayat's activities are very localized. For example, in Sumatra, Fatayat chapters partnered with other groups to help rebuild areas destroyed by the tsunami, while in other regions they are involved with efforts such as educating women about sex trafficking or voter training programs. The program coordinators in the national office visit Fatayat offices around the country to conduct gender trainings or other educational seminars and workshops.

In addition, Fatayat has established about a dozen women's reproductive health centers, called PIKER (*Pusat Informasi Kesehatan Reproduksi*—Center for Reproductive Health Information). These centers provide leaflets and other information on reproductive and sexual health issues—including HIV and other sexually transmitted diseases, family planning, domestic violence, and puberty. Fatayat leaders hope to eventually provide more health services at these clinics. Though they endorse family planning, they argue that government programs do not provide women with adequate choices or information about contraception. Through PIKER, they hope to be able to give women the information they need to make informed choices about reproductive health.

Fatayat also partners with the Indonesian government on programs such as *Desa Siaga dan PHBS* (Prepared Villages and Healthy and Clean Lifestyles). In this program, Fatayat focuses on improvements in three areas: childbirth assistance by medical personnel, exclusive feeding by breast milk, and routine weighing of babies at local health centers.

Fatayat is part of coalitions and alliances with both Muslim and secular women's rights groups. Like Solidaritas Perempuan and Rahima, it has come to be seen as part of Jakarta's progressive milieu, and its leaders are nationally recognized.

THE PROSPEROUS JUSTICE PARTY

The Prosperous Justice Party was founded in 1998 as the Justice Party (*Partai Keadilan*). The Justice Party received just 1.4% of the vote in Indonesia's landmark 1999 elections and reinvented itself in 2002 with a more moderate platform as the Prosperous Justice Party (*Partai Keadilan Sejahtera*—PKS). PKS received 7.3% of the national popular vote in the 2004 elections.[22] In Jakarta, the party stunned observers by grabbing 25% of the vote. Shortly after, party leader Hidayat Nurwahid was elected head of the parliament, giving PKS an important role in national politics. However, in the 2009 elections the party did not achieve its goal of significantly raising its share of the national vote. It received 7.88% of the national vote, and currently has fifty-seven seats in the five hundred seat legislature.[23] Nonetheless, it remains the most popular Muslim political party.

PKS draws much of its support from the urban middle class. Membership is open to anyone who agrees with the party platform. The party's original call for an Islamic state has been dropped, and in 2008 its new platform declared the current Pancasila-based Indonesian state to be "final" (Bubalo, Fealy, and Mason 2008). It held its 2010 convention at the Ritz Carlton in

Jakarta to convey its more moderate, establishment image, as also suggested by its new slogan "Caring, clean, and professional." Nevertheless, observers note that there are tensions between moderate and radical elements within the party. Among the issues is the difficulty of reconciling the party's pragmatic acceptance of the secular state with the continuing desire among many members for a state based on Islamic law (Hasan 2009).

The roots of PKS reach back further than the organization's establishment in 1998. The founders of the party were veterans of the *Tarbiyah* movement, many of whom had studied in the Middle East. For example, the party chair from 2000 to 2004, Hidayat Nur Wahid, earned his master's and doctoral degrees from the Islamic University of Medina, Saudi Arabia (Damanik 2002, 261). Influenced by the Muslim Brotherhood, *Tarbiyah* activists aimed to Islamize state and society, forming *dakwah* groups to educate their peers about becoming better Muslims. *Dakwah* groups became known for their textual approach to Islam and their emphasis on pious practices rather than complex theology (Machmudi 2008). However, unlike some Islamists, PKS activists embraced electoral politics as a way to transform Indonesia.

The Justice Party was founded as a *partai dakwah* (*dakwah* party), and the duty to call others to proper Muslim practice remains central. Unlike most Indonesian political parties, PKS is a cadre organization. Potential members apply and attend trainings to become a cadre, and once they become a cadre they are expected to maintain a relatively high level of involvement.

The party's mission and vision statement is set out in its materials and on its website, yet the specifics of the platform are vague. When I first began studying PKS, their website listed the party's "general vision" as "A *dakwah* party upholding justice and prosperity within the framework of the unity of the *ummat* and nation." The mission statement included:

1. Disseminate Islamic *dakwah* and produce cadres as change agents
2. Develop Islamic social institutions as centers of change and solutions
3. Develop opinions of the *ummat* that are Islamist and a climate that supports the implementation of the teachings of Islam that are a solution and that bring righteousness
4. Develop the political awareness of society, direction, service and empowerment of rights of citizens
5. Maintain *amar ma'ruf nahi munkar*[24] toward authority in a manner that is consistent and continuous in the framework of Islamic law and ethics

However, by 2012, the vision and mission listed on the PKS website had changed substantially. The primary mission is now "Building a civil society that is just, prosperous, and honorable."[25] The statement goes on to declare support for the unity of Indonesia, religious pluralism, and the framework of Pancasila, but also warns that the Islamic *ummat* cannot be separated from politics and will struggle for its principles in a constitutional manner.

PKS cares greatly about matters of religious doctrine. Unusually for an Indonesian political party, they issue *fatwas* and have a set of guidelines for proper behavior and beliefs for cadres. Many of these *fatwas* are trifling; for example, several are about what percentage of income believers should tithe to charity. Another *fatwa* prohibits physical contact between men and women, including shaking hands. These and other *fatwas* aim to regulate the daily behavior of party members.

In its daily activities, PKS functions like a combination of a political party and an NGO. Like other large Indonesian organizations, it has a regional and local branch structure, all headed by the national office of the secretary general in Jakarta. Party branches sponsor activities for cadres, including seminars, rallies and demonstrations, and Quranic study sessions.

PKS emphasizes political reform, anticorruption efforts, and moral concerns. The party's slogan since 2004 has been "Clean, caring, and professional." The anticorruption focus has been credited with winning over voters, but minor scandals have dented the party's clean image. However, most party leaders strive to be professional. For example, when Hidayat Nurwahid was elected head of the parliament, he stepped down from his position as leader of the party.

Despite efforts toward moderation, many Indonesian voters seem to be convinced that the party has a hidden agenda to establish an Islamic state. Hasan (2009) argues that this is because of the party's *dakwah* programs, which he argues are oriented toward building an Islamic state based on the principles of Hasan al-Banna, founder of the Muslim Brotherhood. *Dakwah* activities include religious lectures and study sessions, seminars, and workshops, as well as sponsorship of clubs and associations for high school and college students. At such events the party recruits members, and Hasan maintains that the *dakwah* efforts "represent the shift of the Islamist tactic towards the Islamization of the society from below" (pp. 14–15).

While PKS does not adhere to a specific juridical tradition of Islam, the party has a distinctive approach to Islam. PKS leaders argue that Muslim practices and beliefs should be based mainly on the Quran and the Hadiths, a position that places them within modernist Islam. Other than emphasizing piety, the main characteristic of the PKS approach to Islam is that it is textual. Party members de-emphasize interpretation and claim that religious texts are clear and fixed in their meaning. This approach, influenced by the *Tarbiyah* movement, buttresses a more conservative gender ideology and the goal of stronger regulation of moral life.

PKS has worked with international and national NGOs.[26] The party has participated in trainings and seminars with IFES (International Foundation for Election Systems) and IDEA (International Institute for Democracy and Electoral Assistance). The Division of Women's Empowerment has occasionally been involved in coalitions with women's organizations in Jakarta, especially related to voter education. Yet as I discuss in chapter 4, many of the PKS members I met do not see themselves as part of the women's rights movement. And women's rights activists tend to see PKS as an obstacle to the struggle for gender equality.

THE SETTING OF THIS STUDY: MIDDLE-CLASS JAKARTA

As the capital of Indonesia, Jakarta is Indonesia's cultural, political, and economic center. It is a sprawling city with a population of over 10 million (which may be closer to 28 million if you include the exurbs of Depok, Bekasi, and Tangerang).[27] Like other Asian capitals, it has a modern city center, complete with huge boulevards, upscale hotels and malls, and shimmering office towers. Traffic and pollution are among the worst in the world. Outside the center, much of the city is a maze of alleys and footpaths lined with humble, sometimes decrepit, concrete houses. These dense neighborhoods, known as *kampungs*, are where the majority of Jakartans reside. True slums are rare because the city government bulldozes squatter settlements and impoverished *kampungs*. Gradually, the urban poor are being moved to the exurbs that spread increasingly farther from the city.

In the last decade, Jakarta has become Indonesia's center for activism and NGOs. While the university city of Yogyakarta played this role in the 1980s and early 1990s, by the late 1990s many activists relocated to the capital. Jakarta and its metropolitan area are not only the country's center of wealth but also a stronghold of the urban middle class. With nearly half of its population now residing in urban areas, Indonesia's middle classes are playing an increasingly important role in the expansion of Indonesian cities, as well as in the national imaginary.

The women in this study are mostly members of the urban middle classes, and they permit us a glimpse into Indonesian urban life. They come from modest backgrounds with parents who were civil servants, teachers, or small business owners and have availed themselves of opportunities to enter higher education. Most live in the ever expanding sprawl outside the city. They have cars and televisions, but they lack the financial resources of middle classes in more prosperous countries or those above them on the steep Jakarta class ladder.

But more important, the women in these organizations are self-consciously addressing issues of gender and religion in order to influence national discourses. Their concerns are articulated on a national scale and their activities are covered in the national media and potentially influence women across the country. Indonesia's rapid urbanization and growing middle class mean that the women in this book are increasingly representative of a major segment of the population. And as Islamic piety has become a marker of distinction among the middle classes, these activists have come to embody distinctive ways of being pious and middle class.

As this chapter has shown, Indonesia's democratization has given these women activists greater freedom to organize and express their desires for reforms. Their adaptation of global discourses of Islam and feminism is a consequence of a more participatory public sphere. Yet their visions for Indonesia's future have been profoundly shaped by the intersections of Islamic politics and gender politics over the course of the past century. In the next three chapters, I explore these intersections in detail and I begin with the reformist visions of Fatayat and Rahima.

CHAPTER 3
Fatayat and Rahima

Islamic Reformists

On a sweltering July day in 2003, Fatayat, the women's wing of the Muslim organization Nahdlatul Ulama, hosted a visitor to its Jakarta office, Ziba Mir-Hosseini. Mir-Hosseini is an Iranian-born, UK-based anthropologist who has published widely on women and Islam and had recently made a documentary about divorce in Iran. She had been invited by the Asia Foundation to meet with Muslim women's groups in Indonesia. She was being guided around Jakarta by Lily Munir, a former head of Fatayat and a prominent women's rights activist.[1] Munir introduced Mir-Hosseini by explaining enthusiastically to the small audience that Mir-Hosseini was a Muslim feminist, not a secular feminist. Munir told the women at Fatayat that while many Iranian feminists were secular, Mir-Hosseini believed in the verses of the Quran and did not "reject" religion.

In her talk Mir-Hosseini explained that in Iran, women's rights came to be associated with the dictatorial and secular regime of Mohammad Reza Pahlavi, and that this circumstance contributed to unnecessary discord between religion and feminism. Later, she warned against Islamization in Indonesia, arguing that Iran had shown the failure of ideological Islam, and that its authoritarianism was causing young people to disregard religion entirely. Nevertheless, she added, Iranian women were democratizing Islam by introducing ideas about human rights.

Munir opened the discussion by stating that "feminism is still taboo in Indonesia," but that also there were secular feminists and Muslim feminists in Indonesia. In India and Pakistan, she explained, most feminists were secular and opposed to religion because they saw it as hopeless. Then she added, "But in Indonesia, we say that we are feminists. We work for women's rights, but we are still Muslim."

With those words, Munir summed up the essence of Fatayat and Rahima. Munir's statement captures the refusal of many of the activists in these groups to accept a contradiction between Islam and feminism. Framing feminism in Islamic terms and Islam in feminist terms, they see no reason for women's rights activists to reject religion. They promote a greater role for Islam in the public sphere, yet also advocate keeping the state away from regulating religious behavior. In doing so, they have helped to elevate Muslim women to the status of political subjects. Moreover, they challenge widespread assumptions that religion is inherently at odds with gender equality. Today's outspoken Indonesian women's rights activist often wears a headscarf as she confronts the gender status quo.

Democratization and the increasing power of Islam in the public sphere have opened up space for new social movements in Indonesia, particularly those rooted in Islam. Rahima, a Muslim women's rights NGO, and Fatayat, the women's wing of one of Indonesia's largest Muslim organizations, Nahdlatul Ulama (NU), are part of the new Muslim civil society that emerged in the 1990s (Hefner 2000). As Indonesia democratized in the late 1990s, the national imagination and the role of Islam within it became contested. Women's rights became a subject of debate, partly because the new popularity of Islam was accompanied by the propagation of religious interpretations that restrict women or mandate stricter gender segregation.

Islam and feminism are often considered to be at odds with each other. Western media and some scholars consider revivalist Islam to be a threat to women's rights, while some Muslims see feminism as a threat to Islamic values. A more nuanced perspective proposes that the pious subject is constituted by Islamic norms and embraces submission to norms rather than freedom, while feminism, with its underpinnings in liberalism, presupposes an autonomous internal self that is encumbered by norms that are felt to be external (Mahmood 2005). Others stress that there is a clash between Islamic and secular sensibilities in the public sphere, which arises not just because religion is often perceived as a vestige of tradition, but also because Islamic piety is thought to reject liberal norms such as equality (Göle 2002; Asad 2003).[2]

It is important to recognize that the feminist movement in the West indeed emerged out of liberalism, and the concept of rights is at the core of much feminist thought.[3] Thus, a central question I was eager to explore in my fieldwork was how Rahima and Fatayat activists negotiated Islam and feminism and how Islam influenced their agency. I discovered that the activists of Rahima and Fatayat do challenge the suggestion that Islamic piety necessarily clashes with liberal ideals such as rights and equality. They have developed a pious critical agency that draws on both Islamic and feminist discourses to promote women's rights.

One of the most remarkable aspects of the time I spent with Fatayat and Rahima was learning about their emphasis on interpretation. In interviews, workshops, and meetings, I was struck by how often staff members discussed the meanings of religious texts, emphasizing how they have been interpreted in different historical and cultural contexts. In this chapter, I examine how these acts of interpretation allow the activists of Rahima and Fatayat to seek out Islamic justifications for women's rights and draw on discourses of transnational feminism and Islamic reformism, as well as Indonesia's own heritage of Islam, to make public arguments for social change and religious reform. I show how their contextual interpretation of Islamic texts makes it possible for them to frame women's rights in Islamic terms. In using this approach, these activists demonstrate *pious critical agency*, which involves a critical and public engagement with religious texts, as they make claims for political and social change, including gender equality. Rahima and Fatayat activists certainly also demonstrate *pious activating agency*, in which they mobilize interpretations for political purposes. But what is most distinctive and unusual about Rahima and Fatayat is that they represent women's increased involvement in processes of Islamic interpretation, which is a new role for Muslim women. Only a few women in these organizations actually do formal interpretations of religious texts. However, because interpretation is so central to the work of these groups, all staff members and participants are very much involved in debates and discussions about religious meaning, and they bring these discussions to bear on their organizations' policies and actions.[4]

To understand how Rahima and Fatayat activists have arrived at this position, it is vital to understand their social locations. Women activists' engagements with Islam and feminism are shaped by their trajectories and experiences in the fields of both Islamic politics and gender politics.

Islamic politics is constituted by the Indonesian Islamic tradition, which comprises different interpretive methods, including contextual and textual approaches to religious texts. Pious critical agency is facilitated by the contextual approach, which emphasizes taking into account the contemporary context and/or the sociohistorical context of central texts such as the Quran. In Indonesia, a more contextual approach has recently been fostered by the milieu of Nahdlatul Ulama.[5] Scholars have shown that the emergence of Muslim institutions and networks in the 1980s and 1990s—such as schools, universities, political parties, foundations, and NGOs—facilitated

Muslim women's activism by helping to produce a growing cohort of pious women with middle-class educations and professional careers (Brenner 1996, 2005; Van Doorn-Harder 2008). Rahima and Fatayat activists' trajectories through the Muslim educational system have influenced their political subjectivities and religious approaches. Involvement in NU networks and progressive student activism imbued many Rahima and Fatayat women with a flexible and somewhat contextual approach to Islamic texts. Fatayat and Rahima capitalize on this background to train activists in a more explicitly contextual and feminist approach that supports ideas of rights, equality, and pluralism.

Fatayat and Rahima are also situated in the field of gender politics, which involves political discourses and contestations around gender relations. The gender politics field includes feminists and those who seek to maintain the gender order. However, women's rights activists have been increasingly prominent in this field since the early 1990s. Fatayat and Rahima are in the unique position of straddling the fields of Islamic politics and gender politics in Indonesia. As these fields increasingly intersected in the 1990s and after democratization, Fatayat and Rahima were more influenced by feminist discourses. Their pious critical agency has emerged in the overlap between Islamic politics and gender politics and draws on the norms and values of both.

Fatayat and Rahima activists' ability to frame feminist arguments within Islamic discourse, their pious backgrounds, and their connections with the Nahdlatul Ulama milieu lend credibility to their arguments and help them to mobilize women. The Islamic revival has empowered these activist women by providing them with a means of being authoritatively involved in public debates about the future of the nation.

Their activism calls into question any strict dichotomies between secular and religious women's activism and between pious and feminist agency. Pious critical agency in fact overlaps with feminist agency for these activists. Rahima and Fatayat share many of the aims of self-declared feminists like Solidaritas Perempuan, especially with regard to promoting human rights and women's empowerment, but they frame their arguments within the Islamic tradition, as well as with reference to transnational human rights discourses. This has helped to produce a novel type of activism that creatively mingles influences from Islam and feminism.

After separately introducing the activists of these two organizations, in this chapter I primarily discuss Rahima and Fatayat together. Certainly, the two organizations are quite different. Rahima is a small, Jakarta-based NGO with a dozen paid staff, which carries out projects in various parts of Java. Fatayat is part of the NU, has its headquarters in Jakarta, has a mostly volunteer staff and an elected leader, and has an estimated three million members across the archipelago. It is also important to note that my study of Fatayat was limited to its national headquarters in Jakarta, so my discussion here primarily refers to the activists I encountered there.[6] However, the leaders and staff of both organizations have similar backgrounds in the NU milieu. Most importantly, the ways the activists of these organizations think about Islam and gender are similar because their approach to interpreting religious texts has been influenced by the NU. Therefore, I analyze them together as representing one mode of engagement with Islam and feminism, and a particular kind of pious agency. However, I also discuss the constraints and opportunities faced by each organization.

In the next sections, I explore the pious trajectories that lead women to Rahima and Fatayat. I further examine their understandings of Islam and feminism and how they combine these frameworks in their everyday lives and activism. I also consider how their contextual approach to Islam shapes this activism and the development of pious critical agency. I do this by investigating their interventions in debates over Islamic law, polygamy, and women's bodily autonomy.

The leading women activists of Rahima and Fatayat have much in common with those of Solidaritas Perempuan and the Prosperous Justice Party. Their lives have been equally fashioned by higher education, democratization, and the global Islamic revival. Yet the activists of Rahima and Fatayat embody a distinctive way of being pious, one that combines Islam and feminism with expressive religiosity and respect for religious and cultural difference. They envision a more egalitarian society in which Islam is a force for social justice but not a part of the state. The activism of Rahima and Fatayat demonstrates that Islam provides resources for different kinds of agency for women activists, including those who challenge the contemporary gender order. Moreover, they show that pious and feminist agency can overlap, resulting in new repertoires of collective action.

PIOUS TRAJECTORIES: FATAYAT NU

When I began my fieldwork in 2002, Fatayat's offices were in the prominent NU building in Central Jakarta.[7] Though I was intimidated at first, the warmth of Fatayat staff and volunteers quickly made me feel at home. As I came to know these women, a certain pious trajectory, or a route through particular understandings of religious practices, emerged. From childhood into adulthood, many Fatayat women have been intimately involved in Muslim schools, networks, and organizations, especially those with ties to the Nahdlatul Ulama. Indeed, out of the first eight Fatayat women I interviewed, four mentioned close family members who were active in NU, and two attended *pesantren* (traditional Muslim boarding school) while five attended *madrassah* (modern Muslim school).

This background means that Fatayat women have been schooled in the NU approach to Islam. Like other Muslims, NU *kyais* (Javanese Muslim teachers/scholars) draw on the Quran and Hadiths.[8] However, they are especially engaged with *fikh*, Islamic jurisprudence. Based on the Quran and Sunnah,[9] *fikh* complements these texts with the evolving interpretations of scholars, compiled over centuries. This *fikh*-centered approach to Islam has been influential in Southeast Asia and other parts of the world and is often referred to as "traditionalist."[10] It is taught in the schools and institutions associated with NU.[11] It is an exegetical approach that recognizes complexity of meaning and foregrounds interpretation by trained scholars. By the 1980s and 1990s, some scholars from the NU milieu began to adopt a more explicitly contextual approach, emphasizing the need for interpretations to be relevant to the modern world (Van Doorn-Harder 2006).[12]

Farida was the head of Fatayat during much of my fieldwork. Her involvement in women's rights issues mirrors Fatayat's shift from a women's auxiliary organization to an empowerment and rights agenda. When I first met her, she was in her midthirties and lived with her husband and children in a suburb east of Jakarta. Soft-spoken but articulate and determined, Farida grew up in a farming family in West Java. Her father was a religious teacher who established a Muslim girls' primary school and built a *mushollah* (prayer room) in his field. Farida attended both a *madrassah* (a modern-style Muslim school) and a *pesantren* (traditional Muslim boarding school) and got involved with NU as a teenager, influenced by the *kyai* of her *madrassah*. She got her undergraduate degree at the State Islamic Institute (now known as UIN) in Jakarta in the mid-1980s, where she also joined the NU-affiliated national student group Pergerakan Mahasiswa Islam Indonesia (or PMII or Indonesian Muslim Students Movement). Upon graduation, she took a job with an NU think tank and also joined Fatayat.

Farida told me that in 1990 she attended a gender training for NU staff conducted by Mansour Fakih, one of the first Indonesian Muslim advocates of women's rights. Fakih was an NU activist and worked for Oxfam. The training sparked Farida's interest in gender:

> With the style of a facilitator like that, I became very aware of imbalances for women. I felt that women's rights were something women had to know about.

In 1994, in Fatayat, I was asked to become a leader of a project to raise family income. From there, I became more aware that imbalances in the economic sphere were very apparent.

Farida became more involved with women's rights when she worked with the US-funded Asia Foundation on women's human rights and women's reproductive rights programs. Soon after, she began developing reproductive rights programs for Fatayat. Farida was head of Fatayat from 2000 to 2005 (a paid position), during which time she also completed a master's degree in women's studies at the University of Indonesia.

As head of Fatayat, Farida became a public figure. She served as a legislator for the National Awakening Party (PKB—affiliated with NU) from 2004 to 2006. Since 2010, she has been chair of the Indonesian Child Protection Commission, and she is also currently pursuing a PhD at the University of Indonesia.

The NU heritage was a powerful influence for other Fatayat staff, like Mei, who grew up in what she called "a *pesantren* family." Mei told me that her grandfathers on both sides were NU *kyais* who came to Central Java in the 1950s to spread Islam. They opened the first *pesantren* in an area then known as a "red zone" (controlled by the Communist Party).

Mei's mother was a member of Muslimat, and her father was an NU activist who brought his daughter to meetings and political rallies.[13] Mei attended the State Islamic University in Bandung and, encouraged by her parents, became head of her local Fatayat branch before she graduated. After her mother died, she returned to Central Java to help her father run the *pesantren*. He supported her in 1993, when she ran as the only female legislative candidate in the district. She noted:

> This political education really influenced me. I was very rich with *kyai* politics. That is why I became active politically in the PPP.[14] It also influenced my political activities when I was at university. I was active in organizations that were very religious. So I chose a party which strongly maintained religious principles. At that time, I was very opposed to the government.

Mei became a member of the regional parliament but later moved to Jakarta and became a volunteer at Fatayat's national headquarters. When I first met her, Mei was not married, unusual for a woman close to forty, and it was an issue she was sensitive about. But by the time I left, she was engaged to a fellow NU activist in Jakarta.

Farida and Mei wore *jilbab*, as did all of the other Fatayat staff and volunteers. The women I met all said they felt they were complying with Islamic guidelines on modesty. They explained that they believe Muslim women have a duty to cover their hair completely, their arms to the wrist, and their legs to the ankle.[15] A few dressed in colorful silk tunics with embroidery or beading, while others wore simpler "Muslim clothing" consisting of a tunic with wide-leg pants or a long skirt. They told me that clothing is not supposed to be too tight and that makeup and jewelry are allowed but should be modest. Fatayat has an official uniform of a long green skirt, green blazer, and white headscarf that is worn for conferences. Multiple styles of *jilbab* were exhibited by Fatayat women, with some tying the scarf tightly around their necks, others wearing it loosely around their shoulders, and a few wearing more lengthy styles.

The other staff and volunteers at Fatayat's Jakarta headquarters were nearly all university educated, and some were working on advanced degrees.[16] Like the other women in this study, they were among the first generation of their families to have a modern higher education, and they were far more likely than their mothers to have careers in the formal economy. The women I met lived in the sprawling suburban areas to the east and south of the city. Nearly all worked outside the house, often as university lecturers or teachers. Their husbands were lecturers, journalists, small business owners, or civil servants. They owned modest houses and planned to send their children to universities. They were affluent compared to many Indonesians but lived modest lives compared to Western middle classes. Most of my informants only occasionally ate dinner at restaurants and they traveled mostly to visit kin or for work, and their clothing was often made at a tailor or bought from a market kiosk rather than a department store.

The lives of Farida and Mei represent a common trajectory for Fatayat women, growing up in modest NU families, attending schools where they learned the NU approach to Islam, and becoming involved in the field of Islamic politics. The women I interviewed did not directly participate in the *reformasi* movement of the mid-1990s (because they were already out of school), but they sympathized with the aim of democratization. At university, they also often joined student groups, entering activist social networks tied to NU and becoming exposed to the ideas about human rights and democracy that were circulating through these networks in the 1980s and 1990s (see chapter 2 for more on this). Like Farida, many adopted the headscarf in high school or at university as a symbol of their commitment to Islam. They joined Fatayat to work for Islam and social justice, and this also marked their entrance into the field of gender politics. Fatayat activists are now truly at the intersection of Islamic politics and gender politics.

Like many of the progressive NGOs in Jakarta, Rahima's offices were in a house in a middle-class neighborhood. The house was small and there was an informal and sociable atmosphere. Ranging from their midtwenties to forties, many Rahima staff were married with children and lived in the suburbs. Some younger staff and interns lived with parents or in boarding houses. Some of the most fascinating conversations during my fieldwork came during lunches around Rahima's communal table. It was in these discussions that I began to understand the intriguing pious trajectories of Rahima staff members. Such trajectories often began with NU families and *pesantren* educations. Indeed, of the first seven Rahima staff I interviewed, five had attended *pesantren* or *madrassah*, although only two mentioned family members involved with NU. This trajectory continued through university and student activism into the field of Islamic politics (many Rahima staff attended state Muslim universities and were involved in national Muslim student organizations), and it sometimes included stops in the liberal left milieu of the 1990s and 2000s, where it intersected with the field of gender politics.

When I started my fieldwork, Ayu was in her early thirties and had been a student activist through the 1990s. She was intensely intellectual and pious, a combination I found in other Rahima staff. Ayu was not married and finding a suitable life partner was an issue of concern for her, especially since she hoped to have children (Ayu has since married).

Ayu grew up in Central Java, where her father taught English at a *pesantren* and her mother at a *madrassah*. They were a very Javanese family with respect for parental authority and attention to etiquette paramount. Ayu told me that she still used the honorific form of Javanese, *kromo inggil*, to speak to her parents. She attended *pesantren*, and then, after some time at a state Islamic institute, she continued on to the elite Gadjah Mada University in Yogyakarta. While at Rahima, she finished her master's degree in women's studies at the University of Indonesia, with a thesis on women in Indonesian political parties.

As a student, Ayu joined the Himpunan Mahasiswa Islam (HMI, or Muslim Students Association). In the early 1990s mainstream student groups were beginning to take more oppositional stances toward the government. Ayu worked her way into the leadership of the organization and plunged into Yogyakarta's intense activist scene, where she was exposed to new ways of thinking. In this way, she came to know many of the other activists who were involved in *reformasi* efforts.

Like many activists at the time, Ayu was part of informal study groups that brought students together to read and discuss political and social theory. The reading was eclectic and, because of censorship, often available only in badly translated versions that had been photocopied repeatedly. In her study group, Ayu read Karl Marx, Erich Fromm, Paulo Freire, and Khalil Gibran, among others. When Ayu graduated in 1997, HMI sent her to their office in Jakarta to work for their women's corps. She became head of the women's corps and eventually left to take a job as a program coordinator at Rahima.

Rahima was founded in 2001 by veterans of a progressive Muslim NGO. One was Ika, a dedicated activist who was in her forties when we first met. Married with two children, Ika has a unique background. Her father was the descendant of an Arab who came to Indonesia to spread Islam. Growing up in Central Java, Ika attended an Arab language school, as her father wanted her to marry an Arab Indonesian.

After high school, Ika matriculated at the State Islamic Institute in Yogyakarta. There in the mid-1980s, like many of those who have since become NGO leaders, she found a hotbed of student and women's rights activism. She was part of a group that initiated discussions of Islam and women in activist circles. She and her colleagues produced the first Indonesian translations of articles by Middle Eastern Muslim feminists like Fatima Mernissi and Rifaat Hassan. Ika remembers:

> Yogya was a remarkable city for me. This city contributed many beneficial things to me . . . not only as a gathering place for people from all over Indonesia, but also as a small world, because there were many nationalities. I got to know the world better in Yogyakarta. In this city the concentration of my life also changed, from just religion to a focus on women's issues.

Ika's father disapproved of her activism. Ika rebelled against him by marrying a non-Arab student activist. She got a master's degree in sociology from Gadjah Mada University, and in the mid-1990s she moved to Jakarta with her husband. There, she first worked for one of Indonesia's first feminist NGOs and then for an influential Muslim NGO. Ika now lives in East Java, where she and her husband established an organization that provides multicultural education and events for youth.

During my fieldwork, all of the female staff of Rahima wore headscarves and Muslim clothing, which they said complied with Islamic guidelines for women's clothing. Similar to Fatayat, Rahima activists' *jilbabs* included a range of styles. Younger Rahima staff often sported trendy clothing such as stylish blouses with jeans and a *jilbab*.

Interpreting clothing styles, however, is complicated in Indonesia. A common perception in Indonesia and elsewhere is that more modest (i.e., covering more of the body) clothing means more conservative political views. Indeed, clothing has become politicized enough that certain styles of clothing are sometimes associated with particular strands of religious and political thought. For example, informants told me that women wearing long skirts and socks with sandals and/or the larger white *jilbabs* that cover all of the upper body and arms are usually members of PKS, Hizbut Tahrir (an Islamist student group), or Persis (an older conservative Muslim organization). In contrast, they said, those with tighter or smaller, colorful *jilbabs* are usually from the NU milieu. Nevertheless, I found that these correlations were not always accurate. Some Rahima women adhered to conservative clothing guidelines while expressing liberal political views. Overall, though, Fatayat and Rahima women dressed less conservatively and exhibited more flexibility with clothing than women in PKS, as discussed in chapter 4.

Rahima activists told me that they wear Muslim clothing because they believe it is a religious obligation, although they don't think it should be required by law. Some cited other reasons, including a desire to express Muslim identity. Ayu said that she wanted people to know that she was both modern and Muslim:

> I felt there was an assumption that *pesantrens* were backward, slummy, dirty. Meanwhile, I felt my school was a modern Islamic boarding school. . . . Finally, I thought, for the first time during the Suharto era, I want to talk a lot and be seen. I have to show you all that we are not old-fashioned and conservative. We are not underdogs. That was my motivation. Why? Maybe because it's my identity and dignity. So I wanted to raise up my Islamic identity. I wanted to erase the impressions of orthodoxy, conservatism.

While Ayu said that she wears the veil to comply with Islam, she also sees it as a means of expression. She seeks to demonstrate to the world that pious Muslim women are not conservative or passive. Indeed, she seems to take pride in the possibility that she might shake people's preconceptions by being pious and feminist.

Like Ayu, many Rahima staff attended *pesantren* or state Islamic schools, and several attended state Islamic universities. Several had master's degrees and a few had specialized training in Islamic theology or Islamic interpretation. They were from small or midsize cities and towns, with parents who were civil servants or teachers, and family members involved in NU. However, a few had more unusual backgrounds. One was from a military family and another's father was a bus driver in a small town in East Java.

Some Rahima staff were involved in the *reformasi* movement through Muslim student groups. Others, like Ika, represented an older generation of activists who helped inspire the *reformasi* movement. Their experiences reflect the intersections of Islamic politics and gender politics, and as activists, they bridge these fields. As with Fatayat, most Rahima staff grew up within the NU milieu. However, Rahima activists' individual trajectories, as illustrated by Ayu and Ika, reveal more extensive cross-fertilization with global discourses of human rights, gender equality, and Islamic reformism.

As noted earlier, many Rahima and Fatayat staff have been embedded in Islamic institutions since childhood. But they are also one of the first generations to have the opportunity to be so embedded and obtain a university education and professional career. The first State Institute for Islamic Studies (then known as IAIN) was founded in 1960. At the time, graduates of *pesantrens* could not be admitted to state universities, so the IAIN became an important opportunity for higher education for these graduates. Additional IAINs were established, and in 1989, the government created a unified educational system. *Pesantren* graduates then became eligible to take the exams for state universities (Meuleman 2002).[17] In the 1990s and early 2000s, a number of IAINs were transformed into more prestigious State Islamic Universities (UIN), which teach business, law, and education in addition to the traditional Islamic sciences. The UIN-IAIN system now admits an increasing number of public school graduates (Azra et al. 2007).

At university, many of my informants from Rahima and Fatayat became involved with the national Muslim student organizations PMII and HMI. Participation in these institutions put these young activists into contact with broader social networks of reformists, as well as with ideas of gender equality and democracy. Working for Rahima and Fatayat has enabled them to continue their work for social justice as part of professional careers. These organizations represent the increasing intersections of Islamic politics and gender politics. They are located in the overlap of these fields, a position that shapes their pious critical agency and active engagements with Islam and feminism.

FEMINISM IN FATAYAT AND RAHIMA

In a bustling market town in West Java, Fatayat staff were holding a meeting for local members to introduce the organization's new membership cards. They were designed to be both identity cards and ATM cards, and Fatayat had made an arrangement with a *Shariah* bank to accept an initial minimum deposit of fifty thousand *rupiah* (about five dollars US at the time).[18] The cards were intended to allow Fatayat to create a membership database and help women get bank accounts for the first time.

What caused the most stir at the meeting was the issue of the name on the forms. Dita, a Fatayat staff member, told the assembled women that they should use their individual names on the form rather than their husbands' names—that is, "the name before you were married and you must provide your mother's maiden name too." Traditionally, many Javanese had one name, and married women used the name of their father as their family name. But women are increasingly adopting the Western habit of taking their husbands' surnames when they marry. Dita was asking women to identify themselves as individuals and in relation to their natal families, as opposed to just their husbands. This is just one of many examples I witnessed of Fatayat's subtle approach to challenging gender norms.

When I first met Fatayat and Rahima staff, I was surprised to find them so conversant with the language of gender equality (Figure 3.1). I expected that Muslim women's organizations might be uncomfortable with concepts like equality or that they might simply see feminism as an irrelevant Western discourse (Narayan 1997; Abu-Lughod 2002). But Fatayat and Rahima embraced equality while taking a critical approach to feminism.

Figure 3.1: Fatayat Nahdlatul Ulama, 2005 national conference.

Like many women's rights activists around the world, Rahima and Fatayat advocate for women to have equal opportunities for education and careers and to become more involved in politics, and for women and men to share domestic duties. While Rahima and Fatayat draw critically on transnational feminism, they are adapting it to fashion advocacy for women's rights that is inspired by both Islamic and feminist discourses.

Gender equality is a clear objective for both groups. It appears in Fatayat's vision statement: "To end all forms of violence, injustice and poverty in society by developing a discourse of social life which is constructive, democratic, and based on gender equality."[19] Similarly, Rahima's mission and vision statement states:

> Rahima's goal is to not only strengthen the position of women within Islamic societies (based on equality and justice), but to also assist in laying foundations for the creation of public democracy within Indonesian society.[20]

Since Rahima was established with the intention of empowering Muslim women, this commitment to gender equality was not such a surprise. But as I discussed in chapter 2, the overt promotion of women's rights is a relatively new agenda for Fatayat. Historically, NU was slow to incorporate women. Although the organization was founded in 1926, Muslimat, its group for older women, was established in 1946, and Fatayat in 1950. Both did mostly uncontroversial service and charity work focused on women. But in the early 1990s, international NGOs and donor agencies began to involve members of Fatayat in seminars about gender and human rights issues. Now the language of equality and rights is frequently used at Fatayat and Rahima, but terms such as *feminism* and *feminist* are more rare. Thus, in my fieldwork I was eager to understand what these activists meant when they talked about gender equality and women's rights. And how did they understand feminism?

The Social Construction of Gender

Rahima and Fatayat staff learned about women's rights on the job. While most said they joined the organizations because they were interested in helping women, they also said that they began to understand gender inequality once they became involved in the groups. Both groups have a similar standard curriculum for gender trainings:[21] they learn about the history of the women's rights movement, they are presented with a typology of feminisms (liberal, radical, and socialist), and they are taught that male and female roles are socially constructed.

Rahima and Fatayat have also added religious content to the trainings. For example, Fatayat's Gender Analysis Training Module starts out with a discussion of the work that men and women do. Trainers help participants classify which tasks are related to biological differences and which are related to sociocultural differences. Biological differences are categorized as *kodrat*, a Javanese term meaning nature or natural destiny, while sociocultural differences are considered to be gender. According to this manual, while giving birth and breastfeeding are related to *kodrat*, raising a child and housework are related to gender and are tasks that can be done by men or women. Participants then go on to discuss forms of gender inequality such as domestic violence and women's representation in politics (P. P. Fatayat Nahdlatul Ulama 1999).

This distinction between *kodrat* and gender is key to the training and resembles the distinction between biology and culture that is fundamental to many varieties of feminism. The Indonesian term used for gender is *jender*, though often the English word *gender* is used with Indonesian pronunciation (Bahasa Indonesia does not have a word that clearly denotes the social construction of sex roles). The global discourse of gender is thus domesticated by translating it into Indonesian. *Jender/gender* is used by the entire spectrum of women's groups in Indonesia, but I found it was especially common among Muslim activists. This is because, as discussed in chapter 2, feminism is linked with the West, communism, and secularism, all of which have negative associations for many Indonesians. Muslim women's groups are particularly sensitive to this problem because they feel that such connotations pose the most serious challenges in pious communities. One Fatayat staff member explained to me that people in such communities were suspicious of anything that "smells like America."

In contrast, terms like *gender equality*, *empowerment*, and *human rights* are considered to be more acceptable. Santhi explained that it is important to place ideas within a Muslim framework: "to translate them into local language, so that people feel the ideas are part of their culture and can be comfortable with them." Rahima staff told me that Muslim communities do not object to feminist ideas if they are framed under the rubric of *jender/gender*. Some Muslim women activists even describe themselves as *aktivis gender* (gender activists).[22]

Rahima's and Fatayat's emphasis on gender equality might be expected given their relationship with donors such as the Asia Foundation and the Ford Foundation. The Asia Foundation and the Ford Foundation have long histories in Indonesia. Since the early 1990s, they have funded programs to build civil society and democratization in Indonesia, and women's empowerment is part of this agenda. These donors seek out local NGOs and activist groups to participate in such programs. The transnational women's rights movement, which works primarily through NGOs, has also been influential in Indonesia, with European and American organizations such as the Global Fund for Women and Hivos providing funding for women's rights activists.

Nevertheless, it is not true that feminism is entirely exogenous to Indonesia. As I discussed in chapter 2, contemporary Indonesian women's organizations are building on a history of women's political mobilization that stretches back to the nationalist movement. As Narayan (1997) argues, "third world feminists" embody real and ongoing contestations within cultures, and they respond to the conditions that they experience. Moreover, scholars have chronicled how Indonesian Islam experienced much intellectual revitalization in the 1980s and 1990s, a process that both reached back to reclaim older traditions and was inspired by global currents. An interest in women's rights was a major element of this reformism. As the women's division of NU, Fatayat has certainly been part of such changes, and Rahima, founded by younger Muslim activists, is one of the consequences. Due to their interest in democracy and rights, both of these organizations have an elective affinity with the goals of international donors and NGOs, and they view them as crucial sources of knowledge and resources.

Adapting and Critiquing Feminism

Rahima and Fatayat engage critically and in varied ways with transnational feminism. Some members of Rahima and Fatayat sometimes voiced concerns about feminism. Others said that they agreed with the content of feminism and did not mind being considered feminists, although they were careful about using the term in their work. A few women called themselves Muslim feminists, a term they liked because they felt it emphasized their religious orientation. Others, like Farida and Ika, have fashioned their own feminisms and use the term freely.

Ika said that she became acquainted with feminism in the mid-1980s, after a friend returned from the U.N. women's conference in Mexico. She realized that women all across the world faced similar problems and were victims of oppression. I knew that Ika considered herself a feminist, so I asked her what kind of feminist she was. Ika replied:

> I am closer to socialist feminism.[23] I studied from books, from friends and discussions. I got a lot of theory from discussion groups, socialist theory groups, also because I was close to friends who think in a socialist way. I am happy gathering

with both older and younger socialists. I stay interested in socialist discourse because there is a place for discussing religion, although in the framework it is criticized and not implemented. Religion is a big and influential institution. We cannot reject the growth of fundamentalism. A lot of people still use religion to obtain various kinds of goals. This is one of the reasons I maintain a feminist socialist perspective.

What Ika means is that feminists in Indonesia must grapple with the reality of religion in their society. She seems to feel that socialism offers more flexibility with regard to religion than other left or liberal political ideologies.

Many Rahima and Fatayat activists said that they agreed with some aspects of feminism but disagreed with others. Yet their concerns about feminism were also not what I expected. I anticipated that Indonesian women would be critical of feminism because they saw it as Western or because of its universalizing qualities (Mohanty 1988). Instead, Rahima and Fatayat activists told me that just because an ideology is Western or foreign is not a reason to reject it. Many said that Indonesians should select the aspects of feminism that are culturally appropriate and reject those that are not.

A few women said that feminism was against their religious convictions. Concerns about feminism's incompatibility with Islam stemmed from several issues: the perception that feminism supports sexual liberation and "free sex," the belief that feminism is antireligious, and a concern that feminism discourages women from fulfilling their religious responsibility to marry and raise children. The explanation given by Mei fell into the latter categories:

> M: ...I don't really agree with the pattern of liberal feminism.[24] I struggle for women's rights in accordance with religious principles [and] also within religious principles and cultural norms, especially the Indonesian culture in which women exist. Not too vulgar and harsh. I don't go in that direction.
> R: What do you dislike about feminism?
> M: I think it is not Islamic enough. We as women, within Islam, are already given our own places as men and women. There is no difference, but we are apportioned our places. That is what is said in the Quran. So there is no difference even in politics. Our *kodrat* is to breastfeed, be pregnant, and give birth [which] represents a place for women, so that we must pay attention to it. For example, we have soft skin. Women are given a place that has already been determined, for instance, the worlds of education, medicine, and the spheres that are

not too harsh.... For instance, as athletes, men and women are both permitted to do it, but women can only be in certain sports.... They should look for things that are appropriate for women, because women are actually given advantages by God.

For Mei, equality does not mean that men and women do the same things. But while some Muslims argue that equality in the Quran means *moral* equity rather than *social* equality, Mei wavers between a conception of moral equity and a conception of equality as sameness. She says that there is no difference between men and women but argues for physical difference, referring to the notion of *kodrat*. Yet according to Mei, the physical difference is not huge; men and women can both participate in sports, but women presumably should be in less taxing sports.

Dewi, a young staff member at Rahima, associates feminism with radical feminists who blame men for everything. Interestingly, her concerns echo some of the common American stereotypes of feminism as being "antimen":

> I want to be a woman who humanizes people. Yes, there continues to be injustice which happens to men and women; it is proper to deal with that. We are right to prevent it. And if that is called feminism, I think it is too harsh. It's as if we position men as the ones who are doing something wrong.... On the one hand I agree with the views of feminists who feel that oppression of women has to be stopped. But on the other side, there are radical feminists who think that men are the oppressors of women. In conditions like this, we can't be like that, because anyone now has the opportunity to be oppressive.... I think the gender issue is one of the ways to teach humanity to people.

On the other hand, Ayu argues that feminism is about equality, but also that feminism can be culturally defined. Her concern is that some activists say only certain ways of being feminist are valid:

> There are some who say that they are surprised at Muslim feminists who wear the veil. If the problem is *the meaning* [of the veil], shackles, limitations, you may call me *uncivilized*. But if I feel, *"this is my identity that I have to show other people,"* then you must value this choice and you cannot dictate my path by saying this is false consciousness... because what feminists are struggling for is the issue of equality.... Equality is the basis... because people understand each other's realities. And what is necessary is *how we try to understand each other.*[25]

Ayu is alluding to feeling marginalized by feminists who criticize her for wearing the veil. Only once did I hear an Indonesian feminist publically question the veil. I did not find out if Ayu had had personal arguments with feminists. In any case, she argues that the two sides must try to understand each other better because they are linked by their common vision of equality.

While many Rahima and Fatayat activists adhere to particular understandings of feminism that lead them to distinguish themselves from feminists, a few also proudly claim the label. And most say they are working for equality and rights for women. Though Ayu has concerns about a monolithic feminism, it is clear that she is attracted by the notion of equality that she considers to be at the heart of feminism. While these activists often measure themselves against what they consider to be Western feminism, they are very much engaged in forging their own politics of women's rights that draws on Islam and feminism. They focus on equality in the household and the public sphere and stress the compatibility of these ideas with Islam. In the following section, I probe more deeply into what gender equality means to Fatayat and Rahima activists by exploring how it is implicated in their daily lives.

Feminism and Daily Life

Many of the activists of Rahima and Fatayat that I met were in their twenties and thirties, so not surprisingly, marriage and family came up often in my discussions with them. Their aspirations for their intimate relationships reveal the potent appeal of ideas about equality.

During my fieldwork, a few Rahima staff members were unmarried and searching for partners. Such single women activists reflect a broader demographic shift toward later marriage in Indonesia (Jones 2005). In a society where being married and having children is *the* definition of adulthood, they are in a difficult position. Ayu spoke candidly about this dilemma. In 2003, she told me that several years previously her parents wanted her to get married before her younger sister did. They tried to her convince her to accept an arranged marriage, but she wouldn't. Her sister got married and now has children. Ayu felt pressure from both her parents and her religion:

> Sometimes I think, "I have to prepare myself [to convert to] another faith. I have to get married soon. What for?" Because I think like this: *You should have reproduction and according to your religion you should have to get marriage.* It's not just that. *I don't want to get married with every man, but I just want to marry a man who has the same view with me. I have to find the right person....* My social

awareness, my activities have made me something new. Actually, the problem is not a problem of love or not love; the problem is not because of liking and not liking. We have to have a person who can be invited to work together with us. It's called "partnership." Marriage for me is working together, collaboration. You can divide things up. So I hope. I must find a person who is progressive enough to cooperate with me.[26]

Ayu's busy life made it difficult for her to meet suitable partners. This reality proved hard to reconcile with her belief that a Muslim woman must marry. At the time when I first met her, she hoped to find a man who was both pious and progressive. Since then, she has married.

Women in Fatayat were energized to talk about balancing family life with work. Like other activists, Farida was proud that her husband was willing to share domestic duties, but she admitted that having household help lightens the burden:

At the beginning, we didn't have a maid and so we shared the household chores. Sometimes I washed his clothes, but sometimes he washed my clothes, or he washed our clothes, and I ironed them. We're also very flexible about cooking and serving meals. I never have the obligation to prepare meals for him and accompany him while eating. In this case, I don't follow my mother and grandmother's tradition. If he wants to eat, he'll eat. The first time I had a baby, my mother and parents-in-law often visited us, but I was often admonished by my mother for letting my husband wash our clothes. She thought that it was inappropriate. Then, we decided to have a domestic helper. Now, my first child is already in the third grade of junior high school and the second one in the fifth grade of elementary school, and we take turns to take care of them. If, for example, I have to travel, then he stays home and looks after the children. That's the deal. We also take turns to drop them off at school.

Most the women I spoke to at Fatayat had domestic help, as did some of the staff of Rahima. The supply of cheap labor in Indonesia has aided middle-class women's entry into the professional workforce, though some women activists have raised concerns about the exploitation of poor women and girls in paid domestic work. Yet for many middle-class Indonesian women the role of housewife remains an ideal, if one that is difficult to fulfill. The strategy outlined by Farida demonstrates her desire to have an egalitarian division of labor in the home, a rejection of the widespread notion that cooking and cleaning are women's tasks. And more than that, her career outside the home is taken for granted.[27]

Not all Fatayat women agree. Farida's colleague Wiwit told me that domestic duties are women's responsibility, though she approves of men helping. When I asked her how her family felt about her activism in Fatayat, she said, "I thank God that my husband does not mind; if he did I couldn't go out to Fatayat. So my husband understands [and] as long as the household business is finished, then I can go out to Fatayat." Nevertheless, Wiwit lauds the trend toward equality in Indonesian households and cites her relationship as an example:

> Women are now brave enough to express their ideas to their husbands; they don't just obey them. They are brave enough to express new ideas. In raising the children, certainly, we have ideas, the husbands also do, and we can discuss them. . . . If I look at the highly educated, there are those who have begun to have equality because of awareness. Here is an example. My husband is a better cook. He is better at taking care of the children than I am. We have a maid, but sometimes my husband also looks after the children.

The influence of feminist ideas was obvious in my discussions about marriage and family with Rahima and Fatayat women. These activists, including those who consider domestic work as primarily women's responsibility, emphasize what social scientists call "companionate marriage," a relationship in which men and women make decisions together and in which the relationship is believed to be based on notions of mutual love and romance.[28] In fact, most of the Indonesian women activists I met, across all four organizations, shared this ideal. As I also discuss in chapter 4, companionate marriage is not alien to Muslim thought (Abu-Lughod 1998). However, it is only in the last few decades that it seems to have become culturally dominant among the Indonesian middle classes (Smith-Hefner 2005). Yet there is a subtle and important difference between women at Rahima and Fatayat and the PKS women I discuss in chapter 4. Women at Rahima and Fatayat were more likely not just to speak of a partnership or a team effort in their relationship, but to mention wanting an equal relationship. This aspiration represents a break from the more patriarchal variant of companionate marriage, featuring a devoted housewife and a breadwinning husband, promoted by the Suharto regime (Brenner 1998). Interestingly, the ideals of equality they hope to instill in their intimate relationships were inspired not only by feminism but also by Islam. These activists' interest in women's rights and egalitarian households reflects the recent overlap between Islamic politics and gender politics in Indonesia.

Prayer was woven into the fabric of daily life in the offices of both Fatayat and Rahima. The Fatayat office in the NU building was tiny, with just enough room for three or four desks. There was a small prayer room down the hall, where I sometimes conducted interviews. But most Fatayat women washed in the hallway bathroom and then put on their white shawls and prayed on the floor of the office. Rahima staff were less public about their prayers. They simply disappeared to the back of the house, or if I was with them, they would politely excuse themselves. Yet because of the frequency of Muslim prayers, I was constantly aware of staff members carrying them out.

There were other reminders of the active practice of Islam. Both offices had wall decorations with Arabic writing or motifs, including mementos such as calendars from a visit to the Middle East. Some staff had Arabic names. Such names have become widespread in Indonesia over the past few decades, replacing names derived from Indian mythology. Arabic names seemed to be more common among Muslim activists compared to groups like Solidaritas Perempuan, perhaps reflecting more pious family backgrounds.

Women took pleasure in collective religious rituals such as prayer or communal dinners to break the Ramadan fast while also treasuring the sense of personal transformation they got out of participation in these activities. Santhi told me that she felt Rahima had made her into a better Muslim. In an emotional speech at her goodbye party, Santhi told the gathering that she didn't know if she could be considered a true Muslim, but she is much happier with the Muslim she is now than when she first started working at Rahima. As an example, she said she only started wearing a *jilbab* after she joined Rahima.

As their trajectories show, the lives of Fatayat and Rahima activists have been shaped by the Islamic revival and their involvement in the field of Islamic politics. The NU milieu has structured the way these activists understand and practice Islam. In particular, the contextual approach to interpretation learned through their educational institutions and activist experiences contributes to the development of a pious critical agency that engages actively with religious texts. Moreover, as the intersections between Islamic politics and gender politics have expanded, these activists' unique position in the overlap between these fields has also made possible their embrace of ideas about women's rights and gender equality.

A central tenet of Islam for Rahima and Fatayat members is egalitarianism. Their conception of piety foregrounds not just individual religious practice and personal faith, but also social justice. Other scholars (Brenner 1996; Van Doorn-Harder 2006) have observed that Islam is viewed by many Indonesian Muslim women activists as a counterweight to local patriarchal cultures. Rahima and Fatayat activists frequently cited the Quranic verse that says that all humans are created out of the same material and are the same in the eyes of Allah. Another verse they were fond of citing, especially about the relationship between husband and wife, translated roughly as, "He is your garment and she is yours." Although in some circles the first statement is interpreted to mean that men and women are equal in matters of faith, Rahima and Fatayat members expand its meaning to argue that men and women are equal in general. In doing so, they follow Muslim leaders such as former Indonesian president and former NU leader Abdurrahman Wahid, who also emphasized the egalitarian qualities of Islam.

A few women I met argued that Islam provides a model of gender equality that is preferable to the cultures in which they were raised. Dewi of Rahima explained that at the State Islamic University she attended, her involvement with student groups led her to question her parents:

> Added to this was the climate at IAIN, which was thick with discussion. This influenced my thinking. Truly, Islam is not discriminatory. And there are also new ideas I got from my study group. Maybe in the home it's those that are a challenge for me. In the home, actually, my mother and father are strict. They do not permit me to wear long pants like these [points at interviewer]. That means I would look like a man. If I look like a man it means I won't go to heaven. When I came home from campus with rebellious thoughts, I began to question further.... Maybe the patterns of the house and the campus are opposite. At home I enter into old traditions, with Quranic studies and old ways.

Some women said that Islam gave them ammunition to argue with strict or oppressive families. Tuti, a Fatayat member from conservative South Sulawesi, said that what she learned about gender in Fatayat helped her have a voice in her family:

> Because in my family women were not allowed to be independent, they had to obey. When I was a student, I joined organizations and then got into Fatayat.

After moving to Jakarta, I became aware that women did not yet have their rights.... Now these are free times; we have the right to a voice.... In my family, forced marriages are still happening; like it or not, that is the wish of the parents, the grandparents. So because of that I entered Fatayat and communicated with my family. I said that I have rights.

Not only does Islamic theology provide a framework that allows Fatayat and Rahima activists to argue for equality, but Islamic institutions and organizations have also made it possible for pious Muslim women to attain university educations and go on to have careers. Certainly not all women who have been empowered by Islamic education and organizations become women activists. But confidence in the egalitarian spirit of Islam, as well as their own sense of empowerment through Islamic education, leads the activists of Rahima and Fatayat to insist that the true Islam supports women's rights.

Though members of Rahima and Fatayat say they see no contradiction between Islam and women's rights, they admit that some aspects of the religion can pose problems for women's rights. In particular, they argue that when formally enacted by governments or local authorities, Islamic *Shariah* law usually restricts women or treats them unequally.

At a Rahima conference in 2003, a young *jilbab*-wearing activist from West Java gave a synopsis of recent developments regarding *Shariah* in her city. She started out by saying that Islam in the area is mixed with local Sundanese (West Javanese) customs and values. In this, she was echoing statements by other Rahima activists who argue that traditional forms of Islam are patriarchal. She talked about the efforts to implement laws inspired by *Shariah* in the province, noting that "gender activists get threats from Islamic fundamentalist groups and other religious literalists." In response, a male conference participant asked if there had been a rejection of *jilbabisasi* by the lower class. "Maybe their analysis is different than ours," he said. "Women were very much confined and are now rejecting that, so there may be a reaction."

The young woman responded by saying that the community does not truly understand religious ideas, and therefore, people tend to do what they are told is obligatory for Muslims. "*Jilbabisasi* has occurred not from the government, but from groups opposed to sex workers," she explained, referring to the religious organizations and political parties who had promoted local headscarf laws or nighttime curfews for women, allegedly to discourage prostitution.[29]

Jilbabisasi was a term I heard frequently. It was initially a source of confusion. Thinking activists meant the trend of wearing *jilbab*, I wasn't sure how to respond when I heard this term from women who themselves wore *jilbab*. It eventually became clear that *jilbabisasi* refers to efforts by local governments or other authorities to require women to wear *jilbab*. Fatayat and Rahima staff endorse the *jilbab*, but they oppose attempts to make it a law. The Rahima activist from West Java was suggesting that the promotion of *Shariah* law and *jilbab* regulations are tied to a conservative interpretation of Islam that is at odds with both women's rights and Rahima's activism.

The distinction between *jilbab* and *jilbabisasi* is crucial for Rahima members because it signifies the difference between personal piety and social justice, of which they approve, and publicly enforced morality, which they oppose. Rahima and Fatayat activists were very thoughtful about the subject of piety, and it came up often in my interviews with them. They were united by their understanding of piety as a personal choice, though not one that necessarily must remain in the private sphere. Some scholars argue that the concept of piety promulgated by the global Islamic revival has highly public features (Mahmood 2005; Deeb 2006). As such, it emphasizes visible forms of practice like prayer and clothing as much as faith. Beyond women's rights, the *jilbabisasi* and *Shariah* discussions demonstrate that what is at stake for Fatayat and Rahima members is whether the state should govern by enforcing or regulating pious behavior. The answer is a definite no, although activists do hope that the government will be influenced by religious values such as social justice, and they approve of piety taking publicly expressive forms (such as clothing). In keeping with Muslim convention, Rahima and Fatayat activists say they are implementing and carrying out *Shariah* in their personal lives.

This was explained to me by Ayu. In one of our early conversations, we discussed competing interpretations of Islamic law. She was telling me that NU recognizes the validity of all four major Sunni schools of jurisprudence. I asked her how a person can know what is right, given that there is no central authority in Islam. Ayu replied that, in her opinion, it is up to the individual to decide what is best for him- or herself, and that this is a private decision. This is why one religion cannot be the basis for state law in a religiously plural state, she continued. The important thing, she added, "is to decide what are the universal values that underlie Islam and other religions" and to "socialize" them so that everyone internalizes them.

While Fatayat and Rahima promote religious expression in the public sphere, they differentiate such activity from state control over religion. For Rahima and Fatayat women, religious practices, such as wearing a *jilbab* and carrying out prayers at the proper times, are public practices but are also matters of individual choice—even if they also believe that some choices are better than others.

For Fatayat and Rahima activists, piety is intertwined with a conviction that to be a good Muslim means respecting others as full human beings with rights and responsibilities. This to them includes a commitment to gender equality. For example, Ayu explained that the increasing number of mosques and women wearing the *jilbab* do not necessarily reflect true piety:

> Claiming to be speaking in the name of God is not necessarily an indication of religiosity either. Religiosity is when a person tries to fully comprehend his/her own life and tries to implement the teachings of faith, meaning that he/she knows the position of *Tuhan* [God] and humanity. God has power over humanity and humanity is obligated to make an effort and as long as we try and turn over the final decision to God, that is what I call religious. When parents can give their children rights, when a husband can give rights to his wife and the wife to her husband, when people respect each other, that is where religiosity appears. When a person is moved to empower those who are weaker, that is religiosity. It's not just a matter of giving charity, but about empowering the people who are being helped—that's what I call religiosity.

For Ayu, religious piety not only is about one's individual practices but also is expressed in how one relates to people. Her definition of religiosity includes empowerment of those who have been marginalized. When I asked her if there was a difference between "regular" feminists and Muslim feminists, she replied:

> I always say there is no contradiction within myself in being Muslim and a feminist. I am a Muslim and I am sure of the teachings of my religion. I implement those teachings, but I am also aware that there are social relations in society, including in the Muslim community, that contradict those values. With regard to feminism, Islam teaches us to respect women and to never deny their rights, and so it is in line with feminist values.

In this respect, piety and women's rights are bound together for many Rahima and Fatayat staff.

What Fatayat and Rahima share with groups like PKS, as we shall see in the next chapter, is a conception of piety that involves more than individual religiosity—it also entails a commitment to public life. This is reminiscent of the kind of piety Weber saw as transformative in Western Europe. In *The Protestant Ethic and the Spirit of Capitalism* (2001), Weber argued that Calvinist religious teachings were directly related to the rise of capitalism. The new religious ethos told people not only that they must have faith but also that economic success was a sign of being among the chosen. Instead of drawing inward for religious reflection, increasing numbers of Protestant Europeans began to focus their lives around hard work and investment in business and education.

Perhaps the mark of modernity is this mixture of piety and worldly affairs. However, Fatayat and Rahima also use piety to achieve emancipatory reforms, especially women's rights. As they do so, they manifest a pious critical agency, which involves a critical engagement with religious texts, allowing them to advocate for women's rights within an Islamic framework.

Arguing for Women's Rights in Islam

Arguing for women's rights in Islam poses potential difficulties for Muslim women activists because some verses of the Quran and Hadiths are widely believed to condone male dominance. For example, the Quranic verse Surah an-Nisa 34 is conventionally understood to command men to be rulers in the home and to allow them to beat wives if they disobey.[30] In some parts of the world, patriarchal practices such as stoning, domestic violence, and restrictions on women's mobility are justified with reference to such texts. Whether or not one can find an actual basis for such forms of treatment in the Quran, it is certainly also the case that Islamic law includes provisions that are at odds with gender equality, for example, unequal inheritance regulations.

How do women's rights activists manage this dilemma? This is precisely why the process of interpretation is so crucial for Fatayat and Rahima activists. They have developed a pious critical agency as they seek to interpret religious texts in ways that support women's rights and equality. Key to this agency is a contextual method, which provides flexibility in interpretation and which has been instilled in individuals through the NU milieu, as well as taught by Rahima and Fatayat. As Islamic politics and gender politics have intersected and Rahima and Fatayat activists found themselves in the fertile overlap of these fields, they have sought to frame feminist claims within an Islamic framework. Pious critical agency makes this possible.

The actual work of interpretation is more central to Rahima, which has staff who are involved in the study of texts, but Fatayat's activism is also shaped by the contextual approach. Contextual approaches are well known to Muslims in Indonesia and elsewhere.[31] One of the central claims made by Rahima and Fatayat activists, and that has been influenced by NU intellectual leaders such as Abdurrahman Wahid, is that while the Quran was transmitted directly from Allah to Muhammad, the Hadiths and the *fikh* represent the writings of jurists and scholars over a period of several cen-turies.[32] Thus, interpretation, as well as an understanding of historical context, is necessary to understand the religion. The Indonesian Islamic tradition, with its emphasis on jurisprudence, helps to make this approach possible and culturally legitimate. Fatayat and Rahima therefore capitalize on the NU backgrounds of many of their staff and volunteers and the par-ticipants in their programs.

The contextual approach is at the heart of Islam's meaning for Farida. Mentioning what she sees as an ongoing struggle between conservative and progressive Islam, Farida said she preferred to be in the progressive camp:

> I think the most important thing is to implement the teachings of Islam in our everyday lives, and because life is dynamic, there is always room for reinterpre-tation of texts. That way, the values contained in the texts will be applicable to all times and will always be meaningful. We won't be trapped in one particu-lar interpretation, which in the end makes life difficult. Some people might not agree with me, but I think Quranic texts and the Prophet's statements should be understood dynamically. We should put them into context.

For Farida, it is precisely such flexibility that allows Islam to be relevant and meaningful in the contemporary world. Similarly, when I asked Hasan, one of the founders of Rahima, about the ideological influences on his thinking about women's rights, he responded, "We reinterpret the teach-ings of Islam that are not in accordance with the demands of the era. We have to do this." Later, Hasan continued, "My religion is a living tradition. So I must care for it and undertake renovation and new interpretations so that the religion is not left behind. The function of religion is liberation, so that we can free humanity from difficulties."

Farida's and Hasan's statements demonstrate their renewal of the Indonesian Islamic tradition and their pious critical agency. However, Indonesian Islamic traditions have not necessarily been supportive of women's rights. Indeed, early opposition to women's rights in Indonesia came from the traditionalist Muslim milieu. Nahdlatul Ulama was much slower than its more modernist counterpart, Muhammadiyah, in allowing women to form their own division within the organization. What the new generation of NU progressives has done is to consciously adapt their tradi-tion to ideas of gender and human rights.

Many examples of revisionist interpretation can be found in Rahima's jour-nal, *Swara Rahima*. For instance, Faqihuddin Abdul Qodir (2011) writes about the concept of *aurat*. *Aurat* is an Arabic term for the forbidden, intimate parts of the body that are sinful to expose. In this essay, he seeks to understand the common Muslim expression "women are *aurat*." Qodir quotes the verse that is conventionally understood to use *aurat* as the reason for veiling: "Say also to women of faith: They should restrain from view and guard against shame, and they should not make visible their decorations, except those which usually are visible. And they should cover their chest with a veil." Qodir says that this verse is vague and that scholars don't agree on how to interpret it.

He then goes on to analyze some related Hadiths. One says that Allah will not accept a woman's prayer unless she wears a cloth covering her head. Qodir says that this Hadith is often used to argue that women's heads are *aurat*, but he says the majority of *fikh* scholars say it means that only the head is *aurat*, and that does not include the face. Another Hadith calls for women during prayer to wear a long dress that covers the soles of their feet. Qodir says this Hadith is considered weak, possibly inauthentic.

After critically examining other Hadiths and judging them invalid, Qodir says that verses that use unclear wording and have multiple interpretations cannot be turned into a basis for certainty, much less law. He concludes, "In the time of Nabi, many women went out of the house, prayed, sought knowledge at the mosque, worked, or fulfilled their needs. This means that in the time of Nabi, women were not considered *aurat*, which would have meant that if they went out they would be cursed by Satan. That would have required women to be confined in the house."[33] Qodir employs the texts and the historical record to argue that women are not *aurat*, and that if the term does apply, it may only be in a limited sense, such as requiring a head covering during prayer.

Closely related to this line of reasoning, some Fatayat and Rahima activists employ a more explicitly feminist argument. Influenced by the writings of Middle Eastern feminists such as Fatima Mernissi, Rifaat Hassan, and Nawal el Saadawi, this approach insists that Islam has been interpreted by men in ways that benefit men. This is what accounts for the discriminatory concepts and regulations found in Islamic texts, including the Hadiths and *fikh*. Mutiara, a Fatayat leader, explained:

> When I study religion more deeply, I salute Islam even more, because since the times of Muhammad, Islam has given women a high position. Women finally got an inheritance. But because in Indonesia the culture is patriarchal and the *kyais* are men, all the verses are interpreted as they look and they benefit only men. So my task is to straighten out those wrong interpretations.

The logic of these arguments is that Islam needs to be reinterpreted for a contemporary context to find the true ideas of equality and justice that have been buried under patriarchal interpretations, making new and more egalitarian interpretations are necessary. In advocating this path, staff at Rahima and Fatayat often say that they prefer to focus on the spirit of Islam. Rahima activists often refer to theirs as the "substantive approach." They contrast it to the approach of more conservative Muslim groups, which they describe as "formalist." By formalist, they mean an approach to religious practice that is preoccupied with rules and symbols and understood in a literal way, rather than the deeper meaning implied by the "substantive" approach. Rahima and Fatayat staff sometimes say that the substantive approach is the key to combating "Wahhabism," the catch-all derogatory term for Muslim extremists or hardliners, and a reference to the prevailing school of religious practice in Saudi Arabia.

Rahima activists often spoke about how the contextual, substantive approach to Islam influenced them personally. For example, although her modest clothing might be seen as evidence of formalist commitment to Islam, Dewi told me that she takes a substantive approach in her own practice of Islam. "I think my religious views are still very strong. And they influence my attitudes for living.... I think what is most important is how we are religious and have social piety, because in Islam honor isn't shown by clothing but from devotion. And devotion is visible in how much someone cares about fellow people." Dewi's statement indicates that Rahima's substantive approach foregrounds piety's public aspects of social justice, rather than the rules of religious practice.

Ayu elaborates on the difference this approach makes for Indonesian activists:

> Islam is open to *itjihad*,[34] as we live in a world where history, texts from the past, and other artifacts should be reread for the present context. In the end, the essence of Islam becomes a political discourse.... Looking at Islam as a formality tends to restrict people to concentrate only on legal matters.... Viewing Islam in terms of substance, on the other hand, leads people to explore issues of pluralism, humanism, and gender equity.

Here it can be seen how pious critical agency involves a critical engagement with religious texts to make claims for social and political reforms. In the next section, I examine more closely how Fatayat and Rahima activists use contextual methods to produce egalitarian interpretations of Islamic texts.

Contextual Interpretation and Women's Rights

With a contextual approach, Islamic texts can be understood in manifold ways, including those that support gender equality. This approach allows

Fatayat and Rahima activists to argue for gender equality while framing their claims within Islam, thus maintaining legitimacy as Muslim activists.

Yet the contextual approach sometimes seems to be at odds with many of the articles in Rahima's own journal. These articles often painstakingly parse the meanings and authenticity of texts to answer doctrinal questions. If the substance and context of the religion is the focus, then why devote so much time trying to find the true meaning of a fragment of text?

The reason is that what Rahima and Fatayat are aiming at is nothing less than changing conventional understandings of Islam's teachings about gender and using these alternative interpretations to push for broader social changes. These activists do so as a matter of strategy, in that they think that feminist ideas need to be framed within Islam to gain traction. But they also do so as a matter of belief, and because they are profoundly inspired by their own view of Islam as feminist and egalitarian.

These issues are at the heart of the pious critical agency that can be seen in the intense interpretive emphasis of both organizations. One of Rahima's most important functions is to create and disseminate alternative interpretations of Islam to promote gender equality. While it is still mostly men who do such interpretation, Rahima does have programs to train female scholars. Moreover, discussions and debates about texts are a feature of its work. Though Fatayat does not spend as much time on such efforts, a few staff are involved in interpretive endeavors. For example, Farida has worked with Puan Amal Hayati, which focuses on producing gender-egalitarian interpretations of Islamic texts. Fatayat strives to disseminate these alternative interpretations among its membership base.

This can be seen in the manual that Fatayat uses for gender trainings for its members, which has a section called "Gender in the Islamic Perspective" (P. P. Fatayat Nahdlatul Ulama 1999). Fatayat leaders conduct these trainings for Fatayat branches all across the country using this manual. The final section of the manual lists as the goals for these trainings:

1. Participants understand and comprehend that the essence of the teaching of Islam is the oneness of God. The unity of God as a theology means the liberation of humanity from all kinds of oppression and from all forms of shackles so that humanity realizes that what is proper is to worship Allah.
2. The participants understand that Islam is a religion which strongly respects the values of brotherhood, equality, justice, and freedom.
3. Participants understand that Islam gives women a high position. Women are viewed as the same as men, namely as full human beings, who have certain rights and obligations.

4. Participants realize that some of the teachings of Islam which deal with the relations between men and women have been wrongly interpreted so that they produce the belief that Islam legitimizes gender relations that are not equal.

5. Participants have a critical awareness about the necessity of interpretations that return to the sources of Islamic teachings about the relations between men and women. (P. P. Fatayat Nahdlatul Ulama 1999)[35]

As part of the training, participants are led through a discussion of the concepts of justice and equality, said to be the core principles of Islam, and taught the ideas behind the methodology of contextual interpretation of Islamic texts. The concluding section of the manual includes Arabic verses and Indonesian translations of Hadiths that are considered as "not taking the side of women," as well as those that appear to be about "equality and justice." The leaders end the session with a dialogue on which Hadiths and verses need to be reinterpreted and why. For example, one of the texts presented as not supportive of women is the following:

> The Prophet Muhammad spoke: Women are *aurat*, so when they go out of their houses, the devils will feel happy.... In other stories women are *aurat*, so they should stay in the house. Truly if women go out they will make the hearts of devils happy because they are tempting.[36]

Examples of more positive teachings include:

1. All people, be devout to your God who has created you from one substance, and from out of which Allah created his wife, and from the two of them Allah bred many men and women.

2. The best example for you women are the women of Anshor, they are never embarrassed to ask questions about religious issues.[37]

Although the first quotation seems stronger in its opposition to equality than the next two are in their support for equality, in the manual the "positive" verses are considered evidence that Islam supports women's rights.

Rahima publishes similar analyses of Islamic religious texts in its journal *Swara Rahima*. These alternative interpretations are taught in seminars and workshops, and the scholars who write them often participate in the workshops. For example, Marzuki Wahid, a well known NU Islamic scholar, is on Rahima's board. He has published many articles in *Swara Rahima*, including one about sexuality, women, and freedom entitled "Giving Authority to Women" (Wahid 2011).[38] In this article, Wahid clarifies what he sees as the basic Quranic position on sexuality. He writes that the Quran is not a book of law, but rather "a framework for the breaking down of problems, and a base for us to understand the basic principles of life."

Wahid discusses the Quranic verses that describe the sexual relationship between a husband and wife. He acknowledges that a famous verse uses an agricultural metaphor to describe the sexuality of women as passive and males as active, and that it seems to suggest that women must be prepared to receive any sexual acts at any time from their husbands. Wahid says that this general understanding has proliferated and has led to the subordination of women. He claims that it is a biased interpretation that has arisen from a patriarchal culture. Wahid argues that if one examines interpretations of this verse from a variety of holy books (he does not specify which), the verse can be interpreted to demonstrate the freedom of ways to carry out sexual intercourse. In fact, he continues, "The verse... aims to show that a sexual relationship can be carried out not only for reproduction but for recreation as well. Reproduction is only one function of a sexual relationship.... An equal relationship is a relationship complete with mutual respect and mutual need for a partner to carry out one's sexual desires."

In his conclusion, Wahid discusses the importance of a contextual approach, arguing, "To read the Quran concerning sexuality without reading and understanding the cultural construct of the society of Jazirah, Arabia, at that time, will result in the loss of the vision of emancipation, which is implied in every meaning of the Quran." And in dramatic fashion, he concludes:

> The Prophet Muhammad is a revolutionary, both in his expression as well as in his action. With the inspiration of the vision of God... he proposed an alternative social level that was just and not exploitative or discriminative, as well as opposing slavery and inhumane tendencies toward women. Within this context, is it not true that we can call the Prophet Muhammad a feminist?

Wahid's reinterpretation is reminiscent of Liberation Theology, which interprets Christian teachings in terms of liberation from unjust social conditions.[39] In doing so, it contests the conventional framing of the question of women's rights, which associates equality and emancipation with secularism, and inequality with religion. As Casanova (2009, 18) observes, "At least in Europe, the need to advance and protect gender equality and women's rights has become today the most common normative justification of secularism." Wahid's proposal is that religion can provide support for women's emancipation and equality.

Though they do not put it this way, what these examples demonstrate is that Fatayat and Rahima are engaged in a struggle for believers over what Islam means and how it should be practiced. As reformists, they work to transform their religion and their society, and gender equality is a key aspect of the changes they hope to make.

That is what Lily Munir meant at the Fatayat workshop when she said that "we work for women's rights but we are still Muslim." Munir's statement stakes a claim for being simultaneously Muslim and feminist. Likewise, for Fatayat and Rahima, women's rights and Islam are intertwined. Certainly it is not always as seamless a picture as they would like. The work they do to reconcile these two discourses is crucial not only to their own identities as Muslim women's rights activists but also for their success in disseminating their ideas to others.

Pious critical agency facilitates these new activist repertoires that combine Islam and feminism, relying on contextual interpretations of Islamic texts to do so. In the following section, I investigate how Fatayat and Rahima develop pious critical agency as they engage with texts to advocate women's rights and equality. In their activist interventions related to polygamy and women's reproductive rights, pious critical agency overlaps with feminist agency. Pious activating agency is also visible, as Fatayat and Rahima activists use accepted interpretations to mobilize. Moreover, their involvement in these issues emerges with the overlap between Islamic politics and gender politics, as these dynamic fields of action increasingly influence each other.

ENGAGEMENTS IN THE PUBLIC SPHERE: WOMEN'S RIGHTS IN AN ISLAMIC FRAMEWORK

Polygamy

Since the late 1990s, polygamy has become the subject of contentious public debates in Indonesia. As discussed in chapter 2, polygamy has an extensive history as a subject of argument in Indonesia. The 1974 Marriage Law permits a man to take a second wife if the first is an invalid, infertile, or terminally ill, but court approval is required. In 1983, the government began to require male civil servants to seek permission from superiors before divorcing or taking a second wife. By the 1990s, Indonesia's growing middle class generally saw polygamy as backward. Although there is little evidence that its prevalence has increased, after the collapse of the Suharto regime in 1998, a few public figures became outspoken about their support for polygamy. It came to be seen by some as an authentically Muslim form of family, as well as a solution to a perceived moral crisis (Brenner 2006; Nurmila 2009).

The contextual approach to religious interpretation is fundamental to women's rights activists' public interventions against polygamy. Polygamy is an especially emotionally charged issue for staff at Rahima, which was founded when activists left another Muslim organization after that group's leader took a second wife.

Rahima's cofounder Ika explained that her opposition to polygamy arises partly from her personal experiences. Her own father married a second wife. As Ika told me:

> My marriage has bargaining. It's about how to measure the interests of the man and woman. I am on the side of the woman. My mother did not agree with the polygamy, because she felt it was unjust. My father didn't want to know [about this]. According to him, the person who influenced my mother with antipolygamy thoughts was me.

Displeased with Ika's choice of spouse, her father decreed that if her mother attended Ika's wedding, she would have to leave the house permanently. Ika's mother was miserable and wanted to leave her marriage. Ika went through with the wedding. "But it was difficult and made me ill. I was stressed and sick for a long time because I was expelled from my family and had to bring my mother with me."

At a conference for community activists, Hasan, a cofounder of Rahima, told the audience that Rahima's basic principles of justice and monogamy come from Islam. Later, a representative from a women's rights NGO asked Hasan whether Rahima accepted staff or volunteers with two wives. Hasan, the author of a book on women's rights in Islam, didn't answer directly, but reiterated the importance of monogamy: "Monogamy is a kind of ideal; monogamy is a form of justice."

Fatayat leaders have also helped to popularize arguments against polygamy. For example, Farida has published articles on polygamy in Indonesia's leading newspapers and magazines. In one essay, she writes that the "basic principle" of marriage in Islam is monogamy, and that the Quranic verses about polygamy should be understood in the context of a particular time and place (Ansor 2002). Similarly, she is quoted in a newspaper article saying, "Islam does not prohibit it, but it also does not encourage it. The Quran has a verse on polygamy, but when it is read completely, polygamy is not encouraged. It demands just treatment or we should not have polygamy" (Pambudy 2009).

The polygamy debate exploded into controversy in 2003 with the announcement of the "polygamy awards" contest sponsored by the entrepreneur Puspo Wardoyo. Wardoyo, who owns a chain of fried chicken restaurants, announced an award to promote "transparent polygamy" in which a husband informs his wife of his new marriage. His restaurants adopted a polygamy theme, serving items like "polygamy juice." At the gala, Wardoyo honored thirty-seven men and distributed pro-polygamy books. Hundreds of protesters (including Fatayat members) marched outside the hotel with placards reading "Monogamy yes, polygamy no" (Brenner 2006; Nurmila 2009; Robinson 2009). The award ceremony has not been repeated.

In 2006, the controversy became more polarized with the fashionable Muslim preacher Aa Gym's announcement that he had married a second wife. His popularity plummeted and his commercial empire subsequently shrank dramatically, although it has since rebounded (Hoesterey 2008). Aa Gym's revelations inspired competing street demonstrations by pro- and anti-polygamy partisans.

The polygamy controversy has generated copious media extolling the values of polygamous families or, conversely, arguing that polygamy has no place in contemporary Islam. Indonesia's vast pop culture industry has capitalized on the controversy. The 2008 hit film *Ayat-Ayat Cinta* (*Verses of Love*), which ends with the marriage of its romantic hero to a second wife, helped to spawn a trend for Islamic romance stories and films. While Indonesian president Susilo Bambang Yudhoyono and leaders of Muslim organizations praised the film for presenting the story of a youth getting married in an Islamic manner, many women's rights advocates were uncomfortable with what they saw as the film's gentle treatment of polygamy.

The Quranic justification for polygamy is found in Surah 4:3, which reads: "If ye fear that ye shall not be able to deal justly with the orphans, Marry women of your choice, Two or three or four; but if ye fear that ye shall not be able to deal justly (with them), then only one, or (a captive) that your right hands possess, that will be more suitable, to prevent you from doing injustice."[40] Many Indonesians believe that this verse does not encourage polygamy but allows it in special or emergency situations.

Rahima and Fatayat activists add more historical complexity and a stronger disavowal of the practice in their work. Fatayat leaders do not dispute that the Quran allows men to marry four wives. They draw on historical studies of women in Muslim societies to explain that polygamy was a common practice in the Arab peninsula during the time of Muhammad, and that men sometimes had dozens of wives. They argue that the restrictions the Prophet Muhammad placed on polygamy, limiting men to four wives, were progressive for that era. Moreover, Farida's 2002 article maintains that the Prophet's practice of polygamy was a special right guaranteed for him only. According to Farida, he took several wives because during his lifetime there was an oversupply of widows due to intertribal conflict. According to both Rahima and Fatayat, since Islam at its outset intended to make progressive reforms and was concerned about the well-being of women, it makes sense that polygamy should not be allowed in contemporary society. Fatayat leaders also contend that the wording of the verse on polygamy makes it clear that men are only permitted to marry more than one wife if they can support all the wives equally. They say that accomplishing that is impossible in this day and age, especially when it comes to fulfilling wives' emotional needs.

Fatayat and Rahima activists also have participated in demonstrations and other events criticizing polygamy. In the wake of the Aa Gym case, for example, they helped to organize an International Women's Day celebration with the theme of rejecting polygamy as violence against women and children. In 2009, representatives of Rahima, Fatayat, and other women's rights groups formed Alimat, a coalition that describes itself as a movement for family equality and justice. Alimat has called for a review of the 1974 Marriage Law and other policies it considers discriminatory toward women.

Some activists have also turned to more legalistic approaches against polygamy. In 2003, Muslim scholar Musdah Mulia, a former leader of Fatayat and Muslimat, published the booklet "Islam Criticizes Polygamy." In it, she argued that the Quran aimed to eliminate polygamy, and that those who use the Quran to justify it are misinterpreting its message. Mulia was also the main author of a 2004 document known as the "Counter Legal Draft," which was an ambitious attempt to reformulate Indonesian family law based on a revisionist and feminist interpretation of Islamic law. The "Counter Legal Draft" included support for interfaith marriages and banned polygamy and was almost immediately shelved by the Ministry of Religion (Robinson 2009).

Fatayat's position as the women's division of Nahdlatul Ulama somewhat complicates advocacy against polygamy. Though many NU leaders discourage polygamy and reiterate the view that a husband must have the means to fully support his wives, NU is a diverse organization and there are NU members who are polygamous. While Fatayat has a fair amount of autonomy, they must walk a fine line between their own opposition to polygamy and the tendency of some NU members to accept it.

Rahima and Fatayat activists' stances on polygamy draw on their contextual approach to Islamic texts, as well as their egalitarian convictions. Their activism reveals influences from Islam and feminism and illustrates how pious critical agency overlaps with feminist agency. They frame their primary arguments against polygamy from within Islam, using contextual methods to argue that the Quran should be understood as promoting monogamy and justice. They also contend that a man cannot treat more than one wife in a truly equal manner. Certainly, feminists have criticized the historical inequities of monogamous heterosexual marriage. Nevertheless, in a context where some men proclaim their rights to women's bodies, Rahima's and Fatayat's espousal of monogamy represents a feminist claim that men and women should be treated equally in public and private life.

Bodily Politics

Bodily politics is an area of emerging interest for Rahima and Fatayat. I use this term to describe their activism for reforms that give women greater control over their bodies, including their sexuality. Here again we see pious critical agency in action, as Rahima and Fatayat engage critically with religious texts and use them to support their calls for change. Davis (2007) argues that feminism is not simply a social movement but an epistemological project that invites women to use their own experiences as resources for producing situated, critical knowledge, especially about their bodies. The bodily politics of Rahima and Fatayat aim at women's autonomy, but within the boundaries of conventional Islam, advocating women's sexuality and rights within heterosexual marriage. Mernissi (1992) and others (Boellstorff 2005) argue that sex itself is not stigmatized in Islam; rather, sex outside heterosexual marriage is strongly prohibited. However, a conservative attitude reigns in urban Indonesia when it comes to discussing sex publicly, and there is also a gendered double standard, in which men are considered to have a stronger sexual drive. Being grounded in Islam gives Rahima and Fatayat legitimacy to have more open discussions about taboo topics and to advocate reforms they believe would empower women.

I had the opportunity to observe these dynamics one afternoon when Fatayat held a seminar in the NU building on the subject of female circumcision. Female circumcision is widespread in Indonesia but differs from the way it is practiced in parts of Africa and the Middle East. The most prevalent form in Indonesia is a ritualistic pricking or small cut on the clitoris of an infant just after birth. Many Indonesians believe the practice is mandated by Islam.

The Indonesian government banned female genital cutting in 2006. But many Muslim organizations including NU condone the practice, though advising followers "not to cut too much" (IRIN 2010). In 2011, the Ministry of Health issued guidelines directing health professionals to "scrape the skin covering the clitoris, without injuring the clitoris." Many Indonesian women's rights activists are concerned that the guidelines implicitly encourage the procedure. The prevalence of female circumcision in Indonesia is difficult to estimate because many births occur outside medical facilities. A 2009 study by researchers at Yarsi University in Jakarta found that 12% of female babies born in hospitals, born in birth centers, or assisted by government midwives undergo the procedure, but this does not include the many circumcisions done outside such facilities (Uddin 2010).

The speakers at Fatayat's seminar consisted of a representative from the Population Council (an international NGO), a woman doctor, and a Muslim scholar with a degree from a Syrian university. After we watched an unpleasant close-up video of a baby girl being circumcised in an Indonesian hospital, the doctor presented a list of the harmful consequences of circumcision. She told participants that the more extreme forms of the practice cause women to suffer painful sexual intercourse, and that women have a right to enjoy sexual relations. The participants around the table nodded as she said this, which was notable because for many Indonesians sexual pleasure remains a male prerogative, and sexuality is considered to be for the purpose of reproduction (Blackwood 2007).

Next, the Muslim scholar started out by saying that his own daughters were not circumcised because his wife is not Indonesian. He passed around a document with explanations of various Hadiths, quotations from the Quran and other religious texts, and much use of Arabic terminology. He told the gathering that the Quran does not have regulations for female circumcision, and therefore, the practice is not based on a command from Allah. He then said that various Hadiths mention female circumcision, but they may not be authentic Hadiths. In any case, he continued, they appear only to permit the least invasive forms of female circumcision and neither encourage nor require it. The scholar argued that most of the Hadiths that mention female circumcision are weak and/or ambiguous, and scholars interpret them differently. However, he noted, all the main schools of Sunni jurisprudence allow for the practice. He said that circumcision is definitely required for men in Islam, but scholars are conflicted about whether it is necessary for women. The scholar concluded his talk by saying that he personally was not able to say whether female circumcision is *wajib* (an obligation) or *haram* (prohibited), because he was not sure if it is a sin or not. In the end, he proposed, it depends on medical research. If it can be shown to have negative side effects, then it should not be done.[41]

The participants were riveted by this presentation and it spurred a discussion about whether female circumcision is a religious practice or a cultural practice that is attributed to religion. Those who spoke seemed to assume that if it is a cultural practice, it can be discouraged, and perhaps banned. For example, Lies Marcoes, a well-known feminist and a staff member of the Asia Foundation, observed that according to the handout, the Hadiths only permit an already existing and old practice and don't require it. She argued that in Indonesia, because the Suharto regime became close with Muslim groups, the practice came to be seen as Muslim and therefore necessary. She then went on to argue that even if the practice is done in ways that produce no medical effects, the symbolism is dangerous because it is about controlling women's sexuality. For Marcoes, this was reason enough to ban it.

At the end of the seminar, a young Fatayat volunteer who had been taking notes stood to read some conclusions out loud. She stated that Islam does not seem to require female circumcision, and that female circumcision in Africa and the Middle East is more about culture than religion but is thought of as a religious practice. She said that female circumcision in Indonesia is more symbolic, but medical research has found that there are many problems associated with it, especially infections. She ended with the statement, "We conclude that it's not necessary, but should maybe be up to women. We need more research from social scientists about the reasons for the practice. This is a continuing discussion."

In the seminar, it was clear that while participants were certainly influenced by the doctor's video and her explanations of medical problems associated with female circumcisions, the Hadiths provided what they considered to be more conclusive evidence that Islam does not require girls to be circumcised. For many, this was reason enough to limit or discourage the practice, and some even seemed to conclude that it should be banned. I expected that some people might be concerned about interfering with a local cultural practice. But for those at the table, what mattered most was whether or not female circumcision was an obligatory *religious* practice, and second, whether it had harmful effects. While many participants were already inclined to criticize female circumcision, or at least certain forms of it, the evidence from the Quran and Hadiths gave them authorization to conclude that it is not *wajib*, and therefore, not necessary. Thus, an Islamic scholar who used a complex, *fikh*-based interpretive approach helped to convince Fatayat staff that female circumcision is not required by Islam, and this allowed them to conclude that the practice needs to be researched and perhaps reformed.

Rahima and Fatayat are also interested in other bodily issues. For example, Fatayat emphasizes reproductive rights in its efforts to provide women with better access to information and services about their sexuality and reproductive health. More controversially, Fatayat helped to reopen the debate on abortion in Indonesia.[42] In 2002, Fatayat and the medical faculty of Universitas Indonesia published Farida's book *Abortion in the Perspective of Contemporary Fikh*,[43] which outlined the opinions of the four traditional schools of Islamic jurisprudence. Surprising to many was that some classical scholars permitted abortion up to varying periods of time, usually in the first trimester. In 2004, Farida published the results of her master's thesis, which noted that most of Indonesia's estimated two million annual illegal abortions are sought by married women and, based on her study of Islamic texts, advocated that abortion be allowed in the first forty days after conception. Farida's study caused a stir and earned her the ire of some conservative groups.[44]

Farida went on to press for reforms to Indonesia's abortion law. When I interviewed her again in 2005, after the furor over her master's thesis had died down, she explained why she was interested in the issue. She said that she was intrigued by why Indonesia has so many illegal abortions, despite the fact that religious and cultural norms generally oppose the procedure. Farida believes illegal abortions are implicated in Indonesia's high maternal mortality rate, and that society is obligated to find solutions for those who are already pregnant.

Indeed, reproductive health is a problem in Indonesia, especially maternal mortality (see Table 3.1). Indonesia's 2006 maternal mortality rate was estimated to be 220 per 100,000 live births, which is significantly higher than the Philippines (99) but somewhat lower than Cambodia (250) or most countries in sub-Saharan Africa (UNFPA 2006; World Health Organization 2012). However, some regions of Indonesia such as Maluku and West Papua have much higher maternal mortality rates. Although poverty and geographic dispersion are correlated with maternal mortality, Indonesia's maternal mortality is higher than many other countries with comparable

Table 3.1: INDONESIA'S MATERNAL MORTALITY RATIO (NUMBER OF MATERNAL DEATHS PER 100,000 LIVE BIRTHS)

Year	Ratio
1990	600
1995	420
2000	340
2005	270
2010	220

Source: World Health Organization 2012.

GDPs. While abortion is difficult to obtain, the Indonesian government has long promoted family planning initiatives. However, district health officers provide contraception only to legally married women, and in some cases, they require consent from the husband (Amnesty International 2011).

Farida's examination of *fikh* law led her to conclude that Islam permits abortions in the first forty-two days of pregnancy. While Fatayat does not advocate legalizing abortion, the group joined with a coalition of other women's groups to push for a slight liberalization of the abortion law to allow for abortions in cases of rape or incest. Finally, in late 2009, they had some success—the parliament approved a new health bill which permits early abortions in the case of rape or if the health of the mother or fetus is endangered. However, abortions in the case of rape are only permitted in the first six weeks of pregnancy, a stipulation that prevents many victims from accessing the procedure. Moreover, many health workers are apparently unaware of the exception for rape victims (Amnesty International 2011).

In 2008, I had another chance to observe such activism around bodily politics when Fatayat held a series of workshops on women's reproductive rights for chapters in West Java. The program was meant to train the leaders of Fatayat branches to understand reproduction and sexuality from a gender-sensitive Islamic perspective. Fatayat activists demonstrated pious critical agency in this effort to change their grassroots members' consciousness and promote women's reproductive health and rights.

At the workshop in Bandung, Farida introduced the first session by stating that NU *kyais* are still debating whether the fetus is a human being or just cells. "There is a debate about when the fetus becomes a viable human," she told the audience of about seventy-five women, many wearing their green Fatayat uniforms. "All *fikh ulamas* agree that when a fetus is viable, it is *haram* to do something to it, except in emergencies." However, she said, summarizing her book, the Hadiths give different recommendations about when a fetus should be categorized as viable.

Farida went on to argue that many factors influence unplanned pregnancies, which can result in unsafe abortions. In fact, she said, "People think abortions are done by doctors, but in practice most are done by *dukuns* [traditional healers] and are not categorized as abortions." She didn't explain what she meant by this, but most likely she was speaking of traditional methods of abortion such as ingesting herbs. The women around me nodded their heads in agreement as she talked about this. Farida explained that such traditional methods are dangerous and contribute to maternal deaths. She concluded by saying, "State laws are partly the cause of this. The 1992 laws are very restrictive. We need to open an opportunity for safe abortions that are not expensive. Reproduction needs to be more planned to prevent unplanned pregnancies."

Sexuality outside marriage is not often addressed by Fatayat or Rahima. Nevertheless, this does not mean that discussions about sexuality are absent. Indeed, the workshop featured a raucous afternoon session on the topic of safe Islamic sex. Dr. Prasetyo introduced himself and told the audience that he had been requested by the organizers to "talk about sex that is safe and Islamic and to talk about sexual pleasure and orgasms. How can they be most luxurious?" There were lots of laughs, and he responded, with a smile, "We're all adults, we can talk about this."

The beginning of Dr. Prasetyo's talk was fairly uncontroversial. He spoke about maternal mortality and reiterated Farida's points about abortion, proposing that it is mostly married women who have abortions because they don't want the economic burden of more children, and that society needs to talk about ways to help them. Then the questions began. One of the first was about the difference between men's and women's orgasms, which turned into a lengthy discussion and involved many comical comments from the audience. The rowdiness peaked with the next question: a young woman stood and said, "This is a question for many of us. How can we make sure to have an orgasm at the same time?" After the laughter died down, Dr. Prasetyo launched into a light-hearted reiteration of the difference between vaginal and clitoral orgasms and suggested tactics for delaying male orgasms. The rest of the session continued in this manner. When I spoke with Fatayat staff about it later, they were disappointed that the session had turned into a sex workshop, in which they felt the political content was lost. Nevertheless, it seemed to me that it was also an unusual opportunity for grassroots Fatayat members to talk about sexual health and pleasure and to get accurate information on both.

In this case, we can clearly see pious critical agency in action, as Fatayat uses contextual interpretation of religious teachings to justify more open discussions about controversial reproductive issues like abortion, as well as to advocate for legal changes. The revisions to the health law, while minor, are an indication of the success of arguments that draw on *fikh* and employ contextual interpretation. Fatayat and Rahima activists not only use interpretation as a strategy for winning arguments about women's rights but also develop a notion of bodily autonomy, emphasizing women's rights to knowledge and choice in reproduction. Such activism pushes boundaries in a cultural context where sexuality is considered by many as improper for public discussion, and where sexuality is still generally defined as a matter of reproduction and family, rather than personal fulfillment, especially for women.

CONCLUSIONS: ISLAM, FEMINISM, AND LEGITIMACY IN THE PUBLIC SPHERE

The Indonesian Islamic revival has generated widespread debates about gender and sexuality and women's proper roles and behaviors. In a context where Islam and feminism are often considered to be irreconcilable, these activists have made an unusual choice to combine them. Yet the mounting influence of religious discourse is not necessarily a hindrance to Rahima's and Fatayat's work. For even though they are concerned about the influence of conservative Islam, these activists' unusual location in the overlap between Islamic politics and gender politics has fostered pious critical agency. This agency buttresses a new kind of women's rights activism that resourcefully combines Islam and feminism. However, a crucial question is the cultural status of such activism and the possibilities and obstacles faced by these organizations.

Despite the concerns of Indonesian Muslim reformists that they are losing ground, Rahima and Fatayat have a great deal of legitimacy both in the Jakarta activist milieu and in provincial areas. When I accompanied Fatayat leaders on visits to villages in West Java, they sometimes encountered initial skepticism from locals who were not familiar with the organization. But once they were told that Fatayat was part of NU, the concerns diminished. Indeed, more than once, I saw that invoking NU and its role in "nation building" helped to discursively connect Fatayat to both Islam and nationalism.

The mass base of Fatayat provides a remarkable opportunity for promoting women's rights throughout the archipelago, but it can also be a limiting factor given that so many Indonesians think of feminism as foreign and possibly threatening to Islam. Yet Fatayat's work shows that it is possible to advocate for rights and empowerment for women in ways that are culturally legitimate but still challenge entrenched inequalities. In its work with local communities, Fatayat tones down direct appeals for equality, instead emphasizing contextual interpretation, opposition to extremism, and women's rights as citizens. While this may be less of a frontal attack, it leaves the door open for more reforms inspired by egalitarian Islamic ideals.

Rahima also gains legitimacy through its association with NU because it works through NU-affiliated *kyai*s and *pesantren*s. NU provides the NGO with a natural community and because the NU milieu itself is so broad, Rahima activists feel there is much work to be done within it. Rahima staff's immersion in Islamic texts and arguments makes them credible to these pious communities.

Many of Rahima's programs target local religious scholars. One such program, entitled "*Halaqah* for *kyai* and *nyai*," is designed to enhance Islamic scholars' understandings of issues such as health, sexuality, and HIV. Such activities also aim to produce new female Islamic teachers and scholars. Rahima also has a number of scholars that it regularly uses for trainings, but most are men, such as the distinguished Kyai Husain Muhammad. Former Rahima staff member Santhi says there are advantages to giving platforms to both male and female Islamic scholars:

> If a woman scholar speaks, sometimes it will be more powerful because they have experiences being women. However, male scholars are also important to show their solidarity and for legitimizing, for instance, that the concept of marital rape is not nonsense—it also happens in Muslim societies. So both of them have functions, I think, depending on the context.[45]

My fieldwork showed that some of the participants in Rahima's activities found their involvement to be personally transformative. Siti, a female Muslim scholar who is a veteran of Rahima trainings, told me that her interactions with Rahima had helped her overcome difficult personal circumstances, as well as introduced her to new ways of thinking about Islam. Raised in a conservative family, Siti has an undergraduate degree from the State Islamic Institute in Jakarta, with an emphasis on Arab literature, and a master's degree in Islamic studies from another State Islamic Institute. She explained that her personal experiences with marriage made her interested in women's equality.

Siti's husband took another wife, and Siti divorced him, becoming a single mother of two children. Her friends and family were not supportive. Siti got involved with Rahima, where she learned about the concept of gender, and she was able to tell her new acquaintances that she was a single parent and a victim of domestic violence. At a Rahima training she learned that many religious interpretations were biased against women. She said:

> We were given a historical conception of the role of women in the time of the Prophet. And then with the Hadiths regarding women, we were given more appreciation of women. They have been misinterpreted and given a different meaning. The model is like this—a great deal of reading of classic texts, the Quran, the Hadiths, *fikh* interpretations. That is what we bring to our community. We can then say, look, the Hadiths are like this. It's just that people have interpreted them differently. And we have...the power to reject violence against women.

At a time when piety is hegemonic, the ideas that Rahima activists express have a good chance of being viewed as legitimate. In Rahima's case, the group's working relationships with NU scholars provide credibility, especially given that few Indonesians speak or read Arabic. But the small size of the organization certainly limits its impact.

The deepening influence of Islam in the public sphere and the resources offered by the Islamic tradition make the development of pious critical agency possible for both Rahima and Fatayat. They have delved into with Islamic texts in innovative ways in their struggles for gender equality and empowerment. For some members, this has been a culmination of a long process of such interpretative activism. For example, Ika explained to me how her engagement with Islamic interpretation began while she was an activist in Yogyakarta in the 1980s:

> We became aware of an intellectual and gender perspective with data about women; we made claims about the problems of women more generally, social problems and humanity from the gender perspective. But most people were opposed and scornful of the feminist theories that we put forward and they were forced into a corner. At that time, they used religion as a shield and last defense. They said that those feminist theories were secular and worldly—humans made them. Therefore, they were relative and their truth was not absolute. They said that religion says that women have an inheritance that is half that of men. Religion says that women are not leaders and men can be polygamous. According to them this is religion, and if the discussion entered into religion, we were stuck. We were shocked. We did not yet have rational arguments, did not yet have religious argumentation to oppose this.
>
> Therefore, we tried to dig into the subject. Several friends said that the essence of religion is equality; we had not yet read the articles by feminist theologians. At that time, those appeared in a journal from Jakarta, titled *Ummulum Quran*, about Quranic studies. The journal showed us how to view the Quran and the religion from the perspective of women. We were very happy, this is what we were looking for, but it was still not enough. From there we began, because we were indeed bombarded with those religious arguments. Because of that challenge we studied quickly. We looked for books, then also in that journal introduced by a feminist theologian named Rifaat Hassan. We looked at her articles, and also those of other writers like Fatima Mernissi. These books helped a little bit.

As Ika describes it, once she began to explore religious interpretation, suddenly she was able to argue with people who refused even to listen to her before. Yet this wasn't simply a strategic move for Ika as a women's rights activist. As a committed Muslim, it convinced her of Islam's essential compatibility with feminism. Developing this pious critical agency has allowed Rahima to produce innovative revisionist interpretations that read equality and rights into Islam.

Pious critical agency represents a new way of combining Islam and feminism through critical engagements with religious texts to argue for women's rights and equality. This type of agency distinguishes Fatayat and Rahima from the other organizations in this study. Pious critical agency has been deeply informed by the trajectories of Fatayat and Rahima activists and the organizations' location in the overlap between Islamic politics and gender politics. Rahima and Fatayat activists have been schooled in Islam since childhood. Their university educations and participation in Muslim student groups, often involving networks of Nahdlatul Ulama, introduced them to a flexible, *fikh*-centered approach to Islamic texts, as well as issues of democratization, social justice, and women's rights. Once they joined Rahima and Fatayat, they became educated about women's rights and also learned a more explicitly contextual approach to religious texts, an approach that both builds on the heritage of Indonesian Islam and is also influenced by global reformist currents. This distinct pious trajectory has fostered these activists' agency, which is rooted in discourses of Islam, rights, and equality.

As my fieldwork with Rahima and Fatayat shows, the possibilities for agency are especially rich in the overlap between Islamic politics and gender politics. It is a space that provides resources for inventive combinations of women's rights and religion. In a related way, Rahima's and Fatayat's efforts to promote gender equality in Islamic terms have also succeeded in challenging the conventional association of women's rights and secularism. In the 1980s, the image of the Indonesian women's rights activist was that of an elite woman in Western clothing, typified by figures such as Saparinah Sadli, a psychology professor and wife of a former cabinet minister. But after *reformasi*, the self-consciously Muslim woman, signified by her *jilbab*, joined the pantheon of political subjects. Today's women's rights activist is as likely to be unveiled as she is to be a pious woman in Muslim clothing.

In a similar vein, Göle (1996) argues that the Islamist movement in Turkey enabled the emergence of Muslim women as political actors, who with their own bodies assert their difference from Western modernity:

The more these women enter the urban spheres and educational institutions, the more they become part of the Islamist movement in the name of defending their Islamic identities, in contrast to others' expectations. . . . The increasing

visibility of the image of the educated, militant-Muslim woman in places occupied by Westernist elites signifies a challenge to the old elites as much as it signifies the opposition between the West and Islam. (p. 98)

Like their Turkish counterparts, Indonesian women activists dispute
the idea that modernity means that religion must be relegated to the private sphere. For Rahima and Fatayat, religion in the public sphere does
not mean gender discrimination, nor does it mean a state that governs by
Islamic law. It in fact means quite the opposite to them, namely, Islam as
a challenge to inequality. In this, they resemble the activists described by
Badran (2002) in an influential article on Islamic feminism: "Islamic feminism advocates women's rights, gender equality, and social justice using
Islamic discourse as its paramount discourse, though not necessarily its
only one."[46] Badran maintains that secular and Islamic feminisms should
be understood as overlapping rather than dichotomous. Nevertheless, it
is important to note that Muslim women's activism in Indonesia and elsewhere may include political projects that are potentially disempowering to
some women and/or religious minorities.

Rahima and Fatayat critically mobilize Indonesia's Islamic traditions to
participate in the public sphere and seek reforms to empower women. Their
knowledge of religious texts and their presentation as pious Muslims give
them legitimacy as they argue for reforming Islam and society. Pious critical agency is facilitated by a contextual approach to religious texts, which
helps activists to promote a conception of women's rights that emphasizes
the social construction of gender. This approach also gives them the flexibility to adapt ideas from transnational feminism and integrate them with
Islam. Rahima and Fatayat activists have created a new mode of women's
rights activism that draws on both secular and religious sources, intertwin-
ing ideas from Islam and feminism. Their agency shapes their struggles
against polygamy, for reproductive rights, and against state implementation of Islamic law. They demonstrate that pious agency and feminist
agency can coexist and overlap, and that Islam can enable diverse forms
of agency. In the process, the women activists of Fatayat and Rahima are
forging a new model of middle-class Indonesian womanhood, one based on
piety, social justice and equality, and respect for cultural difference.

CHAPTER 4

The Prosperous Justice Party

Islamizing Indonesia?

As I walked into a banquet room in the Sari Pan Pacific Hotel in Central Jakarta, I was struck by the upscale surroundings. I was here to attend the Prosperous Justice Party's (PKS) seminar on pornography. There was a buffet table heaped with food, coffee, and tea, and the speakers sat at another table under a banner that read *"Pornografi dan Kommitmen Menjaga Moralitas Bangsa"* ("Pornography and the Commitment to Guard the Morality of the Nation"). The environs were a significant step above the NGO meeting centers or budget hotels where the other groups in my study usually held seminars and conferences.

Kadira, at the time a leader of the party's women's division, which organized the seminar, greeted me warmly and showed me to a table. Seated to my left was a middle-aged woman representing Aisyiyah, the women's division of the Muhammadiyah organization. On my right was a young woman who was a member of Hizbut Tahrir, a radical international organization that seeks a return of the Islamic caliphate. Men and women sat at separate tables, and women in their twenties and thirties predominated. Most women wore white or pastel *jilbabs* (Muslim headscarves) that completely covered their shoulders and chests, one of the variations of the headscarf that has emerged in Indonesia over the past twenty-five years. The only other woman not wearing a *jilbab* was from the government's Ministry of Women's Empowerment.

Erna, the moderator, introduced the seminar by saying, "We face the challenge of building an Indonesia which is moral." Erna went on to say that the nation is facing a very complicated issue—pornography—and that today's speakers would explore the commitment to guarding national morality and discuss how effective their efforts have been. Looking in my direction, she added, "Countries as liberal as America have laws on pornography."

Since Indonesia began democratizing in 1998, PKS has emerged as the country's most popular Muslim political party. While it does not advocate an Islamic state, it does call for Islamic values to be the source of national legislation and policy—a very different position from the other organizations in this study. PKS is not the only Muslim political party in Indonesia. It has several competitors, notably Partai Amanat Nasional (PAN) and Partai Kebangkitan Bangsa (PKB), which are both linked to Muslim organizations. There are also several small Islamist parties that espouse the implementation of Islamic *Shariah* law throughout Indonesia. PKS has a more pious image than the dominant political parties, but with its embrace of electoral democracy and civil law, it has a more mainstream platform than the Islamists. PKS claims to have 2.5 million members and up to 8 million supporters (Noor 2011). It garnered 8% of the national vote in the 2009 elections, and this popularity has generated concern among some Indonesians about the PKS brand of pious politics. Women's rights are of concern because many Indonesians believe that PKS supports efforts to implement local or regional regulations inspired by Islamic law.

The women activists of PKS are therefore an interesting contrast to the other activists I discuss in this book. In my fieldwork, I was especially interested to learn how the women activists of PKS understand Islam and feminism. And how does Islam influence their agency and activism? The women I encountered in PKS were demographically similar to the women in Solidaritas Perempuan, Rahima, and Fatayat—they are university educated and part of the urban middle class. But unlike the other activists in this study, PKS women tend to view Islam and feminism as incompatible. In this chapter, I discuss how PKS women develop a *pious activating agency* that guides their struggle for a nation infused with Islamic values.

The speakers at the pornography seminar included Soraya, a female member of the Indonesian Council of Ulemas (MUI), a quasi-state body that issues *fatwas*;[1] a spokesman from the Ministry of Communications; a male representative from an NGO that promotes "family-friendly media"; Mitra, one of PKS's women parliament members; and Abdullah, a young representative from the party's General Secretariat.

Mitra and others were concerned about "American cultural exports," and they contended that the interests of Indonesia's media industry conflict with the country's moral interests. But the most fervent speech came from Abdullah. He began by stating that pornography is the difference between a good community and an immoral community. He said there are two different approaches to the problem of pornography—rational and religious. "We cannot use the rational approach, because things that are *haram*² are not definitely illegal in the rational approach," he argued. And he continued, "We must use the religious approach." As an example of the limitations of the rational approach, Abdullah mentioned the debate over sex workers. He said that with the democratic approach, society is concerned about how such people can make a living, which to him is unacceptable. "There is unusual moral tolerance in society and we have to deal with this," he said. Abdullah concluded his talk with a call to action. "We must raise our tradition of resistance to 'porno' culture," he contended.

During the seminar, the speakers from PKS and MUI argued for a ban on all forms of pornography. Audience members lamented the availability of pornography on the Internet, as well as pornographic videos, which are easily found for sale in street markets. What constituted pornography was not explained, but Soraya mentioned her concern about advertisements that show women without covering their *aurat*. *Aurat* is an Arabic term for impure parts of the body. It is understood by Muslims as the justification for women's modest dress. While the concept is ambiguous, many Indonesian Muslims consider *aurat* to include a woman's hair, as well as the area from her chest to her lower legs. It was hard to know what Soraya meant by *aurat*, but to follow these restrictions in the media would mean not showing women wearing shorts or short sleeves. This would be a significant shift for Indonesia, where not all Muslim women wear clothing that complies with such guidelines.

After lunch, I shared a minivan with several women and we headed a few blocks south for a demonstration against pornography. We joined about 150 people waving flags and banners, all standing on the concrete island at the roundabout in front of Hotel Indonesia and the Grand Hyatt. The women in the rally wore long white *jilbabs*. Young men shouted "*Allahu Akbar*" and pumped their fists into the air. Speakers, mostly men, took turns yelling into a megaphone, but with the roaring traffic of Jakarta it was nearly impossible to hear them. As I left, a speaker accused America of exporting pornography and immorality to Indonesia and other countries.

The seminar and the demonstration were examples of how PKS women's activism is oriented toward building a society with stronger Islamic regulation. The participants considered pornography to be "foreign," "Western," and a result of globalization. Rhetoric about women's dignity was mixed with exhortations to protect Indonesia from immoral influences. Scholarship suggests that anxieties about gender, especially women's behavior and appearance, are often part of struggles over social change and nationhood (Chatterjee 1993; Yuval-Davis 1997). Indonesia's democratization has produced many controversies about gender and morality, of which pornography has been one of the more contentious. PKS women have been important and outspoken participants in these public debates.

The party's political agenda does not prevent some PKS women from expressing interest in women's empowerment. While they emphasize women's domestic obligations, PKS women encourage women to be entrepreneurial and politically active. And while they argue against liberalism, they sometimes refer to concepts like rights and empowerment.

How should we understand the agency of women party members? Social scientists have often struggled to understand the agency of women in conservative religious movements. Some have suggested that women find unexpected benefits from participation, while others argue that women are simply used by such movements. More productively, Mahmood (2005) criticizes the tendency of feminist theory to equate women's agency with liberation. Mahmood argues that women in the Egyptian piety movement manifest agency in their efforts to conform to religious discipline, a choice that gives them pleasure. While this is also the case for women in PKS, I think it is also important to emphasize the work PKS women do to mobilize for their own interests and those of the party. In this chapter, I show how PKS women demonstrate *pious activating agency*, in which they activate the party's religious interpretations as part of their work for social and political changes.

To understand how PKS women have developed this distinctive pious agency, it is necessary to understand their social locations. The ways women activists engage with Islam and feminism are shaped by their experiences and trajectories. The PKS women I met demonstrate a different pious trajectory than activists in Fatayat and Rahima. They usually entered the party through experiences in the field of Islamic politics, including participation in Muslim student study groups, part of the *Tarbiyah* movement. As I explored in chapter 2, the *Tarbiyah* (Islamic education) movement, influenced by Islamic renewal movements in the Middle East, particularly the Egyptian Muslim Brotherhood, has popularized an evangelistic and textualist approach to Islam (Sidel 2006; Machmudi 2008). It emphasizes the concept of *dakwah* (religious calling) to summon Muslims to practice their faith. The movement includes a vast network of study groups on college campuses (sometimes called *usrah, halaqah,* or *dakwah* groups). PKS was founded by former *Tarbiyah* activists, and study groups still provide many recruits.[3] Since the party is a cadre organization, and recruits must go through an application and training process, social networks are crucial for entry. Party members seek recruits on university campuses, inviting potential members to join party study circles and cadre programs (Noor 2011).

The field of Islamic politics is constituted by the Indonesian Islamic tradition, which comprises multiple approaches to interpretation and practice. The *Tarbiyah* movement and the party itself are part of the more textualist milieu, influenced by global Islamic currents. Textualists argue for a strict approach to interpreting Islamic texts. Textualists believe that the Quran should guide Muslims, rather than make concessions to contemporary needs, and that the meaning of the Quran is fixed and universal (Saeed 2005).[4] There is always selection involved in religious interpretation, but textualists tend to claim that it is a more straightforward and direct approach to interpretation.

The PKS cadre training program introduces new members to the study of Islamic values, moral lessons, discussion of proper ethical conduct, and methods of political mobilization. Studies of these programs suggest that they focus more on practical skills and organizing rather than theology, but they do emphasize the development of Muslim character, correct religious practice, and a return to the original sources of Islamic teachings (Machmudi 2008; Noor 2011). As I discuss in this chapter, PKS intellectuals consider the text of the Quran to be relatively straightforward. Through their participation in the *Tarbiyah* movement and the party, women learn that the Quran specifies different but complementary roles for men and women, a conventional interpretation in Muslim societies. PKS women generally reject feminism as incompatible with Islam, partly because of feminism's emphasis on equality.[5] The party's religious interpretations allow women to be active in politics and work outside the home, as long as their husbands give permission, and assuming they keep up with their domestic obligations.

PKS does not espouse the more controversial interpretations of Islamic texts that have been popularized in some parts of the world. For example, the party does not encourage women to cover their faces. And given that the party does not call for an Islamic state in Indonesia, it also stays out of discussions of criminal punishments specified by Islamic law. The party has often been characterized as pragmatic rather than strongly ideological (Hwang 2010).[6]

PKS women activate the party's textual religious interpretations to achieve their goals for political and social change. However, as a result of the textual approach, and also perhaps because many women cadres have not had extensive religious education, the PKS women I met were much less likely to engage in the complex theological discussions that I experienced with members of Rahima and Fatayat. Consequently, PKS women have less scope to use religious knowledge as a tool of empowerment. Nevertheless, they capitalize on the party's interpretations, and particularly its emphasis on public piety, to promote their interests in self-cultivation and fulfillment, as well as to bolster women's involvement in Islamic activism.

Social action fields give rise to different forms of agency, and actors' locations and experiences within these fields shape their subjectivities. Pious activating agency emerges from PKS women's position in the textualist milieu of Islamic politics. Women's active participation in Islamic politics is a recent development, and it challenges male domination of the field. Unlike their counterparts in Fatayat and Rahima, who develop a pious critical agency that enables them to incorporate feminist influences, PKS women are not directly involved in the field of gender politics. Nevertheless, the fact that they sometimes justify their work as compatible with women's rights and empowerment reflects the interactions between Islamic politics and gender politics in Indonesia today.

PKS women take on a role in public life and Islamic politics, but in a way that fulfills their ambitions to be pious wives and mothers. PKS's leadership is dominated by men. Women work to legitimize themselves as party cadres, and they often voice strong agreement with party ideology, even if their daily lives don't completely conform to it. They see themselves as filling a separate but equally valuable role in the party. Indeed, the party's agenda of government and moral reform rather than a broader vision of social justice may also provide women less range for participation compared to women in NGOs or mass organization. Nevertheless, this is also a newly public role for visibly pious Muslim women in Indonesia. The goal of PKS is to infuse Indonesia with Islamic values, and women are eager to be part of this project of Islamization.

Studying PKS women, we can see that Islam is a heterogeneous cultural schema that provides resources for different kinds of agency. The party's textual approach to Islam, along with its promotion of a missionary role for women, means that PKS women embrace political involvement to build a society with stronger religious regulation. PKS's rise to power has given the party a prominent role in defining modern Muslim politics as well as Muslim womanhood. Yet as I discuss at the end of this chapter, their piety is increasingly a cultural boundary marker, and their attempt to Islamize society has the potential to marginalize others.

This chapter begins by examining the ideas and practices of PKS and its women members. I trace women's trajectories into the party and investigate their views on Islam and gender, which draw on textualist interpretations. The second section investigates how PKS women's pious activating agency shapes their political activism. In particular, I examine how PKS women activate the party's religious interpretations in their efforts at promoting family values, including debates over polygamy, and during the Pornography Bill controversy. The final section considers how PKS women's activism transforms the Indonesian public sphere.

PKS WOMEN—TRAJECTORIES INTO THE PARTY

I met PKS women at their workplaces, at party offices, in public spaces, and occasionally in their homes. The houses I visited had up-to-date televisions and cars and ranged from concrete houses in narrow *kampungs* (lower-class urban neighborhoods) to rambling structures in more affluent areas. They tended to live in mixed neighborhoods, rather than in Jakarta's more homogenous wealthy neighborhoods. All of the PKS women I interviewed were married, and only one did not yet have children. Most married before they became party members, and in many cases their husbands also joined the party.[7] They are articulate and outspoken women who have many choices in life. They hold a certain understanding of piety and a vision of idealized household life, both of which are central to their identities. While a few were shy about speaking to a foreigner, many were eager to discuss their views and their experiences.

The stereotype of PKS is that it recruits from Indonesia's university campuses. Indeed, every PKS woman cadre I interviewed was a university graduate. Nearly a quarter had master's degrees. They were married and ranged from their late twenties to midforties, reflecting the youthful profile of the party. A few were housewives, while others worked as lecturers and teachers, consultants, or small business owners. They struck me as characteristic Indonesian urban middle-class women, whose lifestyles are informed by Javanese and Indonesian cultural practices, as well as Islam. Their religious backgrounds ranged from secular to devout, but their trajectories into the party were similar, demonstrating the importance of what I call *pious trajectories*: that is, routes through particular social understandings of religious practice. These trajectories reveal increasing involvement in the field of Islamic politics, mainly through participation in the *Tarbiyah* movement and Muslim study groups, which helped to connect women to the PKS milieu. Along this trajectory, women activists learned a style of Islam that emphasizes a textual approach to the Quran.

Secular Backgrounds: Susanti

I met Susanti at her Muslim clothing shop in a crowded Jakarta mall. Surrounded by colorful headscarves and tunics, she was outgoing and talkative. Susanti grew up in the province of West Kalimantan. In a city known for its ethnic Chinese minority, Susanti's middle-class family was not especially pious. At university, she was trained as an agricultural engineer, but after she finished her degree she decided that owning her own business gave her more flexibility. She had three children and was pregnant with a fourth when I first interviewed her. At the time, she often traveled on business to Singapore, Malaysia, Dubai, and Finland and kept in touch by e-mail with friends around the world. Susanti got interested in activism, especially on the environment, while at university in the early 1990s and became an early member of PKS:

> S: At that time, I was not just at university. During semester four, I was also working in a laboratory as an assistant to my professor. And I began to be active in an institute, Yayasan Ridha Ilahi. Because I thought, "I am a Muslim, I want to deepen my understanding of Islam, I want to know more about Islam, so I should join this institute." Many of my friends from school who were working in this area also joined. We were in a provincial area, not a center. So then we got information, enlightenment, and were also helped in matters of insight. The institute was active in the educational and social and *dakwah* realms.
>
> R: How did you get involved in PKS?
>
> S: I got involved in PKS right when I graduated, met my soulmate, and then my husband was transferred to Jakarta. At that time, the monetary crisis had begun and it so happened that we were in the network of a *lembaga pengajian* [Islamic studies institute]. Maybe you already know that PKS was founded by campus activists. I was one of those, and then we widened our scope so that our vision and mission could be accepted by society. And together we moved out from being campus activists. So when we got to Jakarta we were contacted to join PKS together.
>
> ...Basically, PKS is simple, implementing what is actually there in the community. So although we are women, we think that those politics are not too high, that what we are struggling for is our right and is a part of politics. So my husband and I are part of the community, because our vision and mission are the same as that which is included in the *anggaran dasar dan anggaran rumah tangga* [statutes and rules of association].

When I returned to Jakarta in 2008, Susanti was still involved in the women's division of PKS Jakarta. But with four children to care for, she said she was no longer traveling overseas, and instead was using the Internet to sell clothing. Her husband, once a civil servant, had also started his own business. She told me that her family was now her priority, although she has also established her own foundation to promote economic education and training for low-income women in Jakarta. Nonetheless, her everyday life still struck me as quite busy.

Pious Backgrounds: Yanti

I met Yanti at a private university in West Jakarta, where she was getting a master's degree in psychology. Warm and chatty, she came from a modest family whose children have all become successful professionals. Although Yanti's parents were not involved in major Muslim organizations like Muhammadiyah or Nahdlatul Ulama, they took religion seriously enough to send her to a secular primary school in the morning and a Muslim school in the evening. She said that she began wearing the *jilbab* by choice in her final year of elementary school, a time when it was still prohibited in public schools. When she entered junior high she was not allowed to continue wearing it, and so she transferred to a Muslim school. She said:

> I'm glad that the situation has changed. As a Muslim, I feel that being able to implement the teachings of my own religion brings happiness. Preventing someone from practicing their faith, whether at work or at school, is pathetic and can hinder the development of that person's potential. So I'm glad that Muslim clothing has now become a trend. I hope they wear it for virtuous reasons.

Yanti received her undergraduate degree from the Lembaga Dakwah dan Studi Islam (Institute for Religious Call and Islamic studies), one of many such schools that popped up in Indonesia in the late 1980s and early 1990s. These schools were often established by Indonesians returning from studying in the Middle East. Yanti said that she was also a "mosque activist," which is how she met her husband, whom she married while still in college. She and her husband both joined PKS in the late 1990s. "In 1996–1998, PKS was still in the process of being established," she said. "At the time, I already felt that it was the party that was most congruent with my conscience. So, what I felt at the time was the desire to join the party, and I did."

When I returned in 2008, I again met Yanti at the university, where she was teaching. She was then involved in PKS's Women's Network Institute (Jaringan Lembaga Wanita) in West Jakarta. She described this body as a forum for women's prayer groups and said that it includes other local women's groups such as the government-sponsored Family Welfare Movement (PKK). In addition to these activities, she gives trainings for personal development of Muslim women employees, often at the offices of state-owned companies. And she also told me that she started her own institute, which provides community services for the care of the dead.

The Importance of *Dakwah*: Widyawati

Similar to Susanti and Yanti, most PKS women I spoke with followed a trajectory of religious transformation through involvement in Muslim study groups and Muslim student activism to eventually joining PKS. Although a few of those I interviewed were part of the original core of activists who established the party, in other cases, women came into the party through the Tarbiyah networks. Some also joined with their husbands. Although Indonesia has a tradition of women's religious study (Van Doorn-Harder 2006), involvement in *Tarbiyah* networks helped to school middle-class women like Susanti and Yanti in an understanding of Islam that emphasizes social and political participation.

This politically engaged approach to Islam was noticeable in the account of Widyawati, a Muslim school principal. We met at lunchtime at a McDonald's in a rapidly growing Jakarta suburb. Her explanation of how she became part of PKS illustrates how a personal commitment to Islam inspires many PKS women to become activists:

> The way I was brought up, I was not taught comprehensively about Islam. My understanding of Islam was limited to conducting prayers and worshipping, which had nothing to do with public life. My consciousness emerged when I joined Islamic study groups at university. From there I found out that Islam is not just about worshipping at the mosque, but also about how it gives meaning to all aspects of our lives. After getting this idea, I committed myself to making a contribution to the environment around me. . . . I do my activities seriously in PKS because I know that I can have a major influence on reforming the condition of society in the future. I believe everyone has a role to play in the betterment of society and that is what Islam teaches us and what Allah values. This is my motivation, whatever role I am upholding; I must make a contribution, in my role as a mother with children, as a wife to my husband, as a member of PKS, or at the workplace.

For Widyawati, although her parents were believers, they practiced religion in a more private way and did not connect it to their public lives. Involvement in Muslim study groups helped Widyawati use religion for worldly purposes.

Widyawati came from an educated background. Her mother was a dentist and her father a doctor, and she grew up in Jakarta. The family was affluent enough to send her to high school in Australia, and she later graduated from the University of Indonesia. In 1994, she established a Muslim kindergarten and primary school in the suburb where she lives, and by the time I first met her, the school enrolled over seven hundred students.

PKS was established while Widyawati was living overseas. Nevertheless, her participation in Muslim study groups at the University of Indonesia helped bring her into future PKS circles. After her return, she decided to start a Muslim school and in doing so, she met more new colleagues. "When I returned home, PKS was not yet as popular as today. Then, my colleagues asked me to join the party at the local district," she explained. Widyawati's husband also became active in PKS—by 2005 he was head of the PKS Jakarta branch. When I returned for a follow-up interview in 2008, the school she founded was going strong and seemed to be the center of her life.

Widyawati was talkative, if not warm. But there was an awkward moment at the end of the first interview when Widyawati mentioned that her husband was sitting at another table in McDonald's. She introduced me to him as I left the restaurant, but it was a departure from conventional Indonesian politeness that she had not introduced us earlier. He was not friendly. It occurred to me that he was concerned for his wife's safety with an unknown American.

Pious Trajectories and Islamic Politics

These three women, like others in this study, represent the new pious middle class in Indonesia. With the exception of Widyawati, they emerged from striving, lower middle-class families, and they benefited from the expansion of education during the Suharto era. Like many of their generation, the Islamic revival of the 1980s and 1990s converted them to more pious practice. Their lifestyles, as working women raising children, are much like those of their middle-class urban compatriots. Like many Indonesian women wanting to live up to the national ideal of a wife and mother, PKS women sometimes downplayed their jobs to emphasize their family roles (Brenner 1998). They struck me as typical of Indonesian middle-class culture as they expressed concerns about protecting Indonesia from Western influences and ensuring that Indonesian women have dignified moral lives (Sullivan 1994; Tickamyer and Kusujiarti 2012).

Yet there were subtle but telling differences between PKS activists and members of Fatayat, Rahima, and Solidaritas Perempuan. One theme that emerged from my interviews was that the parents of PKS women were much less likely to have been active members of Nahdlatul Ulama or Muhammadiyah, the two largest Indonesian Muslim organizations. In most cases, PKS women described their parents as somewhat religious, at least to the extent of observing the major religious rituals. But rather than attending religious schools during childhood, most of the PKS women I met attended public schools and state universities.

Widyawati's case exemplifies another difference. The husbands of most PKS women I met are also party members and often have positions of responsibility within the party. Thus, many women are participating in the party as part of a couple.

In fact, a few of the women I spoke to met their husbands through *dakwah* groups.[8] Although Susanti did not describe her marriage as arranged, she told me that she and her husband had not spoken much before the wedding because they had only been briefly "introduced." Similarly, Widyawati said that her marriage shocked her mother because she had only known her future husband for two or three months. She explained:

> I don't quite agree with those who say that dating is a part of the process of knowing someone. I think that when we date, we tend to reveal only the good side of our character. To me, what's important before getting married is to recognize our future spouse's potential, and I saw that my husband was a good and responsible man. We got married, anyway. I succeeded in convincing my mother that I made the right decision.

As Widyawati's story suggests, PKS women's views on marriage, family, and gender are more conservative than the other groups in this study. Women's trajectories into PKS are also different. Susanti and Widyawati attended secular schools and universities, came from families that were not strongly affiliated with Nahdlatul Ulama or Muhammadiyah, and were more involved in the *Tarbiyah* movement than mainstream Muslim student organizations or other forms of social movement activism. Yanti's story illustrates a slightly different trajectory, receiving religious (but not traditional Muslim boarding school) education at a young age and attending an Islamic study institute rather than a university.

Women in PKS, Fatayat, and Rahima are all involved in the field of Islamic politics, and often have been so since their time at university. Within this field, PKS women are part of the textualist milieu. But while Fatayat and Rahima activists increasingly straddle Islamic politics and gender politics, PKS women have largely stayed within Islamic politics. Their pious activating agency emerges from this location. Nevertheless, the two fields interact, and PKS women are at times influenced by ideas of women's rights and empowerment.

WOMEN IN THE PARTY

I was not able to obtain data on the percentage of women in the party, but my visits to PKS offices and observations of party events suggest that they are involved in significant numbers. The PKS leadership has stated that men and women should have equal political rights (Trotter 2006). But there is a division of labor within the party. For example, the members of the 2005–2010 *Dewan Syariah Pusat* (Central Shariah Council)—the body that decides on matters of Islamic interpretation and practice for party members—were all men. The party's 2005–2010 *Dewan Pimpinan Pusat* (Central Leadership Council) had four women out of fifty-one spots. Those women were the heads of the women's division and three departments related to women (Machmudi 2008).

As I explain in chapter 2 and in the methodological appendix, my access to PKS was not as wide-ranging as with other groups, and I was not able to attend meetings or "hang out" in their offices. This is apparently characteristic of the party. Some scholars and journalists have complained about the party's secrecy when it comes to matters of strategy and ideology (Bubalo and Fealy 2008). However, my observations at public events and during interviews at PKS offices lead me to conclude that men conduct the primary intellectual and ideological work of the party, and that they deal with matters related to religious interpretation and practice, while women usually handle issues such as education, health, and family. Similarly, Machmudi (2008) observes that most women on committees of the central board are in a special department of women's affairs.

The PKS milieu produces a profusion of media—books, journals, pamphlets, websites, DVDs, and blogs—with advice for living a more Islamic life and building a more Islamic society. Wandering around the booksellers' stalls at the *Musyawarah Nasional* (the party's national conference) gave me a chance to examine these media, and they reflect the party's division

Figure 4.1: Registration desk at the Prosperous Justice Party's national conference, 2005.

of labor (Figure 4.1). Journals and books aimed at women often depict children on the cover and contain articles about family, relationships, education, and health. Books and pamphlets aimed at men, and nearly always written by men, usually encompass more formal political subject matter: state law and policy, history, Islamic law and interpretation, global politics, and critiques of the West.

PKS has fewer women in the national legislature than other Indonesian political parties. Following the 2009 elections, Indonesia's parliament of 560 included a record 101 women (18%).[9] The Democratic Party has the largest number of women legislators, with 37 out of 150 representatives, followed by the PDI-P (Indonesian Democratic Party of Struggle) with women in 19 out of 95 seats. PKS has 57 representatives, of whom 3 are women.[10] The guidelines published by the party's women's division in 2004 state that men and women have the same duties as Muslims, but different natural roles. A woman can be a legislator if it does not have a negative impact on her family, and she must have permission from her husband to run as a candidate (Bidang Kewanitaan DPP PK Sejahtera 2004). However, women seem to have an important symbolic role in the party. Leaders often told me proudly that half the membership is female. Female participation thus seems to be part of the party's sense of its modernity.

Involvement in PKS is a calling for the women I met, and much of their social and civic lives revolve around the organization. Such attachment seems unusual for a political party, and more akin to participation in a social movement or a religious organization.

When asked about the lack of women in powerful positions, many PKS women admitted that they would like to see women become more involved in the leadership. A common explanation was that most women in the party have young children and cannot take on other responsibilities. But most PKS women also say that women in high positions should be sufficiently accomplished. As a female legislator explained:

> I mean, we don't hope that women occupy those strategic positions if it turns out it is not balanced with their qualities. For example, if we are in the legislature, but there is nothing that we can do except fulfill the 30% women's quota. We are not hoping for something like that....If indeed a woman is qualified, if she is capable and interested, I think there is not a problem. It's just that it sometimes comes from the women themselves. Some positions, like officials or the heads of divisions or whatever, they require meetings at night, and for women this can be a problem, because we are very focused on our families' education, on the children.

Party members do not question or criticize women's responsibility for the domestic sphere, which, as the legislator admitted, often prevents women from being fully involved in the party. Moreover, one of the differences between PKS and secular political parties is that its gendered division of labor is institutionalized in practices of spatial segregation such as marching separately at demonstrations. The party has formal regulations that support such practices. One of these is *fatwa* 20, which concerns shaking hands between men and women (PKS, Dewan Syariah DPP 2006). Party members are forbidden from shaking hands or having other physical contact with the opposite sex unless it is an emergency. Handshaking between men and women is common in Indonesia, though it is frowned on in some pious communities. However, such a regulation strikes many Indonesians as overly strict. PKS women told me that they approved of the regulation because they felt that it discouraged sexual harassment, although they acknowledged that shaking hands between men and women is practiced in Indonesia. Pious practices such as *fatwa* 20 and Muslim clothing for women help to instill in party members a sense of essential difference between the genders, one that is respected through bodily separation. Not only that, but such practices inculcate a sense of difference between PKS and outsiders.

However, the case of former Indonesian president Megawati Sukarnoputri demonstrates PKS's flexibility when it comes to gender and politics. In 1999, Megawati Sukarnoputri was a candidate for president in the nation's first democratic election. PKS released a *fatwa* that said that a woman could only become president if no suitable male candidate was available. (Several other Muslim organizations, including Nahdlatul Ulama, came to similar conclusions.) PKS did not object in 2001 when Megawati was elevated to president from vice president after President Abdurrahman Wahid resigned due to allegations of financial impropriety. When I asked Kadira in 2003 about PKS's objections to Megawati in 1999, she asserted that it had nothing to do with her gender, but with her competence as a leader. Perhaps this is revisionist history, but the 2001 events suggest that conservative ideas about gender do not always take precedence for PKS.

PKS women stressed to me that they feel the party is wide open to them, that their opinions are taken seriously, and that *reformasi* and democratization have freed Indonesian women to participate in politics. As Susanti explained, "We continue to be given freedom (by the party) to state our opinions, our thoughts on policy decisions.... But the decisions stay with the *Musyawarah* (national conference), and usually they are accepted and adopted."

PKS WOMEN AND ISLAMIC PIETY

A particular kind of highly visible piety suffuses the atmosphere at PKS offices and events. PKS women wear *jilbabs* that cover their chests and several layers of clothing, often including heavy socks. Men do not smoke, remarkable in a country where 70% of the male population is estimated to smoke cigarettes. A visitor to PKS offices will note the politeness of cadres, as well as their tendency toward rather formal interactions. PKS offices reflect the party's asceticism. When I visited the party's new headquarters in South Jakarta, I found a brightly lit and exceedingly clean building with few decorations and utilitarian furniture.

In Indonesia and other Muslim contexts, piety and clothing have become closely connected. Not only has the headscarf become the most popular global symbol of Islam, but also it is one that is insisted upon by many Muslims. Indonesian Muslims, and those in PKS, increasingly argue that wearing the headscarf is essential to being a true Muslim woman. Piety is linked not only to clothing but also to personal practices, such as observance of Islam's taboos on alcohol and pork. These prohibitions are extended to cigarettes by some strict Muslims.

PKS activists consider piety a defining personal characteristic and also a method for creating public morality. Susanti and other PKS women I interviewed often used the term *shalehah* to describe their ideal of pious womanhood. *Shalehah* means to be a good and pious Muslim, and it is sometimes used to describe the characteristics of proper Muslim women, with connotations of obedience to husbands. Susanti explained:

> I think the ideal Indonesian woman is intelligent, moral, and on the religious side of things, she is *shalehah*. So that with her intelligence she can develop herself and her family and society, and with her goodness and morality she can influence the lives of future generations, because from her womb will be born the next generation of the nation. What is most important from all this is her morals, because their value is immeasurable. She also must respect the religion she professes, for example, Islam, so that she holds its values in high esteem because they give her direction. Because in this up-to-date technological era, people can do anything, and I am concerned about the high level of immorality.

Shalehah, *dakwah*, and piety are all connected for PKS women. Nearly all of the activists I met emphasized that their work in the party is a form of *dakwah*, and that *dakwah* is an obligation for Muslims. *Dakwah* bridges personal and public piety. Nenen, a legislator for the party, said that *dakwah* was the reason she felt no conflict between being a mother and a PKS activist. "When I first joined PKS, my four children were still very young. However, since I consider being active in PKS as a part of doing good deeds and conducting *dakwah* as an obligation, I don't see it as problematic. My husband shares the same view. So we helped each other." For Nenen, *dakwah* is just as vital as raising children, although she also made a point of telling me she never neglected them.

Islamic revivalist piety may be especially public, but there are differences in how piety is understood. For Fatayat and Rahima activists, piety has both a personal meaning and an aspect of social justice. Activists in these organizations often grappled with the meaning of piety. Piety was not as much a matter of debate in PKS. PKS women rarely deliberated about what it means to be pious during interviews.[11] Instead, as with Susanti's discussion of *shalehah*, they expressed a self-assured view that certain behaviors, such as veiling, are the way to be pious. For women in PKS, piety is especially public, and it is this highly visible piety that differentiates them from women in mainstream political parties and women's groups. Moreover, the public piety of PKS is both shaped by and helps to reproduce notions of gender difference.

We don't often think of class in terms of religious practices. Many contemporary scholars consider class to be a matter of tastes and lifestyles connected to socioeconomic position (Bourdieu 1987). Yet tastes and lifestyles are not just about whether people like modern art or junk food. They may also be religious tastes and lifestyles, such as ideas about gender, or wearing certain styles of Muslim clothing. PKS pious practices are helping to constitute a collective identity, as well as new forms of middle-class subjectivity in Indonesia.

Women's Clothing as Pious Practice

The manners of PKS members are often more constrained, and more rules seem to govern individual behavior than with other Indonesian organizations I encountered. The clothing of PKS women is the most obvious example of such differences, though the contrasts are not so much in actual styles of clothing as they are in the way women talk about clothing and religion.

PKS women do not usually gravitate toward the fashionable versions of *jilbab*, which often feature beadwork or printed silk, and they reject the body-skimming clothes favored by many young women in Jakarta. Indonesian women often wear vibrant colors, and the styles of PKS women set them apart. Their clothing usually has subdued prints and light colors. They do not wear pants and use little make-up or jewelry. However, they also do not wear the faux-Arab clothing styles, including lengthy robes and/or face veils, which are becoming common among more radical groups. Some of my Indonesian friends considered PKS women's clothing to be a uniform, particularly the long white *jilbab* worn with a tunic and skirt, often including socks with sandals.[12] In this sense, PKS women's clothing is a blend of Arabic and Indonesian styles. PKS men's clothing is less distinct. At events or in PKS offices, most men wear long-sleeved shirts, often batik, with dress pants. In daily life, PKS men often sport casual Western clothing.

Women's clothing at public events is one of the most recognizable aspects of PKS. Just as I saw at the pornography demonstration, PKS women march together, forming a phalanx of flowing white headscarves. Women are thus the embodiment of the party's approach to Islam.

Perhaps more significant than the clothing styles are the ways women talk about clothing. In 2008, when I met with Yulia, a leader of PKS's women's division, I brought along an Indonesian friend. The conversation turned to my friend's research on Muslim women who veil their faces, and from there to a discussion about Muslim fashion. Yulia thought PKS women's clothing had become much more colorful, and she brought out photographs to prove her point. Yulia herself looked more stylish than in the past, wearing a white cotton tunic with a long Javanese batik skirt. The photographs showed that some PKS women were adopting a similar style for ceremonial events. Yulia saw this as evidence of women's pride in their local heritage. Yet the majority of photographs showed PKS women in the more typical plain tunic and skirt, nearly always with a long white or pastel *jilbab*.

Yulia reiterated what I had been told before, that PKS does not have rules for clothing except for a uniform worn on special occasions, which includes the long white *jilbab*. However, she added that PKS feels that a proper *jilbab* fully covers the neck, chest, and shoulders and should not simply be wrapped around the neck or shoulders, as has become popular for many Indonesian women. Yulia's remarks were instructive, not only because they demonstrate the party's concern for minor details of dress, but also because they reveal the extent to which Muslim clothing for women remains a subject of debate in Indonesia.

Although PKS women cadres tend to dress alike, they expressed varied views about whether recent provincial laws requiring women to wear headscarves are appropriate.[13] Such laws alarm many women's rights activists, including those in Fatayat and Rahima. Some PKS women argued that if people vote for such laws, they understand the consequences. They maintained that Islam requires women to wear *jilbab*s, so they should be wearing them anyway. A few suggested that society was not yet ready for such laws. Others seemed ambivalent about the regulations but said that women should not be forced to wear headscarves. For example, when I first interviewed Erna, the moderator of the pornography seminar, she explained:

> E: And in the practice once again there is no compulsion. Like in the verse Al Imron 33, if I'm not mistaken, once again I say that there is no force in the religion, so it's invited of each individual. We just explain that this is what Muslim women must do.
> R: What about women who don't wear the *jilbab*?
> E: We have never discussed it here. How can we explain to them how a woman should be? And our cadres have a lot of interaction with women who don't wear *jilbab*s and they have no problems. Like in the service posts we have set up, there is no problem with visitors who don't wear *jilbab*s; in NTT and NTB [regions in Eastern Indonesia where few women wear headscarves] it's no problem.

While women in PKS argue that wearing a *jilbab* is the correct way to be a Muslim woman, some are uneasy about compelling such behavior from women. They view the *jilbab* as a religious practice that should not be forced on people, but they also see the *jilbab* as the only proper choice. PKS women seem to believe that women will themselves choose to do the right thing, in this case to wear the *jilbab*.

For women in PKS, the *jilbab* and modest dress are taken for granted as obligatory. I saw little evidence of the debates among Rahima and Fatayat women, some of whom argued that the *jilbab* is only required during prayer. Yet in Erna's comments, I detected a pragmatic concern for recruitment. Many Muslim women in Indonesia have never worn the *jilbab*. The party does not want to exclude them but hopes they will eventually adopt proper attire. Indeed, during the 2009 election campaign, women without headscarves were prominently featured in PKS advertising, despite the fact that I never saw a woman without a *jilbab* at a PKS event. There is a double message from PKS. The *jilbab* is the right choice, but it should not interfere with recruitment.

PUBLIC PIETY AND THE TEXTUALIST APPROACH TO ISLAM

The ideas about clothing expressed by PKS women reflect a different way of being Muslim compared to the other groups in this study. The PKS way of being Muslim is one in which piety and public morality are closely linked. Carrying out one's religious obligations in particular ways is essential to being a good Muslim, according to PKS. Female cadres publicly embody their piety by wearing the *jilbab*. Their discourses on clothing reflect their aspirations to follow religious obligations completely. PKS members believe that the words of the Quran should be followed precisely, and doing so is what it means to be pious. This conception of piety reflects PKS's roots in the *Tarbiyah* movement. As Machmudi (2008) explains, *dakwah* groups focus on nurturing moral character and instilling proper religious practice, rather than complex theological discussions.

Public piety is facilitated by the textualist approach of PKS, which diverges from the contextual approach of Fatayat and Rahima. As discussed in chapter 2, traditional Indonesian Islam is characterized by an emphasis on the four main schools of Sunni jurisprudence, with exegesis of the Quran, Hadiths, and *fikh* carried out by trained scholars. In contrast, PKS does not adhere to a school of jurisprudence, and PKS scholars emphasize the Quran and Hadiths more than *fikh*. This leads the party to reject contextual approaches.

PKS textualism has been influenced by the *Tarbiyah* movement and the Muslim Brotherhood. The Muslim Brotherhood demonstrates what some scholars call a "purification" approach to Islam, meaning that it seeks to return to the original foundations of Islamic teaching, the Quran and

Hadiths, and eliminate practices that are viewed as a corruption of authentic Islam, such as mysticism and innovation (Machmudi 2008). It is an approach that rejects traditional religious authorities and refuses a distinction between religion and politics. The public piety of PKS is reminiscent of the Muslim Brotherhood's proclamation that "Islam is the solution." However, the influence of the Muslim Brotherhood on PKS should not be overstated. For example, purificationism does not seem to be as strong among PKS. The party recently held its national conference in the city of Yogyakarta, long viewed as Java's cultural capital, and several events mixed Islamic and Javanese elements (Woodward et al. 2011).

Moreover, in the wake of the Arab Spring, the Muslim Brotherhood has undergone significant changes. Its candidate Mohamed Morsi was elected president of Egypt in 2012, and some analysts suggest that the group has become divided between conservatives and reformists, especially over women's rights (Wickham 2011). Others argue that despite the efforts of reformers, the organization still espouses an essentialist and patriarchal gender ideology (Tadros 2011).

Nonetheless, during my fieldwork the writings of Brotherhood figures were still widely read in the party milieu. This was clear at PKS's first national congress, the *Musyawarah Nasional* or *"munas,"* in Jakarta in 2005. In a building adjacent to the conference center, there was a "bazaar" where vendors sold books, magazines, journals, and Muslim clothing. Prominently displayed at many stalls were Indonesian translations of works by Hassan al-Banna, founder of the Brotherhood, as well as translations of popular Brotherhood thinkers such as Sayyid Qutb, Said Hawa, and Yusuf al-Qaradawi. Articles by these figures, especially al-Qaradawi, frequently appear in the journals associated with PKS—*Sabili, Saksi,* and *Ummi.*

PKS women often spoke about the connection between piety and the need to build a more moral and Islamic society. For example, when I asked Yanti about the controversial regional regulations inspired by Islamic law, she responded:

> Maybe it is a good step from those regional legislatures to implement it. It's just that there are shortcomings which they weren't prepared to deal with, because *Shariah* can only be implemented, be practiced, if society is ready. So I think what we need to do is to change society so that it can be aware of and know about something that has meaning and is good for them. If the person is Muslim, are they in accordance with the values of Islam? Or if not, their consciousness needs to be raised and implemented, so they have personal awareness, which can promote a structure of values in society itself.

Yanti does not make it clear who she thinks should be doing the regulation—the individual or society—but it is plain from her words that those who are deemed to not be in accordance with Islam must be helped along in the process of change. Other PKS women echoed this gradualist view. They are less radical than those who would make *Shariah* into national law, but they are not critical of the regulations that have been promulgated so far. And unlike women in Rahima and Fatayat, they do not argue that there are multiple ways to interpret *Shariah*.

For PKS women, piety takes on meaning not just through individual practice, but also through assuming a regulatory quality. This helps to explain why piety seems more visible within PKS, and why there is so much emphasis on rules governing behavior.

The conceptual link between piety and public morality is also the reason PKS, like no other political party in Indonesia, produces *fatwas* Reflecting the prominence of *dakwah*, PKS is not simply a political party, but an organization of people attempting to live fully Islamic lives and transform society. PKS women's piety reveals their concern for the morality of the nation. And this effort for public morality is underlined by the party's textual approach, which does not leave much room for alternative understandings, attempting to strictly follow the text of the Quran and Hadiths, and viewing them as a complete guide for life and politics.

At a time when Indonesian women have many possible lifestyle choices, PKS offers a distinctive way to be Muslim, one that centers on public piety and textualism. The party is pragmatic and attempts to accommodate difference, such as accepting non-Muslim members. But the pious practices help to forge a sense of community, becoming cultural boundary markers.

The practice of such publicly pious Islam demands effort and discipline. The narrative of transformation voiced by many PKS women is an indication of the sense of the agency that women develop through their involvement in the party. Yet the pious Islam of PKS also has a more specific appeal for women. The middle-class women in PKS want to be involved in building their nation's future. Unlike women's groups who challenge conventional gender norms, PKS provides a way for women to fulfill their desires while emphasizing their conventional roles. Their complex views on feminism and gender reflect how Islamic politics has been influenced by gender politics.

PKS WOMEN AND FEMINISM

Women in PKS tend to see feminism as a Western import that promotes conflict between men and women. Erna explained her views:

The West and Islam are two different things, because in the West, they are influenced by the ideology of Christianization, which has also experienced deviation...so that society itself never believes in the church. And when the Renaissance happened, there was a revolution that produced rebellion, including hot-headedness about women's rights. It's different in Islam; values that respect women already exist. It's just that they might not be fully understood. For feminists, men and women are two different entities, which always produces conflict. If I lose, it means he wins and vice versa. In Islam, the family entity is promoted.... So there is no one who is jealous or hateful. The husband and children are proud if the wife advances. So this can be made into an alternative to resolve problems, especially the crisis between men and women.

Putting aside Erna's historical inaccuracies, she blames feminism for disharmony between men and women. Nevertheless, she allows for the possibility of women "advancing," indicating that she is not hostile to women's rights if such a project is not framed as feminist, and if such rights are defined in ways that do not interfere with what she considers to be women's roles in Islam. I was also intrigued by Erna's implication that feminism has caused a "crisis" between men and women in Indonesia. Contrary to Western stereotypes, PKS women were often thoughtful in their critique of feminism, challenging its presuppositions, and not always hostile to women's rights. Their statements draw on the party's textualist interpretations, which allow women to be politically active while also promoting the idea that gender difference is natural.

The Politics of Gender Equity

Views like Erna's, which reject feminism yet to some extent allow for women's rights, have been characterized by scholars as advocating gender equity rather than gender equality. Gender equity, according to Foley's (2004) analysis of Muslim women activists in Malaysia, is a way for those who reject social constructionism and equality to advocate some forms of empowerment for women and permit them to have a public role while not challenging conventional Islamic discourses on gender. The difference between equity and equality resembles a long-standing debate within feminism, in which proponents of equity argue that upholding difference is empowering and proponents of equality argue that reinforcing difference can promote injustice (MacKinnon 1991; Brown 1995; Scott 1999). Yet unlike "difference feminism," Erna does not seem to be arguing for respecting gender difference in the service of challenging the status quo, but rather gender difference for the sake of the natural order of things.

I saw a change in PKS attitudes toward feminism between 2003 and 2005. Women I spoke to seemed less antagonistic to feminists, and they used terms like *empowerment* and *rights* more often. When I asked Yulia, the head of the women's division, to explain the difference between a woman activist and a feminist, she said that there had been a change:

> There has also been a shift; if previously we considered feminists very radical, now they are more realistic. When they [the feminists] faced men by confronting them, they didn't get anything; instead, they [the feminists] were challenged vehemently until they finally are more realistic. If previously they concentrated more on the issue of *public* and *domestic*, now they are looking more at *function*.[14] All of those are shifts and hopefully it is toward the better. The issue of feminist or not doesn't need to be made into a controversy as long as there is a similarity in purpose as to what can be done for the betterment of the people.

Yulia admits some common ground between feminists and PKS women. Yet she criticizes feminists for placing too much weight on the issue of public and private spheres. Yulia seems to be saying that if they drop this aspect of their activism and focus on improving women's lives, there can be more collaboration. Her comment seems to reject the premises of activism for women's rights but interestingly suggests the possibility of *rapprochement* between PKS and feminists.

Women in PKS do sometimes use terms like *women's rights* and *equality*. However, the textualist approach, which relies mostly on the Quran for evidence, means women in the party usually understand these concepts differently from the other groups in this study. When I first interviewed Kadira, one of the founding members of PKS, I asked her about the intellectual influences on her thinking about Islam and gender. She explained:

> Because reading is my hobby, I have gained knowledge. This also created my support for founding Islamic parties, even though previously just one was permitted. I am sure about the Islamic base because Eastern culture is definitely appropriate for Indonesia. I more and more think that in Islam there is no difference between men and women from the time that they are active in the mosque. So also when I read books, I am even more convinced, even though for me some things are too excessive. I mean, the data that many women are oppressed—but actually, I think men are also oppressed because it is difficult to find a job. For me the media reports about the oppression of women are too excessive. For me, men and women in Indonesia are both oppressed. They are not free to actualize themselves.

Kadira's statement ties her support for Islamic political parties to her statement that there is no difference between men and women in Islam. Her final sentence suggests that she thinks the system oppresses both men and women. This sounds similar to feminist scholars who argue that the gendered social structure, while giving advantages to men, also limits men by forcing them to conform to particular ways of being masculine (Connell 2009).

However, Kadira does not use the word equality (*kesamaan*) in this statement. Her avowal that men and women are no different in the mosque is followed by a denial that women face more oppression than men. At other times, she acknowledged that women face discrimination. But she said that she does not think that the practice of Islam limits women. Gender inequality, according to Kadira, can be traced to an incomplete understanding of Islam. She cited the example of Muslim communities in Eastern Indonesia, where men sometimes have numerous wives, far more than the four allowed by the Quran. For Kadira, this unfortunate situation is due to the local culture that predates Islam and the lack of religious education that might help people realize that such practices violate Islamic law. In this account, it is Indonesia's older patriarchal traditions that are to blame for inequality.

This argument is superficially similar to that made by other Muslim women activists, who maintain that the patriarchal practices associated with Islam actually derive from Arab or tribal culture. Certainly there is evidence for this claim, as historians have shown that veiling and polygamy predate Islam. But Rahima and Fatayat members say that while inequality is not inherent to Islam, patriarchal interpretations have become embedded in the religion, and reinterpretation is required. In contrast, Kadira argues that Islam is not the problem.

Kadira and other PKS women argue that Islam specifies different duties for men and women, and that both sexes are judged by Allah on the basis of their piety and devotion. In their view, Islam specifies that men should provide for the household and women should raise the children, and these tasks are equally important. As Yulia explained, "I am convinced that men and women have the same tasks in life. This is written in the Quran. We talk about *amar ma'ruf nahi mungkar*,[15] to make policy and prohibit people from doing shameful things. That is already our obligation together; what remains is how to divide up the tasks. We have to help each other. Women continue to have a major portion in bringing up the children."

Nevertheless, PKS also urges Muslim women to be involved in the public arena. In a 2001 article for a PKS newsletter, one woman party member wrote: "At this time society is in the middle of a moral hemorrhage, far from the holy teachings of Islam that can return social life to an honorable state.... It is certain that Muslim women have a major role in this field, a role that, like it or not, requires going out of the house, a role that requires the husband to permit his wife to play an active role in developing an Islamic society."[16]

While many Indonesian women activists contend that differences between men and women are socially constructed, PKS women refer to the Quran to claim that gender difference is natural. Their argument is for moral equity between men and women, rather than social equality. PKS women's statements about gender draw on the party's textualist approach, which rejects the contextual approaches used by many Muslim feminists. However, PKS women also understand Islamic texts in ways that serve their interests in living modern, active lives. Although PKS women emphasize gender difference, they understand the Quran to allow women to be involved in politics and to work outside the home. The party encourages women's political mobilization. Such views probably reflect the influence of ideas about women's rights and political mobilization. But PKS aims to reform the way Islam is practiced in Indonesia and to convert Indonesia into a society with stronger moral regulation. PKS is not so much disseminating a specific interpretation of Islam as it is promulgating an approach to the religion that foregrounds textual readings of the Quran and the Hadiths, public piety, and the integration of Islam into all aspects of life.

For PKS cadres, Islam is the unquestionable source of authority for understanding women's rights and responsibilities. Nevertheless, PKS women share class and educational backgrounds with other activists in this study. This was evident in the ways they spoke about marriage and family life. When they discussed their lifestyles with me, they did not sound terribly different from women in Fatayat or Rahima.

Marriage and Family

PKS women emphasize that men are the heads of household and that family should be women's priority. Some, but not all, reject the notion of equality between men and women. Yet when they talk about their own relationships, they highlight their husbands' supportiveness and willingness to help with household tasks. In short, their marriages sound like conventional Indonesian middle-class "companionate" marriages. How are we to understand this?

Widyawati, the Muslim primary school principal who spoke about her transformation in the *dakwah* movement, was one of the few PKS women

I met who used the word *equality*. Explaining that Islam says that that male and female are equal in public affairs, she stated, "I implement the concept of equality in the family and at school." Widyawati emphasized her husband's support for her career. She explained that he gave up his PhD program to help her:

> The sacrifice my husband has made for me is proof that he supports my involvement in public life.... He decided not to continue his studies in Birmingham [U.K.] and said that he had changed his goal, that is, to prioritize his wife, family, and community. He said that he didn't want to be a lecturer anymore; instead, he wanted to be an entrepreneur and be more involved in the party. I was so amazed. He rejected the two or three letters from Birmingham, which asked him to continue his studies. Really, what he did means a lot to me. My experience is, in fact, proof that men and women are indeed partners. I have never felt marginalized or harassed.

Widyawati uses her own experiences to generalize about gender relations in Indonesia. I wondered if she had difficulty reconciling her egalitarianism with some of the practices within PKS. For example, like other practices of gender segregation in Muslim communities, the *fatwa* prohibiting women and men from shaking hands is premised on the belief that women's bodies incite inappropriate male desire (Mernissi 1987; Mahmood 2005). Widyawati viewed such rules differently. "The essence of these rules is how to bring goodness to our lives and live in peace. The rules also set our aspects of cooperation and collaboration between men and women. One of the examples of these rules is the obligation to wear the *jilbab* for women. I believe such obligation exists for the sake of women themselves—to protect them from harm and bring them comfort." Like other PKS women I met, Widyawati acknowledged that women are less active in PKS because most are still in their reproductive years and caring for children. While she and her husband can afford a domestic helper, she admitted that not all can do so. "Consequently, some of us have to choose between staying home and being active in public." PKS women seemed comfortable with how this choice influences their lives.

Susanti, the Muslim clothing seller, was proud to tell me about her husband's support for her career decisions:

> I am an agricultural engineer; previously I was an assistant lecturer. But because I wanted to improve my family's economic situation, I entered the business world and my husband supported me. Sometimes I leave the children for twelve days or two weeks and my husband stays in the house, and thanks be to God, he

very much supports me. We communicate about everything. Certainly, without forgetting that my responsibility as a mother and wife is in the house.

But when I returned in 2008, Susanti explained her decision to conduct more business online: "The children are getting bigger. When you met me, the children were still small, and I had enough time to be in touch with my community, whereas now the children are older, but attention to my family is a priority for me, without neglecting the obligation to participate in the community," she told me. Nevertheless, she went on to discuss her work for the party and to describe the institute she has established, which specializes in education and training for low-income women.

Yanti, who came from a less affluent and more pious family, married young at age twenty, when she was just out of high school and studying at an Islamic institute: "I am glad that my parents did not object to the marriage proposal. We had known each other for quite a long time before we decided to get married. We were both mosque activists. Perhaps my parents thought I was mature enough to decide for myself."

Yanti has three children, and she said that her family has not hindered her continuing her studies at university and becoming politically active. Her husband is also a PKS cadre: "I'm very grateful to have such a wonderful husband. He understands my full schedule. I have to attend board meetings that last until midnight twice a month, not to mention the other meetings at the regional level. Before we got married, we agreed that building a family is not just a matter of fulfilling personal interests, but a way of contributing to the community."

In this activist family, Yanti says that her husband makes a real contribution to household labor. "Concerning domestic chores, we are used to helping each other, without having to be asked. That's why I said my husband is wonderful. He is used to cooking, washing the dishes, and taking care of the children." Yanti also argues that women must fight for their rights and empowerment. But she is uncomfortable with the idea of equality:

> I believe feminists should pay more attention to women's issues rather than the issue of equality, regarding men as their rivals. However smart we are, we still need men in our lives because males and females are created to complete each other. God creates everything in pairs: night and day, morning and evening, up and down, men and women, etc. I cannot imagine what would happen in the family if the feminists' ideas that demand equality with men in all areas of life are implemented; wives would probably feel oppressed, and they would fight with all their might to achieve equality, and their husbands, in turn, would be miserable.

In short, PKS women describe their family lives in ways that middle-class, urban women in many parts of the world would recognize. But like Susanti and Widyawati, Yanti maintains that men are the heads of the households, even if in practice decisions are made jointly. Different from the other groups in this study, most PKS women do not express a vision of equality in all spheres or criticize the gendered division of labor. They are more committed to the idea that women and men have different responsibilities in life.[17] When they speak about rights for women, they usually mean in the public realm. Nevertheless, their households sound relatively similar to those of other activists in this study: both spouses have busy lives, children's education and development are a priority, and families own middle-class consumer goods like computers and updated televisions.

All of the PKS women I interviewed spoke highly of their marital relationships, and they often described their husbands as partners (*pasangan*). Such language is common in Indonesia, and Javanese gender ideology tends to stress complementarity (though not equality) between husbands and wives. Yet coupled with the discussions of supportive husbands, I also detected the influence of more egalitarian notions of marriage. Nonetheless, the uniformly positive answers made me wonder about women with less idyllic marriages. The party's emphasis on wives needing their husbands' consent for activities outside the house renders PKS women dependent on their husbands' goodwill. However, educated Indonesians are aware of Western styles of marriage, and some women may have been trying to convince me that their marriages live up to these standards. PKS women may also simply have different expectations of their husbands. Moreover, couples often avert their eyes from the gendered division of labor in their household, in Indonesia and elsewhere (Hochschild 1989). As Tickamyer and Kusujiarti (2012) show in their study of rural Java, many couples say that husbands contribute to domestic work, but when observers break down the household tasks, it turns out the contributions of husbands are quite minor. Importantly, as already noted, the ability to afford domestic help lightens the load for some PKS women, as it does for other middle-class Indonesians.

The PKS approach to the Quran allows for women to pursue careers and active lives, especially in the pursuit of Islamic transformation. PKS women accept that men and women have different roles, but they also understand the Quran to allow women to be politically active. And public piety means a role for women in helping to create a moral society. Second, we should consider PKS women's statements about gender in the context of a party in which men dominate. There are many women party members, but few have positions of intellectual or religious leadership. Voicing strong support for party ideology and party notions of piety allows women to legitimize themselves as committed party activists, even while maintaining more conventional or even relatively egalitarian practices at home. And indeed, many women don't see any contradiction between the ideologies they espouse and their lifestyles. Their statements indicate that they see themselves as fulfilling the Quranic obligation for different and complementary gender roles both at home and in their party work.[18]

PKS women expect to play a role in their communities, to influence the nation through their activism, and to raise the next generation of activists. They feel themselves to be the authors of their own lives (Giddens 1991). Aside from these aspirations, the Indonesian middle classes face the constraints of global capitalism. Living comfortably in major Indonesian cities often requires two incomes. Many Indonesian women generate significant income for their families, even if it is not defined as a "career." And in the past few decades, the percentage of women in the Indonesian workforce has risen, just as it has in many parts of the world.

Other scholars have noted this paradox of Indonesian women's economic empowerment coexisting with attitudes that insist on male superiority (Brenner 1998; Tickamyer and Kusujiarti 2012). Javanese middle-class culture upholds women's roles as wives and mothers and idealizes them as self-sacrificing helpers to their families, although it does not prevent them from working outside the house (Tickamyer and Kusujiarti 2012). Indeed, Brenner observes that Javanese women often do not describe their jobs as work or career but instead emphasize their household contributions.

Javanese gender ideology has been reinforced by state policies. As I discussed in chapter 2, the Suharto regime emphasized the housewife role for middle-class women but also incorporated them into state-controlled organizations. Some of the activities of the PKS women's division are similar to those of the state organizations, which taught women about nutrition and health, as well as instilling conservative ideas about womanhood (Suryakusuma 1996; Brenner 1998). PKS, with its emphasis on women's contribution, harks back to Suharto-era discourses depicting women as mothers and wives, building the nation's future. But such activities can also create space for more women's mobilization.

Comparisons with other religious traditions reveal some important similarities in this regard. Many American Evangelicals maintain that wives must submit to husbands. However, some sociological studies find that men in Evangelical households contribute about the same amount of household labor as men in other religious groups and are more involved in childrearing activities (Gallagher 2004). Gallagher contends that the commitment to male authority is a matter of symbolic marker of identity as an Evangelical. Similarly, the commitment to male authority among PKS women can be seen as part of a collective identity that draws on conservative norms of gender and piety.

Another intriguing comparison is to India's Hindu Nationalist Party, the BJP, which also draws many women. Jeffery and Basu (1997) maintain that the BJP's gender ideology is at times conservative, at other times progressive, but often used to denigrate Indian Muslims' alleged treatment of women. The party offers lower middle-class women opportunities for self-expression and gives voice to their ambivalence about social and economic changes. However, it does not challenge sexual inequality or conventional gender roles.

As the Indonesian middle class expands and people seek to create meaningful ways of life, piety has become a marker of distinction. Middle-class PKS women use norms of gender and family to consolidate a pious identity and a moral vision of idealized household life. They are forging a new way of being middle class, embodied by a public piety that draws on Islamic textualism. They disagree with the goals and premises of feminism but seek an active role for women in the Islamic transformation of their society.

ENGAGEMENTS IN THE PUBLIC SPHERE: PKS WOMEN AND POLITICS

How does the textual approach to Islam shape PKS women's agency and activism? In this section, I explore PKS women's public interventions in the realm of "family values," including their views on the contentious subject of polygamy, and return to a discussion of their involvement in the controversy over pornography. Such activism demonstrates PKS women's *pious activating agency*, which uses the party's textualist interpretations to mobilize for a more Islamic nation. This is a new agency for Muslim women that differs from feminist agency in that it does not seek to confront gender inequality. Yet within this activism, the weight of ideas of women's rights can be felt, both as an influence and as a reference point.

PKS women, along with those in Muslim organizations such as Nahdlatul Ulama and Muhammadiyah, have helped to bring outwardly pious women into the public sphere. The increasing emphasis of the party on issues like family, as well as its attempts to forge a more inclusive public image, may well be a result of greater female participation.

Family Values

One of the signature events for women at the PKS national conference in the summer of 2005 was a talk show on women and the family. It was held in a huge room, with an audience of about 150 women, all sitting on Middle Eastern carpets. On the stage was a banner stating "*Keluarga Surga yang hampir Hilang*" ("Heavenly Family which is almost Disappearing"). The emcee was a minor celebrity, an actress who was known for recommitting herself to Islam. She wore a *jilbab* in the fashionable style of a tightly wrapped headscarf and long slim skirt.

Siti, from the organizing committee, made a brief statement welcoming everyone and mentioning me as an honored guest. She reiterated that the family in Indonesia is being lost, and that PKS hoped this program would improve all of our motivations to make our families better. She then introduced Ibu Retno, a psychologist, and Haji Fatma, a female representative from PKS.

Ibu Retno wore Muslim clothing but, like the emcee, had a tightly wrapped headscarf rather than the long one worn by PKS women. She started by proclaiming herself a PKS sympathizer. She went on to say that women are delaying marriage, partly because of their careers, but also because of fear of commitment. But, she said, the normal life course is for women to be married, have children, and be alone again when they are old. Independence is important, she said. Ibu Retno also said that some people at age thirty-five are not ready to marry, and that many women need to work to provide income for their families. Some women in the audience looked uncomfortable with these statements, but they did not interrupt.

Ibu Retno observed that contemporary life puts a lot of stress on families. She cited problems with money, divorce, violence, stress, and boredom. She added, "If women ask me whether they should be at home or at work, I tell them, it's your choice; just make sure the quality of time with the children is good. You can be home all the time and the kids will be bored."

With this last statement, Ibu Retno turned to Haji Fatma to ask if she agreed. Haji Fatma looked skeptical but responded politely, "Yes, it's both the time and the quality of the activities." Ibu Retno concluded by saying that the essence of a good society is good families. "If heaven is to return, it must come back to the mother," she maintained. She repeated, with the audience chanting along: "*Rumahku, keluargu, surgaku*" ("My home, my family, my heaven").

Ibu Retno was more socially liberal than many PKS members, with her talk about marrying late and careers. Her appearance hinted at ambivalence about such subjects among PKS. She was the invited speaker, but Haji Fatma seemed unhappy with her remarks. The event suggested the influence of the field of gender politics, particularly changing ideas about women's roles in family life. Such ideas are not fully embraced by many in the party but perhaps reflect the actual experiences of PKS women, particularly in Jakarta.

The party promotes "family values" through events like the talk show. Family is not simply a niche for women, but a frame for many of PKS's public sphere activities. Not long after the talk show, I asked Yulia why PKS had become so interested in the family. She responded:

> Because the family is the foundation for building a good society. The society is composed of families. So how can we build a strong society if the family itself is not strong? Secondly, we believe that the best education exists in the family—be it education about religion, politics, social, or emotional. Children are our assets that we need to take care of. They are the biggest assets of a nation.

Yulia's statement suggests that it is the connection between family and society or nation that animates PKS. Feminist scholars argue that traditional conceptions of the family and its relationship to the nation reinforce the gendered division of labor (Yuval-Davis 1997). In fact, this is the case in Indonesia, where the family is defined by Indonesian law, and by PKS, as composed of a male head and a wife who oversees the children and the running of the household.

While the Suharto regime promoted the nuclear family as a centerpiece of its development efforts, PKS family values do not exclude the possibility of polygamy.[19] Although it is not widely practiced in Indonesia, polygamy has resurfaced in recent years as a number of public figures began to promote it as an expression of Muslim masculinity and authentic Islamic family (Van Wichelen 2009). The ensuing debates have generated copious media extolling the values of polygamous families or, conversely, arguing that polygamy has no place in contemporary Islam.

As I discussed in the previous chapter, some Indonesian Muslim women's groups oppose polygamy. Fatayat and Rahima acknowledge that the Quran allows men to marry four wives, but they maintain that the verse about polygamy needs to be understood with regard to the historical context of Arabia in the sixth century. They argue that the Prophet Muhammad's limitation of men to four wives was intended as a reform, and that the caveat that wives must be treated equally is impossible to fulfill in today's world, where marriage must meet material and emotional needs.

PKS women express a different view of polygamy. Party leaders argue that polygamy is in the Quran and therefore must be allowed with certain stipulations. And as Hidayat Nurwahid, a longtime party leader, argued in a recent newspaper article, "If the state doesn't prohibit it, why should we?"[20] But the perception that PKS approves of polygamy has made the party controversial with the Indonesian public. In 2003, Kadira told me that none of the leadership was polygamous. But when I returned for additional research in 2005, other party members told me that some PKS leaders, including Anis Matta, then the party's secretary general and currently its president, had more than one wife. Since then, other party leaders in polygamous marriages have gone public or have been "outed" by women's rights activists (though politicians from secular parties were outed as well). Many observers say this hurt the party in the 2009 elections.

I did not meet any PKS women who admitted to being in polygamous marriages. The PKS women I interviewed held diverse opinions on the practice, but nearly all argued against what they saw as efforts to ban it. However, many shared Kadira's view that polygamy should be seen as a provision for special cases.

> Islam, I think, represents rules from Allah. This is what we call *Shariah*. Allah knows the weaknesses of humanity and makes rules for this. Therefore, for humans for whom one wife is not enough, Islam opens the opportunity for polygamy.... If a man really wants to have children, but his wife has been told by a doctor that it is not possible for her to have children, then Islam permits polygamy. Also for a man who has high sexual needs, Islam permits polygamy. Because it is not possible for a woman to serve the man all day long, a man may take another wife.... In practice, we have to pay attention to the context of the polygamy. If it is only to satisfy desire, it is in contradiction to Islam. Unfortunately, in Indonesia, many people don't understand that.

Other PKS women acknowledged that they did not like the idea of polygamy but felt that as Muslims they had to accept it. It is this view that is the key to understanding PKS women's stance on polygamy—their textualist approach to the Quran does not accept the historicized contextual of Fatayat and many Muslim reformists.

For example, Susanti told me that Muslims cannot simply pick and choose what they like from the Quran:

> The problem is that we can only place our trust in Allah. Certainly for a husband who wants to be polygamous, there must be many considerations. He must ask permission from his wife and his children, whether they are ready for it. Individually, as a Muslim I accept it. This is because I want my Islam to be full, comprehensive, and not choosing just what is nice and leaving behind what is not so great. I want to be like that.

A few PKS women were more willing to defend polygamy, arguing that it can work in some relationships. Overall, however, given that polygamy has proven to be politically unpopular in recent years, especially with Indonesian women, it is surprising that PKS women are reluctant to condemn it. While few PKS women can be categorized as proponents of polygamy, their opposition to limitations on it comes out of their textualist approach, which for Susanti and others means not rejecting aspects of the Quran that they find inconvenient. While PKS women did not mention influences on their ideas about polygamy, their statements about their Islam being "full and comprehensive" echo Muslim Brotherhood founder Hassan al-Banna's insistence on Islam as a "total system, complete unto itself" (Mitchell 1993). Nevertheless, PKS women express nuanced views, as is evident in their stress on polygamy as an emergency strategy rather than as an appealing form of marriage. This is an example of women's strategic and selective use of the party's religious interpretations.

A very different example of the party's family endeavors is its community service posts in Jakarta, known as *Pos Wanita Keadilan* (Justice Women's Posts). These posts are intended to provide services such as job trainings, discussions about health issues, and practical skills. The posts are aimed at strengthening families and communities. Although the posts are run by PKS, the party sometimes works with other organizations such as the government-run Family Welfare Movement (PKK), which has long provided similar programs.[21] These posts were first established in the early 2000s. However, in 2011, PKS relaunched the *Pos Wanita Keadilan* program as part of its contribution to achieving the Millennium Development Goals.[22]

Widyawati explained how the *Pos Wanita Keadilan*s are a way for the party to develop relationships with local communities:

> Certainly first we must take charge of our public map, get to know and understand their issues. . . . Our targets are the grassroots that are around the *pos keadilans*, maybe beginning with a *charity* program, like we often hold a *Bakti Sosial* [social services check]. We do health checks, social services that are empowering, in which we develop their economic empowerment, give them capital, skills. And certainly the primary key must be to comprehend our society correctly: what it is like, what are the conditions geographically, topographically, demographically, so we really know it, so that what we offer can be appropriate to the hopes of the grassroots community? To run a *Pos Wanita Keadilan*, one of the skills is how cadres understand the neighborhood, understand the public image of women in the area where they are working, are able to analyze the things that are most needed, because each district has different needs.

The *Pos Wanita Keadilan* is a vehicle for PKS women like Widyawati to help instill family values in urban communities, as well as to recruit supporters through promoting economic development. This suggests that the *Pos Wanita Keadilan* is part of a cultural mission in which PKS members seek to change Indonesians' religious ideas and practices. This and other efforts by PKS women to build family values draw on the party's interpretations of Islam, especially the idea that men and women are naturally different. As I discuss in the next section, PKS women's interventions in the debate over the pornography law reveal that stronger regulation of moral and cultural life is also an aim for PKS. PKS women demonstrate pious activating agency as they use the rubric of family values and the rhetoric of protecting women in their arguments supporting the law banning pornography.

Pornography

The Bill against Pornography and Pornographic Acts (*Rancangan Undang-Undang Anti Pornografi dan Pornoaksi*), passed in 2008, represents one of PKS's legislative successes, and also demonstrates the centrality of national morality to party ideology. The statements in support of the law by PKS women reveal their conception of morality as a public good, one that requires regulation by the state and religious authorities. They utilize the party's textualist approach to make their claims. But their involvement in this issue has brought PKS women into conflict with activists who argue that the legislation harms women's rights.

Pornography emerged as a major issue after the Suharto regime fell in 1998 and media censorship was lifted. While older laws restricting pornography remained on the books, after 1998 some Muslim groups became increasingly vocal about the need for more regulation.

The furor that erupted over the popular singer Inul Daratista in 2002 was one of the first indications of the push for new legislation. Inul's performances were often televised, and her costumes were skin-tight, with moves seemingly lifted from strippers. Some Indonesians, especially those in PKS, felt that Inul symbolized an increasingly sexualized culture, one in which kids were watching pornography at Internet cafes and buying pornographic videos on the street. Muslim politicians began to call for laws that would restrict such entertainment.

Not all Indonesians agreed. Some women in the other groups I studied told me that Indonesian traditional dances are as erotic as those performed by Inul. Others opposed censorship, which they saw as a return to the Suharto era. In 2003, activists from Solidaritas Perempuan and several

Figure 4.2: Activists demonstrate against the censorship of pop star Inul Daratista, 2003.

other groups held a rowdy demonstration in support of Inul (Figure 4.2). In the ensuing years, Inul significantly toned down her style, but other notorious entertainers emerged in her place.

I opened this chapter with a description of a 2003 seminar and demonstration against pornography. At that time, a new bill with stronger prohibitions on pornography was being written. In February 2006, PKS members introduced into parliament draft legislation, written in collaboration with MUI and other religious authorities. As originally written, the bill was broad, and opponents feared that it would be used to outlaw kissing in public or wearing bikinis at the beach. Public outcry forced its return to parliament for revision and it was stalled there for over a year. Through 2008, there were debates in parliament and demonstrations for and against the bill. In November 2008, the parliament passed a revised version that made exceptions for "sexual materials" as part of traditional culture and fine arts.[23] Women in PKS strongly supported the legislation, while women's rights activists (including Fatayat and Rahima), artists and entertainers, cultural traditionalists, and religious minorities opposed it.[24]

In early 2008, I asked women from PKS about the bill, which was still generating much opposition. They blamed the ongoing hullabaloo on media interests, as well as on supporters who hadn't explained the bill well enough so that people would understand it properly. Widyawati, who was confident that it would soon pass, explained:

> I think it is maybe because of the communication factor, which isn't always easy. Sometimes there are obstacles, debates on various sides, which are not clearly communicated and so we don't understand each other, are not open with each other. But the main thing is that we supported it because it protects society from the bad effects of pornography and porno activity. . . . In terms of our position, we have already been very clear that our support for it is related to how the next generation of children can be protected, so that our society will be morally better, because morality is very important to improve ourselves.

Like Widyawati, PKS advocates of the bill linked discourses of virtue to anxieties about national progress. For example, in a statement in 2006, a PKS member of parliament declared Indonesia a "full pornography country," arguing that pornography and "porno-activity" would "trigger free sex, adultery, prostitution, abortion and its side effects, all of which would insult and lower the honor of Indonesian humanity, which is religious."[25] The statement blamed liberalism for social evils: "It is proper to be on guard against the ideological motive behind the rejection of this bill, namely, the dissemination of liberal thinking and behavior in a country that is majority Muslim. The fact is, the principle of liberalism reaps a bitter pill. High levels of abortion, rape, sexual harassment, broken households, and other side effects."

As the bill was revised in 2008, PKS legislators argued that it was essential to combat moral decadence. PKS Deputy Secretary General Zulkieflimansyah was quoted saying, "We are only giving voice to our constituents who are concerned with what they see on television and a sense of moral degradation."[26]

Such concerns are also embedded in the text of the law itself. Section 3 of the law, titled "Purpose of Pornography Rules," states: "A. To shape, protect, and maintain the social order of the community and community ethics, supremacy of privacy, the priceless value of God, and admiration and respect of the dignity and worth of humans. B. To cultivate and instruct a moral and ethical community." Despite the legislators' comments about liberalism, the law contains language about the supremacy of privacy and the dignity of humans. Nevertheless, the law clearly seeks to cultivate a moral community.[27]

Women in PKS echo such arguments about moral degradation. But rather than divisive claims about liberalism, they tend to employ religious discourses about modesty, as well as protection of women and children. Their statements reveal their conservative views on gender yet attempt to speak to the concerns of women's rights activists. For example, Widyawati said, "Pornography and porno-activity in the context of protecting children—that is an issue for all people. But I don't know how in the process it got blown up. It's like it is something controversial and connected to unrelated things." For Widyawati, morality is an issue of protecting women and children from negative influences.

In an interview with the Australian Broadcasting Corporation, female PKS legislator Yoyoh Yusroh, a member of the parliamentary committee that wrote the legislation, maintains that the bill protects women. "You don't need to worry too much about this bill because it is aimed at increasing respect. If people don't wear respectful clothing, it has implications for other situations. For example, it weakens the ability of the opposite sex to study."[28] Yet even as she claimed universality for the bill, she implicitly drew on widely known Islamic discourses that position women as inciting inappropriate male desire (Mernissi 1992).

Guarding future generations also was a common theme in PKS women's support for the legislation. When I asked Yanti if she thought the law would be ratified, she replied: "Yes, hopefully it will be ratified, as it truly is representative. By representative I mean that it's for the good of women themselves and also for the common good. It's not just for women, but also for the family, our children, future generations." Again, morality is linked to the common good, and children and future generations must be protected.

National identity was also a vital theme for many PKS women. In my interview with her in 2008, Susanti's answers reminded me of the way pornography was discussed in the 2003 seminar, as a negative Western influence. She told me: "I look at it this way: we are an Eastern culture. Maybe we can absorb all kinds of knowledge and technology, but we should not leave behind the special characteristics of Indonesia. . . . If we leave our culture behind we will change. I don't mean that we don't accept modernity, but modernity can be a pattern of thinking, knowledge, a level of education that we should achieve."

The impact of the pornography bill is not yet evident. There will no doubt be disparities in enforcement. Yet the fact that it is on the books gives anti-pornography partisans the power to regulate media and entertainment if they choose to do so.[29] And it is often the case that simply the threat of using such powers is enough to provoke self-censorship.

The debate over the pornography bill demonstrates the intersections of the fields of Islamic politics and gender politics. National Islamic values were to be promoted by protecting women and children from sexual immorality. PKS women's arguments in support of the bill mobilize the party's religious interpretations but also attempt to appeal to women's rights activists. However, PKS women's statements about modesty and protecting women employ the same logic as calls for mandatory veiling. They urge restrictions on women's bodily presentations to protect them from male arousal, and in this way to protect the virtue of society in general. Women in PKS are certainly not the only Indonesian activists concerned about pornography. The panic about morality is widespread in contemporary Indonesia, and such concerns are voiced by women's rights advocates, as well as PKS women. Yet many women's rights activists are more wary of state intervention into private behavior. PKS women's interventions in public sphere debates on pornography grow out of their highly public conception of piety, which calls out for increased regulation of behavior. They mobilize their party's established interpretations of Islamic texts to participate in democratic processes and to promote the PKS vision of a greater role for the state and religious authorities in determining the moral order.

Islamization and Public Piety

The party's public piety and textualist approach emphasizes its struggle for a moral society, in which the family is central. In this sense, the party's activism is an example of "Islamization from below," a strategy that attempts to forge a more Islamic society from the grassroots upward, rather than through revolution (Kepel 1994). Growing out of the *Tarbiyah* movement, PKS sees itself as more than a political party, and cultivating Islamic character and fostering piety are central goals.

Carrying out one's religious obligations in particular ways is essential to being a good Muslim according to PKS. More good Muslims will produce a moral society. This project to Islamize Indonesia promotes an important role for women in PKS. Women are the most visibly pious party members due to their clothing, and they are heavily involved in party campaigns around issues like family and pornography. Women are attracted to PKS because they view it as a modern and pious Muslim party. While these women do not necessarily seek gender equality, they do seek the opportunity for meaningful political involvement. Islamization gives PKS women a vital niche within the party, as well as a public platform. Moreover, the party's textual interpretive approach facilitates the emergence of pious activating agency for women cadres.

Nevertheless, because of the relative simplicity of the textual approach and the concomitant acceptance of gender difference, women in PKS are constrained in their involvement in the party. With a seemingly narrow range of critical debate about Islam within the party, PKS women do not have as much ability as women in organizations like Nahdlatul Ulama or Muhammadiyah to adapt religious texts to further their interests.

Just how much of an influence PKS has in Indonesian politics is not yet clear. The party is most popular among Indonesia's middle class, though it has not succeeded in raising its share of the national vote. It attracts voters who are tired of the major parties but put off by more extreme Islamists. The women of PKS enthusiastically use the public sphere to promote political and social change, but rather than advocating egalitarian gender reforms they aim to build a more Islamic nation-state.

CONCLUSIONS—PKS, ISLAMIZATION, AND MIDDLE-CLASS WOMEN'S PUBLIC SPHERE MOBILIZATION

The women in PKS share a great deal with women in Rahima, Fatayat, and Solidaritas Perempuan. They are educated and outspoken, forging middle-class lives in a chaotic Asian megacity. They seek personal fulfillment and social change. Mostly under fifty, they have been inspired by the Islamic revival, as well as by Indonesia's democratization.

What distinguishes the women in PKS from the other activists in this study is their vision for Indonesia's future: a society with stronger moral regulation and a state guided by Islamic values. PKS women's activism is shaped by a textual approach to interpretation and a highly public conception of piety. The primary consequences of this approach are (1) an understanding of gender that stresses essential differences between men and women but allows women to participate in the public sphere and (2) advocacy of a guiding role for Islam in the state and society. The paths followed by PKS women mesh with the party's approach to Islam to produce a moral vision of gender equity and Islamic nationalism.

Many scholars (Moghadam 1994; Ong 1995; Chong 2008) have argued that anxieties over women's bodies and behavior are central to conservative religious movements. It is surprising, therefore, that when it comes to their daily lives and career aspirations, the women in PKS are not as different from the activists of Rahima, Fatayat, or even Solidaritas Perempuan. In fact, when it comes to sexual morality, there is little disagreement between the groups in this study. These similarities demonstrate that a middle-class *habitus* stressing education, moral cultivation, and family structures all of the lives of the women in this study.

In contrast to the other activists I came to know, the women in PKS struggle for Islamization rather than gender equality. Many said they were led to PKS because of their experiences of pious self-transformation while involved in *dakwah* groups on state university campuses. Certainly, not all of those in *dakwah* groups join PKS or continue to be pious. And many Indonesians also attend state universities and do not join *dakwah* groups. Nevertheless, PKS women were part of a particular Islamic milieu and share a pious trajectory that leads them to understand Islam as an all-encompassing way of life and to consider the text of the Quran to be straightforward.

PKS gives such women the opportunity to be involved in national politics while still emphasizing their positions as caretakers of the family. The Islamization project promotes a certain kind of inclusion for women. It encourages their participation while upholding gender difference. It is this aspect of the party that appeals to women who have more conservative beliefs about gender yet also desire to have an impact on their society. Through the resources provided by the party, PKS women construct themselves as modern political actors. They embody a distinctive fusion of being pious and middle class, which also draws on Javanese and state gender discourses. Indeed, they are creating a new norm of middle-class Muslim womanhood. While they do not confront conventional gender norms or advocate for new interpretations of Islamic texts, their increased presence in the textualist milieu of Islamic politics nevertheless challenges men's domination of the field.

Some social scientists view the agency of Islamist women as "paradoxical" (Ong 1995), focusing on the irony of educated women choosing to participate in a patriarchal religious movement. I agree that there is an irony in this, but it is important to admit that seeing such a situation as ironic stems from a belief that education and modernity free women from patriarchal constraints. If we disentangle these concepts, it becomes more possible to grasp how educated middle-class women may want to participate in a movement that seemingly constrains them.

A better way of understanding this decision is to follow the lead of recent scholars and distinguish agency from liberation (Jeffery and Basu 1997; Mahmood 2005). Mahmood argues that pious Muslim women in Egypt find agency (and pleasure) in choosing to conform to religious disciplines. However, it is also important to keep in mind that religious movements are not necessarily conservative and do not necessarily constrain women. Indeed, women in PKS do not use the language of submission that Mahmood heard in Egypt.

I build on Mahmood's argument that agency is more than simply resistance or co-optation, and that agency is not separate from social structures. If social structures and trajectories constitute the horizons of people's imaginations, we should expect that their actions would reproduce rather than challenge the status quo. Although some women seek radical transformations, women's agency has no necessary connection to liberation. Indeed, from this perspective, it is not the women who perpetuate patriarchal structures who require explanation, but rather, those who defy such structures.

PKS women's agency involves the activation of party interpretations to legitimize women's activism for a more Islamic society. It arises from the textualist milieu of Islamic politics, which is premised on a *strict* interpretive approach that leaves little room for flexibility or innovation. Thus, PKS women help us see that pious agency takes different forms. Their *pious activating agency* is different from the *pious critical agency* of Fatayat and Rahima because the latter relies on a *flexible* interpretive approach that more easily incorporates influences from feminist thought. Fatayat and Rahima women also exhibit *pious activating agency,* but the crucial difference is that unlike PKS women they are activating their own critical interpretations of Islamic texts. PKS women, however, do not view adherence to the party's readings of religious texts and pious norms as constricting but instead as an opportunity to fashion themselves and their community as modern, devout Muslims. Women in PKS take on a public role as Muslim subjects and as examples of moral virtue. It is a politicized and missionary role for women, common to many Islamist movements (Göle 1996).

In this sense, the women of PKS have a different position in relation to the fields of Islamic politics and gender politics. Unlike Fatayat and Rahima activists, who are positioned squarely in the overlap of these two fields, PKS women are located more exclusively in the field of Islamic politics. But seeing PKS women's agency as constituted only by Islam misses a great deal. As I have shown, women's class and educational backgrounds direct them toward particular pious trajectories. Compared to Fatayat and Rahima activists, PKS women do not have the same latitude to apply the cultural schemas of both Islam and feminism in new ways or in different settings (Sewell 1992). Yet within narrower limits, they selectively adapt Islamic interpretations to meet their needs—for example, arguing that polygamy is allowed but only for special cases, or maintaining that gender difference is mandated in the Quran but that women can still participate in politics. Here, there is evidence of influence from ideas of women's rights, a consequence of how the fields of Islamic politics and gender politics have interacted with each other in recent years. This further demonstrates that the ways people engage with religion and feminism are strongly influenced by context. Like the other women in this study, PKS women's social networks and activist experiences have shaped their pious trajectories and their styles of engagement with Islam and feminism.

The consequences of PKS women's agency are complex. Along with women in other Muslim organizations over the past two decades, PKS women have helped to open up space for pious women as political actors in Indonesia. Yet the very processes that empower PKS women threaten to marginalize others. In their study of India, Jeffery and Basu (1997) warn that women in the Hindu nationalist movement empower themselves while dehumanizing Muslims. Indonesia is much less religiously polarized than India, and PKS emphasizes Indonesian national unity. However, the party's gendered piety and textualist approach to Islam construct a distinctive identity. They telegraph the message that they represent the right way to be a Muslim, and indeed, that Indonesia's identity is Muslim.

PKS women use their public platform to influence debates about religion, morality, and the nation in specific ways. They have been profoundly influenced by the new emphasis on piety and Islam as a way of life. The Islamization project provides PKS women with a niche within the party and an opening to express their ideas for Indonesia's future. But the future that PKS women activists seek may not appeal to all Indonesians. It is a vision of Indonesia as a nation that is distinctly less concerned with diversity and equality than the visions of the nation promoted by Fatayat, Rahima, and Solidaritas Perempuan.

CHAPTER 5
Solidaritas Perempuan

Feminist Agency in an Age of Islamic Revival

At their office in South Jakarta, members of Solidaritas Perempuan (SP; which translates as Women's Solidarity) were preparing leaflets, buttons, and stickers to hand out to the public at malls. It was part of an international campaign these activists were participating in to end violence against women. I took a taxi to the popular Blok M with several young staff members. As the taxi stalled in one of the city's massive traffic jams, they peppered me with questions. The most assertive was Lilia, who wore a white headscarf with jeans and looked to be in her late twenties. She asked me about the other groups in my study. When I listed them, Lilia said proudly that there were many women's rights groups in Jakarta but SP was known as the most militant. This remark drew laughter all around.

I was captivated by this image of young Muslim women in headscarves bragging about the militancy of their feminist group. As I got to know Lilia and her colleagues, I came to understand more about their commitment to feminism, as well as their Muslim identities.

Given that many Indonesians and Westerners view Islam and feminism as incompatible, it may seem surprising that these young Muslim women were self-proclaimed feminists. As I discussed in chapter 2, Indonesians often associate feminism with communism and secularism, and these ideologies are widely considered "anti-Islamic" (Budiman 2008).[1]

For many Indonesians, secular means being against religion. As Islamic rhetoric in Indonesia has taken on a more nationalistic tone, one of the easiest ways to marginalize an idea is to characterize it as foreign or Western.

Feminists in many postcolonial contexts face this very same problem, in many cases because nationalist movements have successfully valorized patriarchal cultural traditions as authentic and central to their idea of nationhood (Narayan 1997). Despite Indonesia's history of women's activism, feminism is sometimes tarred as foreign because of its association with international NGOs. Self-described feminists face real challenges to their legitimacy as political actors in Indonesia.

At a time when the relationship between Islam and feminism seemed to be especially fraught in Indonesia, I was curious to learn how SP activists engaged with these discourses. How does a secular feminist NGO maintain legitimacy in an increasingly Islamic Indonesian public sphere? And what kind of agency did activists in SP demonstrate?

In this chapter, I examine the contours of SP's inclusive type of activism and what I see as their *feminist agency*. This type of agency encompasses three key features that distinguish it from the pious critical agency of Fatayat and Rahima and from the pious activating agency of the Prosperous Justice Party (PKS). *Feminist agency*, as I discussed in chapter 1, is an agency that aims at empowering women and challenging their subordination relative to men. SP has an explicit commitment to feminism, infusing feminist ideals throughout its activism. Second, adaptation of transnational feminist and human rights discourses is at the heart of its work.[2] And third, SP's activist interventions demonstrate a critical feminist perspective on social problems tied to the global economy, such as migrants' rights and environmental justice.

This feminist agency emerges from the organization's position in the field of gender politics, a field in which activists working for women's rights have been influential since the early 1990s. SP occupies a position that overlaps with several other activist fields, as many SP staff have strong connections to human rights, labor, and environmental movements. SP's most significant interactions are with other women's rights and migrant advocacy NGOs. The feminist agency that SP activists embody is secular in the sense that they do not usually employ religious frameworks to make arguments for women's rights. However, this feminist agency increasingly incorporates Islamic piety. SP activists do not see Islam and feminism as inherently opposed, and some staff are pious Muslims who are not shy about expressing their faith in public. This sets SP apart from some other Indonesian feminist groups who avoid public piety and from feminists in many Muslim contexts who distance themselves from public religious life (Karam 1998; Sadiqi and Ennaji 2006). SP includes pious activists who argue for women's rights on a generally secular basis. In contrast to the other organizations in this study, religious arguments are not central to

SP's activism. Instead, their work is rooted in the ideal of universal human rights. While Fatayat and Rahima demonstrate the promise of Islam as a force for social justice, the experience of SP shows how the rise of Islam does not preclude feminist activism. However, my fieldwork with SP also illuminates the risks of the Islamization of the public sphere in Indonesia.

Influenced by feminist and socialist thinkers, much of SP's activism is predicated on adapting transnational discourses, especially human rights, to press its claims for social reforms and gender equality. SP activists are mediators of such global discourses (Merry 2006), transforming and localizing human rights and feminism by interweaving them with discourses on local culture and histories.

Reflecting the increased intersections between gender politics and Islamic politics, SP activists position themselves not only in relation to transnational feminism but also in relation to the increased role Islam is playing in Indonesian politics. As my fieldwork reveals, this has important consequences for SP's activism. In a study of civil society and political apathy in the United States., Eliasoph (1998) observes that American activists downplay structural social problems and collective identities, instead emphasizing rhetoric about self-interest and personal experiences. The net result is that activists gain mainstream credibility at the cost of being able to incite debates about systemic problems. This makes them unable to push for more radical changes. For Eliasoph, this is an example of how activists' reliance on shared cultural norms constrains the possibilities for political debate and activism. A similar dynamic emerges with SP. Conforming to the norms of the Indonesian public sphere sometimes requires SP members to downplay their feminist identities. Simultaneously, the performance of Islamic identity by individual SP members helps to bring the organization more mainstream legitimacy. While this dynamic benefits SP, it sometimes circumscribes its feminist activism and risks affirming the gendered status quo and reinforcing the expectation that Islam must be at the center of public sphere politics.

SP's global feminism, with its emphasis on transnational discourses, has sometimes kept it on the margins of debates over gender and religion. Increasingly, however, SP has begun to struggle against intolerant and extremist interpretations of Islam, taking on projects in places where there are ongoing efforts to regulate women's bodies and behaviors. SP's evolution is therefore indicative of the shifts in power occurring in contemporary Indonesia and the complex overlap of the fields of Islamic politics and gender politics.

This chapter explores how women in SP understand feminist politics and religious piety. Tracing the trajectories of some of the organization's leaders,

I show how SP activists' feminist agency has been shaped by participation in progressive social movements and through exposure to feminist ideals while in SP. I then investigate how SP activists negotiate Islam and feminism, both in their work and in their personal lives. Finally, I explore three political issues in which SP has been involved—migration and trafficking, environmental justice, and Islamic fundamentalism—to understand how feminist agency shapes SP's activism in a context of Islamic revival.

The experiences of SP activists illustrate the costs of a public sphere becoming dominated by one particular discourse, and how resourceful activists navigate such a situation. Just as women in Rahima, Fatayat, and PKS are interpreting religion in different ways, so do SP activists critically engage with Islam and feminism. Profoundly influenced by feminist ideals of equality and rights, SP promotes a contextual approach to Islam, one that positions Islam and feminism as different yet compatible discourses. Women in SP primarily adapt global feminist and human rights discourses to make their arguments, but some also negotiate Islam and feminism in their political work and their personal lives. They combine these with a focus on economic equality and a critique of neoliberal capitalism. Their activism and robust ties to other progressive social movements show that the rise of pious agency has not undermined feminist agency in Indonesia. Moreover, some SP activists are constructing modern selves that are informed both by a sense of feminist agency and by being devout Muslims. This new feminist subjectivity is less elite and more able to cross class boundaries than that cultivated by earlier generations of Indonesian feminists. Sewell (1992) proposes that putting existing cultural schemas to use in new contexts can drive social transformation. In this sense, SP's global feminism represents an unconventional approach to both feminism and Islam, one that suggests that a public sphere dominated by religious discourse can still accommodate different arguments for egalitarian social change.

ACTIVIST TRAJECTORIES

When I first visited SP, the organization's office, like many Indonesian NGOs, was a house in a leafy, middle-class neighborhood in South Jakarta. The modest building belied the organization's reputation as one of Indonesia's most activist NGOs. It was established in 1990 to advocate for the rights of female migrant workers and for women's rights more generally. Since that time, Indonesia has become one of the world's largest exporters of migrant workers. According to the International Labor Organization, some 700,000 documented people leave Indonesia to work overseas each year. It is esti-mated that 78% of Indonesian migrants are domestic workers.[3]

The Jakarta office had about two dozen paid staff members, all women (in subsequent years there were male staff).[4] While the women I had met the previous day at the offices of Komnas Perempuan (National Commission on Violence against Women)[5] wore Western clothing and one intern sported pink hair, at SP I saw several women wearing *jilbabs*.[6] I was attracted to SP because of its reputation as an outspoken feminist group, but as early as my first few forays to the office I noticed with some surprise that SP staff seemed more likely to wear Muslim clothing than women in other secular women's rights groups.

When I began my fieldwork in late 2002, most of the staff members of SP were a generation younger than those who founded the organization in the early 1990s. Mostly in their twenties and thirties, the women I met were just old enough to have participated in the *reformasi* movement against the Suharto regime. By the time I returned in 2008, there were many new staff who were no longer personally connected to the social movements of the 1990s, though they had other similarities with their elders. A closer look at two women who rose to SP leadership, Lilia and Danita, illustrates the trajectories of many SP women in the 2000s. They demonstrate a simi-lar pathway through state universities and progressive activism, leading to positions as SP staff members and thus entrance into the feminist milieu within the field of gender politics.

Lilia, who I first met in the taxi, told me that she grew up in a city in South Sulawesi. Her mother taught middle school and her father was a civil servant in the Ministry of Health. She attended public schools and a state university in Makassar, the capital of South Sulawesi. She fortuitously moved to Jakarta to continue her education at the University of Indonesia just as the *reformasi* movement was peaking. She had been involved in the national Muslim student group Himpunan Muslim Islam (HMI) in Sulawesi. She described herself in this way: "I am one of those student activists with a Muslim background who has a moderate ideology.... When the Indonesian nation was authoritarian under Suharto, there were many activists who became moderate up to radical and opposed the government. I am one of them."

In Jakarta, Lilia became interested in the women's movement and con-tinued to be active with HMI. She was part of the student occupation of parliament that precipitated Suharto's resignation. She also volunteered at women's rights NGOs and eventually was offered a job with SP.

When I first interviewed Lilia in 2003, she was living in a hive-like dor-mitory and finishing her master's thesis in sociology. She said that her parents did not know much about her life in Jakarta outside school. They were not pleased to find out that she was an activist when they saw her in a demonstration on national television:

> My parents are actually very patriarchal. To them, public spaces are not important for women. What is important is that the children are in school, not so that those children can become activists. Gradually I convinced them that I am an activist to socialize important women's problems, that it is part of the teaching of Islam...that we represent humanity, we must do things for humanity. In Jakarta, I am a woman activist, working in an NGO, and when I go home I assure my parents that I am an activist for the interests of many people....Slowly, slowly they understand. I try to convince them that my schooling is good....I think then that my parents support me.

By 2008, Lilia had risen into the leadership of SP. When we talked again, in her typical frank manner, she expressed anxiety about what she saw as a rise in fundamentalism in Indonesia. She was especially concerned about the consequences for women and religious or ethnic minorities. Though she acknowledged that Islamists were not likely to take over the national government, she was concerned about their power in many of Indonesia's provinces. "The *reformasi* era gave me many experiences," she told me, "especially that the New Order was a time in which women were totally not empowered....And so today I am very critical of how political interests, ethnic groups, and so on are limiting women's political space in the name of religion." As of 2012, Lilia had stepped down from her leadership duties but remained on SP's national advisory board.

When I first met Danita, she was the head of SP's migrant worker program. Tiny and slender, she stood out from the group with her artistic clothing. Her outfits were creatively assembled from various styles yet conformed to the guidelines of Muslim clothing, covering her arms and legs, and usually including a matching headscarf or headwrap. Danita looked fragile, but like Lilia, she was plainspoken and very much in charge. She also became a leader of the organization but left in 2008 to pursue grassroots work and start a family. She remains on SP's national advisory board.

Danita's parents came from the eastern Indonesian islands of Maluku, but she was raised in West Papua, where her father worked for the national police. Her mother was Catholic and, against the wishes of her family, converted to Islam to marry Danita's father. Danita attended public school and when she was in high school her father was transferred to national police headquarters in Jakarta. Danita studied law at a state university in East

Java and later worked for an NGO in Surabaya on labor and environmental cases. In 1996, she returned to Jakarta to look after her younger siblings and was hired by SP to handle migrant worker cases.

Danita entered SP via the emerging labor movement. Like most staff, while she supported SP's aims, she learned about feminism on the job. Nevertheless, she said that her open-minded father gave her a progressive foundation:

> In Maluku tradition, men are very "violent," so it's usual for men to hit their wives. And in Papua, there is also a high level of domestic violence. I remember once my neighbor hit his wife till she bled. He struck her with a bottle until her head was bleeding, and she ran around the complex calling for help. And then my father mobilized; he pulled the woman into our house, and because he was a policeman, her husband was scared, not brave enough to shout at her again. That was an ordinary event in the community, the place where I was raised; only luckily my family and my father weren't like that, maybe because when he was still young, he had already gone away from home to work, he had been to other provinces, so he was spouting new values from other regions. He was an adult in a different situation, so he did not have habits like that.

Danita's parents were aware of her activism and during the Suharto era they were anxious that she would be arrested and jailed. Like many staffers' parents, they had a hard time understanding why their daughter would use her university degree to work for a low-paying nonprofit rather than a private company. But she felt they supported her commitment to human rights and helping exploited women. After a decade with SP, Danita married and moved to East Java.

Like Lilia and Danita, nearly all of the Jakarta staff I met attended university and some had master's degrees. Most attended secular public schools, and some are graduates of Indonesia's most prestigious state universities—University of Indonesia (Jakarta) and Gadjah Mada University (Yogyakarta). The women I met mostly grew up in urban areas. They were often the first generation in their family to attend university and did not have strong links with religious organizations.

What most SP women have in common is experience in Indonesia's broader liberal left milieu.[7] Whether as part of secular or Muslim student groups, *reformasi* demonstrations, environmental groups, or labor rights organizations, most SP women had some experience with liberal or left-wing activism. As is often the case with social movement organizations, SP women were usually not very knowledgeable about feminism before taking jobs with the organization.

As Lilia's story shows, it was often at state universities that SP women became involved in student groups pushing for democratization and other kinds of social change. As I discuss in chapter 2, the founders of SP were involved in the student movement of the 1980s and early 1990s, and several met through the movement against the Kedung Ombo dam in Central Java in the late 1980s. This was a time when Indonesian student activists attempted, with some success, to organize peasants and factory workers against the government (Aspinall 2005). Lilia's remark about militancy alludes to this earlier activism, as students who sought to organize the *rakyat* (people) often identified proudly as radicals. Many were inspired by socialism or Marxism, as well as by regional events such as the People Power uprising in the Philippines.

Most of the SP women I interacted with were of a younger generation. Their experience in progressive social movements introduced them to ideas about social justice and equality, which made them receptive to SP's feminism. Most important, their student and early activist years coincided with the height of *reformasi*.[8]

Although SP played a role in *reformasi* activities, most of the women I met were not yet involved in the organization in 1997 and 1998. But their participation in the milieu of the *reformasi* movement helped to further politicize them and contributed to their building networks that include NGO activists, journalists, academics, and even politicians. Lilia told me how she and Ayu of Rahima got to know each other during the student occupation of the parliament that culminated in Suharto's resignation. SP women indeed emerged from somewhat similar backgrounds in the expanding Suharto era middle classes. Their moral visions and activist practices have been forged through a generational experience of progressive social movements and, as we shall see, through schooling in feminist ideals while working for SP.

FEMINISM AND AGENCY IN SOLIDARITAS PEREMPUAN

At the heart of Solidaritas Perempuan's work is an inclusive feminist agency that is shaped by the adaption of transnational feminist discourses. SP activists tend to understand feminism as an idea that originated in the West, but they also cite Indonesia's record of women's mobilization and female historical figures to argue that struggles for women's rights are authentic to Indonesia. As one longtime member of SP told me: "The history of women's struggle in Indonesia has to be dug up again so that it can become a reference point for the women's movement, even though feminist awareness has indeed come from outside." Importantly, SP maintains

Figure 5.1: Break time at Solidaritas Perempuan's national congress, 2008.

connections to activists in fields such as human rights, labor, and environmental activism, as well as to Muslim women's rights organizations. This position within gender politics, but also as part of a horizontal network, also influences SP's feminist agency (Figure 5.1).

Some SP women have mixed feelings about calling themselves feminists because of the baggage associated with the term. Others said that it was too narrow to capture their humanistic passions. Krisna, a quiet woman in her early thirties, explained her perspective this way:

> Since a long time ago many people have struggled for equality, and they were never called feminists. I prefer to be known as a person who struggles for justice, justice for women....Now many people are scared to be called feminists and define feminism narrowly, as if we were only struggling for women, even though what we are struggling for is so much and it is about lives. But those lives are not only women but also men, nature, life itself.

Nevertheless, many SP women embrace the label of feminist. Lilia told me:

> I often use *bahasa feminis* [feminist language] because my experiences previously showed me how *seorang feminis* [a feminist], a woman who understands

feminism as an idea, ideology, a frame, believes that the problems of women, like issues of discrimination, violence, oppression, stereotypes, and so on, can be answered with a feminist approach. And because I am one of the people who does that, it is not wrong to say that I am a feminist, because I am directly implementing that. And I maintain that feminists must be real feminists, namely, a woman who can reflect on her ideas, concepts, or paradigms of thought in that way, to make noise about the problems experienced by women.

Lilia argued that feminist identity is crucial to SP. She continued, saying: "I am from an SP background, because I have *banyak berkiprah* [been very activist]. Feminism is all of our activities, ways of thinking, ideology—we always use a feminist approach. The ideology is feminist."

Danita also emphasized SP's feminism. She told me:

Before, a long time ago, there were not many organizations who said 'we are going along the feminist road.' There were many who said, 'we are developing' or 'we want to advance gender equality,' because the word gender is more comfortable. But since the beginning, SP declared itself to be a feminist organization, meaning we use feminist values as the principles and philosophy of the organization.

SP's written materials also clearly articulated feminist goals for the organization: empowering women with feminist politics and perspectives; building the women's movement in Indonesia and cooperating with women's movements around the world; advocating for the rights of all women, but especially those who are marginalized; and organizing women to change patriarchal ideologies and behaviors. SP's primary work is advocacy for women migrant workers who encounter exploitative treatment when they go overseas for work. SP has also expanded into related issues, such as advocating for migrant workers with HIV/AIDS, and it also has an environmental focus. The organization is concerned about privatization of water and other natural resources, as well as "food sovereignty," a term activists use to mean the ability of people to produce adequate food for their communities rather than for the export market. More so than the other groups in this study, SP points to neoliberal economic policies and global capitalism as primary sources of women's marginalization.

One of feminism's most important contributions to social theory is the insight that inequities in the domestic sphere buttress inequality in the public sphere, famously encapsulated in the slogan "the personal is political." Solidaritas Perempuan staff are well educated in this regard, although unlike many feminist groups around the world, their activism does not revolve around bodily politics (Davis 2007). This is partly because Indonesia has other well-established women's organizations that deal with issues like domestic violence. SP emphasizes experience as the basis of feminist politics; however, activists interpret this feminist epistemology in their own ways. SP leaders emphasize economics and politics as the main sources of women's oppression. But SP activists also stress how these issues are manifest in daily life, for they see this as the realm in which women experience economic marginalization, environmental pollution, and religious fundamentalism. In this way, SP women connect the personal and the political, challenging conventional boundaries between private life and public politics, and also contesting the masculinity of formal politics.

Most SP staff applied for jobs at SP, or were recruited, on the basis of their work in the activist/NGO milieu: student groups, environmental organizations, or anticorruption NGOs. All new staff undergo a feminist training program in which they learn about the history of women's movements in the West and in the developing world. They study human rights, and it is emphasized that women's rights are part of the human rights struggle. Like the trainings at Rahima and Fatayat, SP's training materials introduce participants to varieties of feminism, including liberal feminism, Marxist feminism, radical feminism, socialist feminism, and third world feminism. Yet outside of the trainings, SP staff did not appear to read much feminist writing. I almost never saw staff take advantage of the well-stocked library, which included both scholarly and popular literature from all over the world.

When I first met Ninik, she was in the leadership of the organization and in her forties, one of the oldest staff members and a veteran of progressive social movements. Seeing that the library had titles by Maria Mies and Vandana Shiva, I asked Ninik if these feminists influenced SP's ideas. She said that only a few staff read them. She explained:

The basis that we see...is the basis of experience. Feminists [like Mies and Shiva] draw on [and] validate the problems facing women and nature, so actually they are studying from life. So if you look, their concepts are actually born from experiences and the result is they write about those experiences and develop them into theory. Meanwhile, our friends here, there are some who talk about it, but I don't think there are any who read, I think it's just their experiences that make them similar.

The main point of SP's feminist training is that differences between men and women are socially constructed and the only real difference between them is biological. Reading the materials and talking to participants further revealed that the training justifies feminism on the grounds of women's experience and knowledge, relating this to ideas of fairness and equality. Younger staff told me that the feminist training was their introduction to such ideas. One young staff member, Mita, was inspired by the training and other activist experiences to stand up to her authoritarian father. She said, "I was very impressed with the feminist training. When there was the question, 'What do you want as a woman?' it turned out that our desires were all for other people, not for ourselves. Our desires were already contaminated."

In addition to feminist trainings for staff, SP also conducts gender trainings for women in the communities in which it is working. SP staff consider rural communities to be deeply conservative, particularly when it comes to gender, and they are cautious about using the word *feminism* in these communities.

On one of my early visits to the SP office, I discussed the gender trainings with Alia, a staff member originally from the province of Aceh. Alia was one of the few staff to wear a long *jilbab* and rather bulky clothing, complete with thick socks. But she told me with satisfaction that SP was one of the only organizations that truly incorporates feminist ideas into gender trainings and discussions. When I asked her if they used the actual term *feminism*, she said no, because the women wouldn't understand it, or worse, might have "misperceptions." Alia said that SP has a hard time getting women even to come to the trainings because they are not used to going about on their own. She said they often bring their husbands with them the first time.

Alia explained that the trainings focus on trying to help women understand that they have a voice in the household. She said that many rural women are not used to making decisions about major issues, like where to send the children to school. One of the first steps in the training is to talk about a typical woman's daily schedule and a typical man's daily schedule and compare them to show how much more work women do. The group moves on to ask why women don't get paid for their work like men do. Alia remarked that the discussion gets women talking and that after a few sessions, women become much more assertive. Indeed, at SP events I often met women from small towns or villages who had attended gender trainings or other workshops and were excited to become more involved with the organization.

This stress on feminism as lived experience is instilled in SP staff through the feminist training and other events in which staff are encouraged to connect their lives to feminism. As Yuli, a young staff member, recalled: "I often heard about gender equality and women's rights. I didn't understand.

But now I know that equality means that women can also do the things that men do. I grasped the essence of equality between men and women, because we are all human, the same."

Another staff member, Mita, told me that working for SP helped her to reflect on her experience with an abusive father:

> My interest in women's rights is because I had a personal experience, because my father is very authoritarian.... So I felt oppressed, but I wasn't brave enough to resist. My anger was because of his treatment of my mother. That was what made me angry and rebellious. I often left the house and was asked to come back. I am unhappy if things like that are happening around me. This is why I joined SP.

Mita said that her experiences with activism, especially SP, inspired her to stand up to her father. "I became an agent for change in my family. Before, I was often grumbled at, hit, and chased away by my father. I thought he didn't want me to come back. Then I thought, 'why can I speak outside, but in my own house it's very difficult?' Finally, I returned home because I felt that I had a responsibility to make changes."

When I first met Mita in 2003, she was ambivalent about feminism. She wore a *jilbab*, usually with a tunic and jeans. As we sat on the floor of SP's library, she said she agreed with feminist ideas about equality but didn't necessarily like the label. Mita said she used to think that feminists wanted to overtake men. "But really, feminism isn't like that. We don't want to mistreat people and we don't want to be mistreated; we are struggling for equality." When I asked her if she thought of herself as a feminist, she said, "I am struggling for equality. It wouldn't be wrong to consider that a feminist concept. But feminist concepts are different for each person. So maybe I am a feminist."

When I returned in 2005, Mita was thirty-three and more confident about feminism and about her life. She was engaged and was looking forward to marriage. Remembering her discomfort with feminism, I asked her if she thought of herself as a Muslim feminist. She said she didn't want to be trapped in the category of Muslim feminist. "But there is a space that unites us in the sense that we understand our rights and we understand that there is discrimination and our desire to struggle against it. Yes, we are automatically feminists whether we are Muslim feminists or not. I think it's up to the individual what kind of feminist you want to be, as long as we are still struggling for women's interests." Mita was also concerned that people still think feminists are opposed to men. "I myself don't agree with that. Feminist for me doesn't mean that we are better than men, but that we believe in equality between men and women." Mita's shift reveals that she has become inculcated with feminist ideals, and her realization that feminism can be defined in multiple ways seems to have made her comfortable with taking on a feminist identity.

Feminist trainings and discussions are only part of SP's activism. On a daily basis, Jakarta office staff are engaged in administrative work and in the service activities that take up much of the organization's time. If anything, dealings with state agencies often seem to take priority. But SP activists' social service work is motivated by feminist concerns, and through negotiations with government officials and the legal system they are able to assist individual women caught up in migration scams or who are abused and exploited by employers overseas.

This is a substantial shift from the early days of the organization. Early SP members risked arrest, jail time, or worse for their activities. Sarita, a middle-aged SP member who is a professor in East Java, recalled: "Before *reformasi*, our activities were hidden. We weren't brave enough to come forward with things that were so opposed by the government. Now we are already used to bringing those things to the fore, and there is no pressure we experience for doing that. For academics like us, this is amazing. From having to cover up our thoughts, now at least on the academic side the liberation is really extraordinary."

SP activists develop feminist agency through their experiences in SP. They identify feminism as a foreign discourse that emphasizes women's equality and rights, but they also come to believe that it is connected to Indonesian women's historical struggles. They highlight lived experience as an organic, authentic link between women, and one that helps to bridge this distance between the transnational and the personal. SP draws heavily on transnational discourses of feminism, stresses the global dimensions of the feminist movement, and works on global issues such as migration. There are three additional significant aspects of SP's feminist agency. First, SP activists connect women's rights to democratization and economic equality; second, SP insists on making the women's rights movement part of the public sphere in Indonesia; and third, SP activists tie ideas about equality to their intimate relationships. All of these characteristics are woven together in a distinctive and inclusive feminist agency, and each is discussed in more detail in the following sections.

Democratization and Economic Equality

SP activities reflect the organization's stress on women's individual and collective experience as the source of authority, rather than religious teachings. They focus on national policy, advocating for migrant workers, and trying to build a broader women's movement. And their analysis of gender inequality connects feminism with democratization and global capitalism.

SP's 1995 mission statement articulates these ideas: "To build social structures that are democratic, based on principles of justice, ecological awareness, value pluralism, and against violence, based on a system in which the relationship between men and women is equal and in which both have access to and control over natural resources, society, culture, economy and politics in a manner that is fair."

At a weekend conference SP held on the subject of trafficking of women workers, the featured speaker was a noted feminist who is on SP's executive board. The audience was riveted as Eka explained the factors behind the rise in trafficking, singling out gender-based violence, as well as globalization. She argued that the situation was caused by "structural injustice" and the exploitation of the south by the north. "In the 1980s Indonesia was opening to external investment and the government was looking for commodities to replace oil. What they decided on was tourism and workers." According to Eka, this promoted capitalism and the commodification of women's bodies. Eka urged SP activists to understand how globalization shapes gender and class inequality, describing how women are freed from social reproduction at the local level and thrown into international social reproduction (as servants, nurses, and sex workers). The first world benefits from the poverty of the third world and gender inequality in the household, Eka said. She concluded, "I use feminist theory to understand globalization, not just because I myself am a feminist."

Politicizing Feminism

Mita's story about resisting her abusive father is a classic example of how feminism challenges the gendered boundaries between public and private. However, SP activists often spoke about feminism and women's rights in rather abstract, general ways. For example, when I asked Yuli about how her ideas about gender changed after joining SP, she said: "This world of ours is patriarchal, so it harms women. Awareness of women's rights is becoming more apparent."

This abstract style draws on cultural conventions. Indonesian rhetorical styles often use generalities rather than personal opinions or experiences. But speaking of feminism in broad and general terms may also reflect SP's interest in appealing to women of different socioeconomic strata. More significantly, it helps to position SP as legitimate in a public sphere in which politics is still generally understood as a male pursuit and political discussions are characterized by formal and impersonal discourse (Fraser 1990). For example, Danita explained to me that SP was trying to shift Indonesian politics toward a broader understanding of rights: "In the past the women's movement rested on political rights. But now I think that sociocultural rights are the challenge. Fulfilling socioeconomic rights is so difficult, like the right to schooling, to health services, to housing, to work. I think we need to look for a strategy for these rights."

SP members seek to politicize feminism and transform politics. As part of this effort, SP activists mobilize transnational discourses such as human rights and equality. These frameworks are predicated on the idea that there are basic similarities among all people.[9] SP activists adapt these broad discourses, rendering them in local terms to reach across class lines and address a broad community of women.

SP's global feminism thrusts feminism into the public sphere, but its inclusiveness and generality help to defuse confrontation.[10] In a context where feminism remains taboo, SP activists stress women's experiences as an axis of connection. They do not shrink from doing social service work or from criticizing the state. In fact, SP's feminist critique of the state led the group to oppose the Suharto regime. For SP, feminism is intimately connected to the struggle to transform Indonesian politics and society, but also to women's daily lives and experiences.

Daily Life and Activism: Marriage and Sexuality

Joining SP spurs staff members to think critically about their lives. Indeed, it is in the realm of daily life that we can see the more intimate aspects of feminist agency for SP activists.

Married women who worked for SP were eager to talk to me about their efforts to share domestic work with their husbands. One explained that she chose to have just one child, unusual in Indonesia, because of concerns about the costs of childcare and education. Another told me that despite loving her work, she regrets the lengthy commute that makes spending time with her children difficult during the week (a common situation in Jakarta).

Women who were unmarried spoke of hoping to find a partner who shares their commitment to equality. In 2005, Mita said that what she liked best about her fiancé was that he is not at all like her father. "He wants to listen to me. He is also patient, democratic. I mean, he can discuss everything and he wants to do that." She said that she wanted their marriage to be a partnership. "We will discuss everything and talk about things together, like what consequences will happen if we make a decision about something. For me, there is nothing that would be felt as discriminatory."

Single women at SP spoke of the family pressure to find a partner, as well as of the difficulties they face in finding one they consider suitable.[11] Alia, the Acehnese staff member, said that the most important characteristic of a husband would be to have the same religion, Islam. "As a Muslim who is carrying out religious *Shariah*, I have a desire to marry," she told me. She too expressed a desire for egalitarian marriage. Her ideal: "Like a friend, meaning that I am equal and not subordinate to my husband. We can divide the household work. Up till now, women are always positioned in the domestic space and men in the public sphere. So I want something balanced and equal between men and women."

Feminism deeply influences SP women's ideas about their intimate relationships. Their varied viewpoints are evidence of the distinctive ways each woman negotiates feminism in her own life. Their statements show the importance of ideas of rights and equality. Yet Islam is also an important aspect of many SP activists' daily lives. I now turn to a consideration of the ways SP activists' feminist agency coexists with Islam.

ISLAM AND SOLIDARITAS PEREMPUAN

During my fieldwork stints in 2002–2003 and 2005, all but one of the SP staff were Muslim (since then there have been more Christian staff members, and some of the branch communities include more Christians). Like others of their generation, SP women were much affected by the wave of Islamic revival that swept Indonesia beginning in the 1980s. Many SP women were university students in the 1990s, as the resurgence fed into the democracy movement. Many told me that they attended Islamic study classes in high school and some adopted the *jilbab* as teenagers, joining a national trend that has dramatically altered Indonesia's fashion landscape.

While some Indonesian feminists are resolutely secular, SP's feminist agency is increasingly open to Islam. I found that about a third of the SP staff wore the *jilbab*, though often idiosyncratically. Since the office was almost entirely female, some staff wore headscarves only outside. Others wore the *jilbab* on some days and not on others, an atypical choice in a place where taking on the headscarf is generally seen as a serious decision and a symbol of piety. A few conformed to stricter guidelines of Muslim clothing, wearing long tunics and baggy skirts. Many downplayed the significance of their headscarves, insisting that they wear them simply from habit or because they like the style. They saw the headscarf as an individual choice, and they also defended the choice not to wear Muslim clothing. Indeed, when I returned in subsequent years, Lilia and Danita often went without headscarves in public, a change from 2003. By 2010, Lilia had actually stopped wearing the *jilbab* because she felt that it had become a political tool for conservatives.

Religious piety was evident in the office. A downstairs closet was designated as a prayer room, which bustled with activity during the noon prayer. Staff often greeted each other at this time of the day by asking, "*Sudah sholat?*" (Have you prayed yet?). During Ramadan, staffers who were still at the office often broke the fast together with food ordered from a local hawker's cart. Yet there were also staff who exhibited little interest in religion. It was difficult to broach the matter with them. In a political environment where even leftists hesitate to call themselves secular, it is not surprising that women who are not particularly interested in practicing religion are also not eager to discuss it. Nonetheless, SP activists have developed innovative strategies for negotiating Islam and feminism as they forge their inclusive feminist agency.

Negotiating Islam and Feminism

Mely was a graduate of the University of Indonesia who came from a middle-class but traditional family in Central Java. She struck me as cosmopolitan, with her stylish Western clothing and jokes about *nongkrong* (hanging out) at the mall or trendy cafes. Yet she told me, "Since junior high I have gone to religious study. If I didn't go to the classes I would be hit. I was taught by a *santri*[12] who said that women must bow down to their husbands. This became a debate in my life. This doctrine took root in me when I was small. Up till now I still study a lot."

Most women at SP believe that the true spirit of Islam is egalitarian. But they also say that patriarchal understandings of Islam are widespread, and they themselves have grappled with such interpretations. Like others, Mely argues that men have interpreted the Quran in a patriarchal way, and that female interpreters could make the religion compatible with women's rights. She maintains:

> I see that many of those Hadiths that are taken are just fragments. It turns out that in other verses, it's written that if a woman doesn't want it, or if she is tired, then her husband may not force her to have sex. Up till now, there are mostly

male interpreters, so that it benefits them. These fragments of verses from the Quran ultimately indoctrinate women, especially in the villages. So we really need female interpreters, from the perspective of women.

Perhaps the clearest expression of this view came from Danita:

I think I have experienced a lot of transformations in my religious convictions since I have been in SP, because many of the religious rules that I accepted before misinformed me about the position of women. And when I came to work at SP, I came to know they were not correct. For instance, many verses of the Quran that are widely socialized, they are only the verses that are, first, interpreted wrongly, and second, those in which women are positioned as subordinates. Now, getting to know more women, I have access to find out about other verses, or other historical facts about when the Quran was sent down, when the Prophet Muhammad was alive, how actually Islam corrected social behavior toward women that was wrong. So, earlier, I only knew that Islam was a religion that was very oppressive and marginalized women. Now, that's altogether incorrect, because, for instance, there are many verses in which it is revealed that women may not be treated roughly. The husband may not force the wife into sexual relations and the wife who experiences being hit by her husband may separate herself from him, divorce, or demand recompense for what her husband did.

Some are less convinced about gender equality in the Quran. Alia initially said much the same as Danita about interpretations of the Quran. But when I questioned her further about how her religious beliefs affect her ideas about gender, she admitted she was unsure about different understandings of the religion. "If I base my ideas on religion, I am uncertain about women's roles. I think men and women are actually the same, but the difference is just because of culture." SP staff sometimes take a more critical stance. One woman told me that if Hadiths are unfair or unjust, they need not be followed. Another, Dian, explained that she was still overcoming her traditional upbringing. "I swallowed the idea that such were the teachings of religion. Because of education, I realized that religious teachings shouldn't be swallowed that way. I must be critical, analyze their correctness, and so on."

Lilia articulated the sharpest criticism of Islam's role in gender inequality. She said that her beliefs about gender do not rely on religion. This is despite her strong Muslim identity, which made her inclined her to wear the *jilbab* for many years. In 2003 she explained:

My beliefs take off from reality.... There is a system at work; there are cultural values that up till now curb women. Those values are patriarchal. There are also religious values which are misinterpreted in the interests of certain people, men's interests. In Islam, men are very dominant. Those who regulate life and death are men. It is men who wrongly interpret religion.... The Indonesian nation, beginning from its culture, religion (religious interpretation), and state policy, marginalizes women. Activists born in Indonesia oppose these three things that shackle us.

While many women in SP like Lilia believe that Islam has been interpreted with a patriarchal bias, this does not stop them from being pious and, in many cases, from embracing symbols of Muslim belief such as headscarves. This is because many SP staff believe that the true spirit of Islam is justice and equality, and that Islamic teachings need to be understood contextually. As Danita told me:

> I think all of the Quranic verses were sent down [by God] into a particular context, which cannot be compared with the current era. For me, for example, that verse was probably just for that time, when women could not be inheritors but were part of the inheritance. The Prophet Muhammad raised women's position by giving them the right to inherit. So I think that if now a person is not happy with the 2:1 division of inheritance, then we should reinterpret it and give them equal shares.... I have never seen the Quran as something rigid, with which nothing can be done. It's not a dogma that must be accepted just as it is.

As Lilia also asserted, religion does not determine SP women's views on gender. While many staff practice Islam in an orthodox way—praying five times daily, observing taboos on alcohol and pork, fasting for Ramadan—they do not expect that all should do so. SP staff stressed their respect for different kinds of Islam, as well as for adherents of other religions and nonbelievers. They see religious belief as an individual choice in which the state should not interfere.

Though many SP staff fervently claim that equality between men and women is part of the true spirit of Islam and they are aware of global debates about women's rights in Islam, they usually argue for women's rights on a secular basis. While a few women said that Islamic teachings about equality and justice motivated them, it seemed that for many staff, such as Danita, religion and feminist activism are two different spheres of life:

> I am not inspired by my religion. In the beginning, I was influenced by the reality that I experienced in which I saw so much violence against women. I feel that Islam is not a religion that legitimates violence against women, and I am not a person who focuses special attention on translating the verses of the Quran. That's not my area. I only know that Islam is there for the kemaslahan [benefit]

of the *ummat* [Islamic community]. So if there are groups who harm society in the name of Islam, I think their conception of Islam is mistaken.

Despite their general separation of religion and feminist politics, SP recognizes the importance of Islam in the communities it serves. Danita said that one of the problems of the Indonesian women's movement in the past was a tendency to view Islam as an obstacle to women's rights. By the mid-2000s, it was becoming more common for SP to invite progressive Muslim scholars along for gender trainings. According to Alia, this is to counteract the perception that SP's feminist ideology challenges Islamic values and to provide a "feminist perspective as observed from Islam." But as we shall see, SP is sometimes hemmed in by conservative or extremist Islamic groups in communities where it works. Muslim scholars are brought in not only to show that gender equality is compatible with Islam but also to serve as a hedge against suspicions that SP's feminist politics are a covert way of promoting secularism, communism, Christianity, or other "foreign" ideologies.

For example, SP has brought the Muslim feminist scholar Siti Musdah Mulia to speak at trainings and workshops, and other prominent Muslim women's rights activists have given talks at SP conferences. SP also distributes books and pamphlets arguing for interpretations of Islam that emphasize women's rights.

SP staff are concerned about the ways Islam is interpreted and practiced yet convinced that at Islam's core is a message of equality between men and women. For some women at SP, feminism drives an interest in reinterpreting Islam to find gender equality within one's own religious tradition. For others, Islam shapes the boundaries of feminism. And some do not see feminism as having any particular relationship to religion.

SP activists have developed a distinctive feminist agency that incorporates Islam. This is a change from recent generations of Indonesian feminists, who not only tended to frame their activism as secular but also presented themselves in a more secular manner in the public sphere. In contrast, some SP women wear headscarves and talk about gender equality. Yet, as we shall see in the next section, their activism is at times constrained by the hegemony of piety and the growing power of more conservative discourses of Islam.

ENGAGING IN THE PUBLIC SPHERE: MIGRATION, ENVIRONMENTAL JUSTICE, AND FUNDAMENTALISM

How does SP's feminist agency shape its activism in an era of Islamic revival? A closer examination of SP's work on three major issues—migration, environmental justice, and fundamentalism—demonstrates how SP activists mobilize feminism's emphasis on lived experience and human rights and then combines these with appeals to local culture. SP's shifts in focus over time also illuminate the changing nature of power relations in Indonesia. The organization has moved from opposition to the state to negotiation with the state, from exploitative migration being its primary concern to a growing emphasis on environmental justice, and from prioritizing economic marginalization to concern about religious fundamentalism.

Migration and Trafficking

Stemming from its understanding of feminism as growing out of experience, SP emphasizes practice in its promotion of human rights. This reflects SP's somewhat ambiguous status as an NGO with a strong activist identity.[13] SP's interventions are driven by core concerns for equality, but they are pursued in a pragmatic manner. This is particularly visible in the centerpiece of SP's work—programs on migration and trafficking.

One of the most interesting days I spent with SP involved a lengthy meeting between an SP staffer, a representative from one of the companies that sends women to work overseas as domestics, and the government agency that is supposed to regulate them. Yulia, from SP's legal aid division, was trying to help the families of two women from rural West Java. The women were supposed to be sent to Singapore and Malaysia to work as maids, but because of the SARS breakout they had remained at the migrant worker company's dormitory in a Jakarta suburb for three months. They were not free to leave the building, and the company was demanding that the families each pay two million *rupiah* (about $225 dollars) for the women to be released.

We went to the Department of Manpower and met with a government official and two representatives of the company (the husbands came with us but did not attend the meeting). The official was an unctuous man whom I had encountered at a previous SP meeting. He wore an expensive watch and invited me to drive to Yogyakarta with him the following week.

Yulia told the official that the families could only pay 600,000 *rupiah* each (about $70). Even that was a stretch, as one husband earned only 300,000 a month as a motorbike taxi driver. The official and the company representatives asked Yulia and me to leave while they talked, ostensibly, to the company president. When we returned, the official told us the company president would meet with SP and the families the next day.

Yulia wanted to resolve the case right away. She insisted that SP would only accept a three-way negotiation between SP, the government, and the company. The government official said he wasn't sure how that could happen. Yulia insisted that he call the company boss to invite him to come meet with them right now. The official stalled, saying that his cell phone was out of minutes and that the office phones could not call outside the building. Annoyed, she dialed the number on her own cell phone and handed the phone to the official. The company boss agreed to 600,000 *rupiah* for each of the women. Yulia handed over the money to the company reps and they wrote out elaborate receipts.

SP had won, but the day was not over. Yulia and I took a taxi with the husbands to the company offices and dormitory, which were an hour's drive away in a tangle of tiny streets. The building had a security post outside and we were not allowed further than the lobby. Finally, the women emerged, and they were so relieved to be released that they spent several minutes kissing our hands. Within a few minutes, the women and their husbands jumped on motorcycle taxis and disappeared into the evening. In the taxi on the way back to SP, Yulia told me that she was sure there was collusion between the government and the manpower companies, and that one of her colleagues had seen company representatives hand over money to government officials.

Without a mention of feminism, equality, or human rights, Yulia worked to free these women. SP not only put up the families in its guesthouse in Jakarta but also paid for the women's release. Yulia loathed the government official, but she also felt that he was SP's only leverage to resolve the case. He was at least somewhat sympathetic to SP's concerns, and she knew the case would flounder in Indonesia's corrupt courts.

Although it was a remarkable day for me, it wasn't unusual for Yulia. Episodes like this reveal the importance of social service work for SP and reflect the organization's stress on practice. Moreover, it reflects a critical shift in SP's work over the last fifteen years. From opposition to the state and having to hide much of its activism, SP now negotiates with state agencies directly, sometimes achieving the tangible results it seeks.

Scholars and activists have long debated about feminists becoming involved in state bureaucracies. Some argue that this necessarily involves co-optation and forestalls more radical changes. In this case, SP is not joining the bureaucracy but negotiating with it. Staggenborg (1988) points out that professionalization can help to maintain a social movement because it enables interplay between feminist bureaucrats and activists. Similarly, SP staff balance social service work with consciousness raising and grassroots mobilization.

SP and other organizations spent many years pushing the Indonesian government to ratify the International Migrant Workers Convention, which was adopted by the United Nations in 1990. They finally succeeded in 2012. The state is now expected to monitor the implementation of various protections for migrant workers outlined in the convention. SP's work on migration and trafficking has also had results for the women and families who have been directly assisted. They have helped women who have been abused or victims of violence overseas obtain medical care and transition back to their communities. And they have helped to raise awareness about the forms of exploitation women encounter overseas, as well as about employment scams.

As an example of such activism, on a typical day at the SP office, I reported in my field notes:

> X went on to say that some people from SP had just come back from Batam Island where they rescued a 16-year-old girl who had been trafficked to Singapore and Malaysia. I asked her how SP found out about it, and she said the girl went to the police, and the police told some NGO people in Batam who knew someone who knew SP, etc. So, SP went there to fetch her and return her to her family. She is from Karawang, West Java. On Sunday, they're planning to go to her family's house to meet with them and explain to them what legal recourse they have.

SP has become well known as one of Indonesia's main defenders of the rights of women migrant workers. The goal of assisting women migrants is shaped by a feminist critique of the global economy. SP activists argue that women's migration is driven by global economic changes, and their interventions take place both in the global arena (as part of transnational networks of women's groups) and the national arena. SP women are motivated by concerns for equality and social justice but pursue these issues pragmatically, through negotiations with state agencies.

Environmental Justice

While migration has always been a focus for SP, in the last decade the organization has expanded its work on the environment, food issues, and natural resources. This environmental justice activism illuminates how SP's feminist agency intermingles the universalizing discourses of human rights and feminism with local traditions.

Human rights has been criticized most prominently by Asian leaders such as Suharto. In the early 1990s, Suharto, along with Singapore's Lee

Kuan Yew, promoted "Asian values" as an alternative. Asian values were said to include social harmony, concern for socioeconomic well-being, and respect for authority. Western notions of human rights have also been criticized from scholars and activists on the Left for an emphasis on individual rights at the expense of collective rights or socioeconomic equality.

But as Aspinall (2005) argues, human rights became one of the most important claims in the Indonesian democracy movement by the mid-1990s: "The twinned themes of *hak asasi manusia* [human rights] and *demokratisasi* became the public themes par excellence of the *keterbukaan* [openness] period" (p. 43). As a reaction to the Suharto government's authoritarian rule, the concept of *hak asasi manusia*, referred to by the acronym HAM, helped to unite students, women's groups, NGOs, and Muslim activists.

SP activists frame women's rights, migrant issues, and environmental justice within the rubric of human rights. This can be seen as an effort toward legitimacy, as well as a way of adapting and broadening the concept of human rights. For example, I attended a press conference that SP held to publicize the deaths of two women who had been working as maids in Hong Kong and Saudi Arabia. The mistreatment of such workers was repeatedly described not as violence against women, but as a human rights violation.

One afternoon, I sat in on a strategy discussion with SP and an environmental NGO with whom SP frequently cooperates. It was about a case of environmental pollution, linked to mining in Sulawesi, that SP was bringing to the attention of the National Commission on Human Rights. When I asked Ninik why SP was involved, she explained that it was part of SP's agenda to include economic, cultural, and social rights as part of human rights rather than accepting the conventional emphasis on individual rights, which she saw as too narrow.

Two representatives of the affected community were at the meeting with a book of photographs that showed skin diseases that were rampant in local households, as well as horribly distorted fish. They had never been to Jakarta and were clearly overwhelmed. Ninik began talking about how to connect their community's problems to the global discourse of human rights. "The *hak asasi manusia* model is from the West, and it means that people must talk about their individual cases as important," she coached them. "Our pattern is to talk about other people or the community in general. We must talk about our individual experiences to make an impact. 'I have experienced this, I saw this, my child,' always 'me,'" she said.

Ironically, Ninik's remarks echo Eliasoph's (1998) account of American activists being careful only to speak about self-interest rather than collective issues while in public. Eliasoph sees this phenomenon as a reflection of the normative constraints on discourse in the American public sphere but argues that in cooperating with such limitations activists help to reproduce them. Similarly, for strategic reasons, Ninik was urging the victims and SP to use a more personal and individual, Western style of discourse rather than the general terms they often use. Yet the stakes may well be different in this context. Drawing on Western liberal ideals, human rights does indeed privilege the individual subject. But human rights is a new discourse in Indonesia, and one that arose out of contestation. Ninik and SP are melding the global human rights discourse with feminism and social justice. She wanted the victims to use the language of individual rights so that they would be credible to the Human Rights Commission and, in doing so, call attention to the community's right to be free of environmental exploitation.

Another way of adapting universalizing discourses emerged at SP's encampment and conference on food sovereignty in 2003. Held on Jakarta's outskirts, the conference focused on environmental and food security and was inspired by movements opposing neoliberal economic policies. Indian activist Vandana Shiva's book on water privatization had recently been published in Indonesia and was widely discussed among activists at the conference.

SP staff discussed the transnational dimensions of the issue, talking about the battles over water privatization in Bolivia and emphasizing the global links between movements. But they also framed it as one of local communities battling global economic forces. In particular, the organizers of the event strategically called on local culture and knowledge to mobilize women.

A feminist Catholic nun from Yogyakarta served as conference moderator. Something of an earth mother, she successfully bridged the gap between urban and rural women at the gathering. Speaking to the group of about one hundred women, all sitting cross-legged in a large circle on the floor of an open pavilion, Ratna declared, "Usually it is men who talk, but today we begin from women's own stories." She continued, "Experience is reality; it cannot be wrong. We have come to witness what is happening in various places." She wrapped up the end of the first session saying, "So, our problems are the same all over. Are women's lives getting easier or harder? Who is it that needs clean water every month? Women...need clean water and vegetables to produce clean breast milk for our children." And finally, she concluded by referring to *ilmu perempuan*, women's knowledge or women's science, a phrase she repeated throughout the conference. "We have *ilmu perempuan* and *filsafat perempuan* [women's philosophy]; we have to take care of nature....Feminism understands women. We are not like politicians, we discuss, and then we act. We have the right to take care of our own clean water and food resources. Our experiences as women must be turned into *pijat* [pressure] for action."

SP's respect for cultural and religious pluralism is expressed in this attention to local cultural practices. They draw on such traditions, as well as Indonesian historical and mythological figures, to talk about women's rights. For example, at the conference a group from West Java performed a traditional dance about women planting and harvesting rice. SP activists frequently wear Indonesia's batik cloth for public events, and they were doing so before it was a fashion trend. Danita explained why:

> Because those who work a lot, in almost every region, who produce weavings, cloth, who create batik, are women. Now the style of dressing has a modern tendency; we wear jeans, t-shirts. It's definitely nice, practical, but if we all tend toward modern clothing, then these women can't continue their specialties. Then, traditions, the skill of making batik, weaving, embroidering, it will all be lost....In the community it is only owned by women. It is usually not handed down to male children, because male children aren't painstaking enough; these [fingers] are very small, so one of the ways we try to further or ensure that the strengths of women are not lost is by using them.

Thus, SP grounds women's knowledge in local cultural traditions. Notwithstanding the essentializing aspects of Danita's comment, SP activists do not necessarily romanticize local culture. For example, SP staff members were often critical of the traditions of their regions of origin, describing them as patriarchal and hierarchical.

As was evident at the food security conference, SP staff draw strategically on ideas such as *adat perempuan* (women's *adat*).[14] What they mean by *adat perempuan* is women's local culture and practices. Batik making is an example of women's *adat*, as are the dances or music often performed at SP's conferences. *Adat perempuan* is distinct from the more typical meaning of *adat*, which usually involves men in decision-making roles. The concept of *adat perempuan* helps SP relate critically to rural culture, validating practices that are seen to be beneficial for women without having to embrace patriarchal or intolerant practices.

Women responded enthusiastically to the invocation of *adat perempuan*. During a group discussion at the conference, a woman farmer from Tangerang, a fast-growing exurb of Jakarta, talked about the reasons pesticides have become popular and the pollution they are causing. But she claimed that she and other women she knows are returning to organic farming and growing their own medicinal plants. Moreover, she continued, "mixed farmers' groups are dominated by men, and so women's groups are necessary." When another woman suggested that separation of men and women might be a bad thing, several others argued that women need their own organizations because they have less access to government and aid than do men. Others spoke passionately about the need for women's knowledge to produce nutritious local foods that are being neglected in favor of cheap imports and industrial products like instant noodles. As one woman asserted, "We have our own products that we can grow; we don't need to eat products from the free market like apples from Washington."

SP activists' inclusive feminist agency can be seen in their mobilization of *adat perempuan* and strategic adaptation of human rights and feminism. They emphasize equality and rights but place them within the context of local histories and cultures. Similarly, SP's insistence that environmental, social, and cultural rights are part of human rights is a significant reworking of the human rights discourse, one that challenges conventional international understandings of human rights, as well as the discourse of Asian values.

When it comes to environmental issues, SP has had some success. At the conference, there were women farmers who were already growing food organically, and participants were very much aware of pollution of air and water in their communities. Environmental issues in Indonesia are difficult to pursue because of corruption in the court system and ties between local governments, the military, and extractive industries. But at the very least, SP has raised consciousness among women in the activist milieu and in the communities where it works about pollution, pesticides, land rights, food sovereignty, and resource privatization.

Campaigning for environmental justice, SP activists develop their feminist agency as they meld global discourses with local traditions and ideas of social justice. Moreover, the struggle for environmental justice is motivated by a feminist critique of global capitalism, which SP activists view as responsible for destruction of natural resources and the impoverishment of women.

Fundamentalism and Feminist Agency

In the last decade, SP activists have been working for women's rights against the backdrop of increasingly vocal Muslim conservatives and extremists. Like most women's groups in Indonesia, SP is anxious about what activists view as a rise in religious fundamentalism.[15] Certainly, extremists have been involved in acts of terrorism and sectarian violence. However, these latter events peaked in the early 2000s with the Bali bombing in 2002, the Jakarta Marriott bombing in 2003, and the bombing of the Australian embassy in 2005. Since then, members of terrorist groups have been arrested. Moreover, the Indonesian parliament rejected bills aiming to institute Islamic law on a national basis, and parties with Islamic law in their platforms were not popular with voters in the 2004 or 2009 elections.

On the other hand, progressive activists are concerned that religious intolerance that seeks to subordinate women and minorities is spreading. There has been an upsurge in violent attacks on the Ahmadiya sect as well as Indonesia's Shiite minority, with little response from the state. Moreover, as I discuss in chapter 2, between 2000 and 2006, numerous provinces and towns instituted local regulations that were inspired by Islamic law. Such regulations, known as *Peraturan Daerah* (PERDA—regional regulations), commonly require Muslim women to wear the *jilbab* or prevent women from going out at night without a suitable male escort. According to a report by the national women's organization Komnas Perempuan (2010), the text of nearly half of the bylaws stipulates the importance of the regulation for maintaining the region's Islamic identity. The report identifies 154 local bylaws, of which 63 are said to discriminate against women. Many bylaws were pitched by politicians as measures to curb the sex trade, but they draw heavily on certain interpretations of Islamic law. In some areas, bylaws also require children to attend Quranic study lessons or couples to answer questions about the Quran before they can marry. Aceh's special autonomy has allowed it to institute more laws that are inspired by Islam. Muslim women are required to wear the *jilbab* and modest clothing, and Aceh is the only province to have instituted *Shariah*-prescribed criminal punishments such as caning.

While the trend toward passing such bylaws is in decline (Bush 2008), they remain on the books and are not trivial. Even if symbolic and unevenly enforced, they target women, positioning them as the upholders of collective Islamic identity. As Lilia from SP argues:

> Power in the New Order was dominated by the military and business. Decentralization has opened spaces for the politics of ethnicity and religion. This is a threat to the women's movement and to women's lives. Women are used in these mobilizations to close access off to women. Laws on the *jilbab*, restricting mobility—it's control in the name of religion over women's thoughts, body, mobility, access to economic and natural resources. This is a threat to women's empowerment.

The emergence of Islam-inspired PERDA reveals how much more significant public Muslim identity has become for many regions in Indonesia. Opponents argue that PERDA contradicts Indonesia's constitution, which guarantees equal rights to all citizens.

While there is an effort to challenge PERDA in the constitutional court, SP has taken a more grassroots approach. An example of this is the 2006–2009 action research project called Women's Empowerment in Muslim Contexts (WEMC), which included sites in several different countries and was directed by scholars at the City University of Hong Kong. The Indonesian arm of this study was coordinated by SP along with other women's rights organizations. Funded by Britain's Department of Foreign and International Development, SP activists traveled to West Java and South Sulawesi to gain a better understanding of the conditions governing women's lives and to bring about some measures of empowerment. SP's role included initiating *kampung* discussions and trainings with local women and appealing to local governments to argue that PERDA regulations are discriminatory.

Entering villages was not an easy task for SP activists. The SP members chosen to work in these communities were usually not from the central headquarters in Jakarta, but from its local offices in various regions. Siti, who coordinated SP's research project in a village in South Sulawesi, explained:

> First we need to develop people's faith in us, and one of the issues that SP activists face when they enter into a new region, sometimes they think that we are outsiders. And one of the tricks, based on the experiences of my friends, first is that they take a preventive approach, meaning they live there; they stay there. And what is most important, the SP activists must know who their friends and enemies are, because if they are misjudged, they will be chased away. That's a very big risk.... So we have an approach there. We also look for friends at the grassroots [level] who can link up with us.

As with gender trainings, SP activists appeal to women's sense of fairness and equity, rather than starting off with talk about unfamiliar concepts of human rights or women's rights. As time goes on, Siti said:

> Women at the grassroots [level], up till now, consider SP activists as their friends. I mean that they also talk about their problems. And finally they introduce women's rights; the women begin to want to know more. But sometimes, it's not that they don't like them, but sometimes they feel strange because it's like we bring new things there. But we actually don't bring new things. We only

want to help women to know, minimally, what it is they want. So they have empathy, they influence them, and finally they are aware. There are actually some who become members, and then they participate in the various actions.

Aside from the WEMC project, another significant development for SP was the emergence of SP Aceh, now one of its most active branches. Coming together in the immediate post-tsunami period, when aid agencies rushed to the province, SP Aceh focused on women affected by the terrible natural events. Now that significant reconstruction has occurred, SP Aceh continues to develop programs to empower poor women in the context of Islamization. The SP activists I met from Aceh were impassioned about the impact of the province's adoption of *Shariah* law on women and gender equality. For some of the SP activists, these issues were personal ones that had touched their own lives.

For example, I met Nur, a staff member from SP Aceh, at a national conference in 2008. She told me that she grew up in a middle-class family in the city of Banda Aceh and attended the state university. She is one of few Acehnese Muslim women who defy the regulation requiring women to wear headscarves. Nur told me she had never worn one and that it was just not the way she understood her religion. She took a risk any time she stepped outside her house, and indeed, by the time I met her, she had been arrested three times by the religious police. The most recent time, she told me between laughs, she tried to tell her captors that she was too fat to fit into the Muslim outfits sold at local shops. She admitted that she is lucky to have a liberal and supportive husband who is ready to retrieve her whenever she is stopped. Nur and the other Acehnese SP members saw their province as a warning for the rest of Indonesia should Islamic law become more widespread.

The fears of SP staff that local communities will accuse them of spreading ideas that are opposed to Islam reveals that a key aspect of SP's legitimacy is the ability of individual members to project a Muslim identity. For a group that is not organized on the basis of religion, the task of projecting Muslim identity without framing the group's work in religious terms is a delicate one. Lilia outlined the obstacles:

> SP activists in the *kampung* are seen as secular, Western feminists. This is a big challenge. It can be used as a tool by fundamentalists to label SP *kafirs*.[16] My colleagues who are doing research get threats from fundamentalists because they are seen as bringing in new Western influences. After a while in one place, after a year or so, it's OK. They see that we pray and fast. This is just about giving information, empowering people. They become used to us after a while.

Tactics such as bringing a Muslim scholar to demonstrate that women's rights and Islam are compatible, as well as distributing books and pamphlets that make the case for women's rights within Islam, lend SP Muslim credibility. SP staff view such tactics as simply another way of presenting their arguments, but also as an expression of their belief that Islam is compatible with gender equality. As Alia explained, "It's sometimes hard for SP's feminist perspective to be accepted because it is thought to be opposed to Islamic values.... Islamic experts are needed to give a feminist perspective from Islam."

Even without a Muslim scholar in tow, the Muslim appearances and practices of many SP staff are helpful in this regard. SP staff acknowledge this, although they consider their self-presentations as pious Muslims to be their own personal expressions of identity and piety.

Nevertheless, the WEMC project and the SP communities in cities outside Jakarta have met with some resistance. Sarita, the professor and SP member in East Java, described how she and her colleagues dealt with the growing presence of the radical Islamist organization Hizbut Tahrir on campus. She said that she sought to avoid open confrontation, but rather to convince with words and evidence:

> Previously, they often sent text messages, invited us to discussions, and we just listened politely; it wasn't a big deal. In formal or informal forums, the issue of abortion, pornography, the things we talked about on our live show on TV, we do those as usual; it's not a problem. But I always say, I don't force you to believe our ideology, and we also will not be forced to accept your ideology. So we keep doing our separate functions and we don't need conflict.

In the current atmosphere, as the experiences of SP demonstrate, challenges to male dominance can sometimes be considered anti-Islamic. Ironically, SP women with their *jilbabs* are themselves deeply influenced by Islam. With their words and actions, they demonstrate that there is no inherent connection between Islamic piety and gender inequality.

It is important to note that SP's work on fundamentalism is a significant shift for the organization. For many years, SP activists' transnational focus kept them on the sidelines of national debates about veiling, *Shariah*, polygamy, and other matters pertaining to gender and religion. By 2005, however, when I asked Danita about her perception of the most important political challenges for Indonesia in the coming years, she listed four main *musuh* (enemies) for women activists to oppose: political and economic globalization, militarism, patriarchy, and fundamentalism.

The newer emphases on environmental justice and fundamentalism are indicative of shifting power configurations in Indonesia. In the 1990s, Indonesian women were subjugated by an authoritarian state. In the 2000s, many faced marginalization by global economic forces. By the mid-2000s, in the minds of women activists at SP, there was another major factor at work in bolstering inequality—the growing influence of religious intolerance in many parts of Indonesia. SP's decision to work on this issue at the local level suggests activists see the local as crucial to this struggle. In their view, it is not at the national level that extremists win their battles; instead, it is in the local arena where they enforce changes intended to make Indonesia a society governed by Islam.

The WEMC project has helped draw SP closer to Muslim women's organizations. SP's work on this issue feeds into a broader, if somewhat belated, effort among Indonesia's progressive activists to tackle religious extremism and promote a more pluralist and egalitarian society. Importantly, not only has SP been drawn into struggles over how Islam should be practiced but in recent years Muslim groups like Fatayat have also established programs to deal with trafficking and protection of female migrant workers. That is, political reform projects central to SP have also been adopted by religious women's groups, a testament to SP's influence in the broader activist milieu.

It is also significant that projecting Muslim identity has become an essential form of legitimacy for SP. Such an identity, especially if visibly displayed in the form of clothing such as headscarves, can help to validate activities that otherwise might not be palatable, especially to the men in a community. The piety of SP staff is genuine but it is also helpful for SP's relationships with people in the communities where the group is active. The strategic value of staff members' displays of Islamic piety reveals the growing power of Islamic religiosity in Indonesia. This is a significant change from the peak of the Suharto regime, when religious discourse, while growing in importance, came second to the rhetoric of nation building and support for the state.

SP's global and inclusive feminist agency shapes its interventions against fundamentalism. SP activists are educated, urban women like those in Rahima, Fatayat, and PKS, but their trajectory has led them to a more secular form of progressive activism. Women in SP adapt feminist and human rights discourses to make their arguments, but the organization's contextual approach to Islam also encourages staff to negotiate Islam and feminism in their own ways. This reveals that SP's feminist agency is flexible enough to incorporate religious piety. This new feminist subjectivity is less elite and more able to cross class boundaries than some previous forms of Indonesian feminism.

In the past, SP's secular framework meant that it was often sidelined from contentious debates over religion and gender. However, as SP begins to confront ways of practicing Islam that marginalize women, they are articulating a global feminism that accommodates religion and situates human rights in local terms. SP activists' work toward challenging fundamentalism demonstrates their recognition that Islamic piety constitutes a growing mode of power in Indonesia. However, their successes also indicate that increasing religious piety need not immobilize feminist activism; indeed, feminist and pious agency coexist within SP itself.

CONCLUSIONS: GLOBAL FEMINISM AND THE INDONESIAN PUBLIC SPHERE

Despite the fact that SP is one of the most outspoken feminist organizations, it has become a legitimate participant in the Indonesian public sphere and a key actor in the field of gender politics. It is involved in the usual workshops, seminars, and public events held by various NGOs and collaborates with many different organizations. Its activities are covered in the mass media and SP staff can meet with government officials and members of parliament who are compelled to take them and their concerns seriously. This is a crucial difference from the early 1990s, when activists openly critical of the government, including those at SP, faced state repression. SP has not felt the violence sometimes encountered by gay rights activists or advocates for the families of people who disappeared during the New Order regime. Such groups have had their offices attacked and staff physically harmed by members of militia organizations with ties to the military and extremist groups. As Danita acknowledged:

> Society can accept us openly, maybe also because our name is friendly: Solidaritas Perempuan [Women's Solidarity]. People like to hear it; they're not scared of it. Later, after we've been active for a long time, the husbands of the women who participate in our activities, they protest because their wives are constantly going to SP, constantly at discussions. But their wives say, "Indeed, going to SP makes me smarter." We have never had difficulties or been approached by people who want to harm our offices. We have not experienced things like that. Previously, maybe it was like that during the Suharto era, but after *reformasi*, no longer.

SP is attempting to transform Indonesia's public sphere through its promotion of a liberal, democratic, and egalitarian society. While they have not had major policy successes, they are helping to keep space open for secular social movements in Indonesia. There are many ways by which a feminist organization could come to be considered marginal, or even illegitimate, but SP works to maintain credibility and to speak to both middle-class activists and lower-class women. SP has certainly helped to bring the exploitation faced by poor women into the mainstream, calling attention to the rough underbelly of globalization.

As this chapter shows, SP activists mobilize and adapt global discourses, particularly that of human rights. Since the United Nations Beijing Women's Conference in 1995, activists around the world have increasingly framed women's rights as human rights. SP activists use human rights to position women as full human subjects who deserve all the rights and protections of other humans, rather than emphasizing their distinctiveness from men. Yet SP's use of human rights puts emphasis on the local as a source of resistance to global economic forces such as neoliberalism.

The women of SP have developed an inclusive feminist agency as they creatively engage with global feminism and Islam. Their activist trajectories, which brought them through state universities during the *reformasi* movement, introduced them to networks of Muslim and secular activists working to bring about a democratic transition and a more egalitarian society. These social networks led women to SP, where they learned about feminism, human rights, and equality. There is no single way of combining Islam and feminism for the women of SP. Diversity thrives because the organization sees piety as a matter of freedom and choice and respects it as a framework for a person's daily life.

It is also notable that despite the common perception that feminists are members of the elite, SP activists have been relatively successful in appealing to lower-class women. This is certainly a function of the organization's emphasis on economic equality and the rights of poor women. But it may also be because SP activists' personal lives are less elite than those of much of the older generation of feminists of the 1980s. They are not bound to powerful government officials, nor are they well-known intellectuals or artists who move in posh circles. Perhaps women in rural Indonesia may also identify with transnational discourses like human rights precisely because of their cosmopolitan qualities, which echo some Islamic discourses in their emphasis on common humanity. And unlike the women of Rahima and PKS, SP women's practice of Islam is not so conditioned by involvement in major Muslim organizations. They are identifiable as Muslim in most cases, but not tied to a particular way of practicing the religion.

Through this activism, we can see a moral vision emerging of a liberal democracy with economic and social equality. According to SP women, the state should not be involved in religious affairs, yet they certainly see a role for religion in the public sphere. However, they espouse a more private and personal conception of religious piety than that expressed by the women of Fatayat and Rahima who more overtly link their religiosity to their political activism.

With the New Order gone, the state is no longer the only focus of SP's work. SP recognizes that after natural resources, people, especially women, are now one of Indonesia primary exports. The days of large-scale state-led development and infrastructure initiatives are over, and so the state may no longer wield overwhelming power over women's lives.

Yet not long after it became clear to SP that the fate of many poor women in Indonesia is closely tied to global economic forces, new forms of gender inequality and discrimination emerged. The growing power of intolerant interpretations of Islam unsettles many SP staff. By 2008, some SP women, like other women activists I met during my visit, no longer wore the *jilbab* daily, and they voiced frustration about how the *jilbab* has been imposed on women through peer pressure. For these women, piety is an individual responsibility that has little to do with the state. This is not an uncommon view in Indonesia, but it is at odds with those who see morality, including religious behavior, as a collective responsibility.

SP's feminist agency is shaped within the possibilities and constraints of contemporary Islamic piety. This demonstrates how actors in the field of gender politics have been influenced by the rise of Islamic politics. The lengths to which SP women sometimes go to show that Islam and feminism are commensurable in their own lives demonstrates the power of religiosity in contemporary Indonesia. In this sense, the hegemony of piety in the public sphere unquestionably influences SP's activist practices. If SP does not project a sufficiently Muslim identity in the communities where it works, it risks being marginalized. The fact that SP must sometimes use religion to argue for women's rights suggests that it is becoming necessary to invoke Islam when speaking about controversial issues.

Conforming to the norms of the new Indonesian public sphere, particularly the pressure to display Islamic piety, can be a challenge for SP. SP activists' feminist agency, with its emphasis on economic equality and global justice, makes the organization distinctive. Yet conforming to the emerging norms of the public sphere sometimes requires SP activists to downplay their feminist identities and emphasize their religious identities. SP activists' ability to present themselves as pious Muslims helps to legitimize the organization and makes it possible to work in a somewhat hostile climate.

This dynamic benefits the organization in the ways I have described, but it risks affirming the norms of the public sphere, which remains dominated by men and formal discourse, and increasingly excludes those who do not present themselves as Muslims. It is therefore worth remembering Eliasoph's (1998) critique of how shared cultural norms can constrain the possibilities for debate and thereby work against social change. This begs the question: by sometimes downplaying feminism and emphasizing Islam, do SP activists surrender claims for more radical social change?

At a time when Islam and feminism are widely viewed as contradictory, SP's feminist agency transforms the public sphere by insisting on inclusion. They demonstrate that it is possible to be a pious Muslim and a feminist. And perhaps more radical in this context, they quietly suggest that religious devotion does not have to be a matter of public regulation. It remains to be seen whether Islam will eventually eclipse the authority of other discourses in Indonesian politics, or if SP's approach to incorporating Islamic piety within global feminism can retain its legitimacy. For now, Solidaritas Perempuan's inclusive feminist agency and continuing struggle against economic and gender inequality represent an important mode of mobilizing women in the Indonesian context.

CHAPTER 6

Conclusion

In the decade after 9/11, the headscarf became a renewed focus of global debate, and nowhere more so than in Europe. In these contentions over Muslim dress, concerns about immigration and assimilation were expressed through the language of women's rights (Bowen 2006; Scott 2007). When France in 2004 banned women from wearing the veil in public places, defenders of the law argued that the state had to protect the rights and dignity of women. In 2011, several more countries, including the Netherlands and Belgium, were moving toward banning face-veils, which they argue are not in keeping with national culture and pose a potential security threat. Although few women actually wear face-veils in these countries, women have become the justification for Islamophobia. In the United States, the headscarf has not become such a central issue, but allegations by some political figures that Muslims intend to establish *Shariah* law have similar resonances. It has become acceptable to exclude or marginalize Muslims because of their allegedly misogynistic and illiberal gender practices (Joppke 2009).

This discourse is the latest in a long history of attempts to cast Islam and feminism as opposites, with Islam standing in for all that is backward and traditional and feminism symbolizing the modern and liberal West. It is an argument that has a corollary in Muslim societies, with many Muslims arguing that feminism is un-Islamic because it is secular and liberal. This holds true in Indonesia, where a grassroots Islamic revival and democratization have resulted in a surge of women identifying themselves as pious Muslims. As one observer wrote about a recent conference of Indonesian women university students:

For these women, Islamic morality is a pressing matter of public and political concern, and is central to all considerations of Indonesian social order. Moral reform is, for them, a struggle in which female sexual behavior forms an important and highly visible front. In this thinking, sexual morality is framed as a step toward the creation of a prosperous, happy, civilized society. They do not regard the sexual behaviour of young Muslims as a matter of personal choice or preference. (Nef 2011)

For some Indonesian women of this generation, feminism is a Western, secular, and morally suspect ideology that does not fit with this effort to live a pious lifestyle in accordance with Islamic law.

In a politicized global context where Islam and feminism are viewed as opposites, the Indonesian Muslim women activists who are the subject of this book negotiate such tensions carefully and thoughtfully (Figure 6.1). The women in Solidaritas Perempuan, Rahima, Fatayat, and the Prosperous Justice Party (PKS) represent different modes of engagement with these global discourses. SP is the most publicly committed to feminism of all these groups, while Rahima and Fatayat innovatively combine ideas from

Figure 6.1: A typical view from a neighborhood in South Jakarta.

both Islam and feminism. The women of PKS reject feminism while pushing for greater women's involvement in their party. These differences are all the more striking given that these women activists are nearly all middle-class and college-educated urbanites. How they adapt and synthesize these frameworks in their activism tells us much about women's agency in an age when religion and politics are increasingly intertwined.

Indonesian women activists' engagements with Islam and feminism are shaped by their personal trajectories and experiences, which lead them into organizations that approach these discourses in very different ways. The organizations in this study have developed distinctive kinds of agency that are informed by transnational and national influences, including Islam and feminism. These forms of agency emerge from a dynamic Indonesian public sphere that is characterized by increasing interaction and overlap between the fields of gender politics and Islamic politics. Gender politics includes not only those advocating feminist politics but also those who seek a return to more "traditional" gender arrangements. Islamic politics comprises different Islamic milieus that have diverse interpretive approaches and practices.

Since the end of the Suharto dictatorship in 1998, these fields have increasingly intersected in Indonesia. This is partly because of personal connections between activists, some of which were forged during the democratization movement. But this intersection also arises because Islam and feminism are ethical frameworks that are often mobilized in ways that affect each other. For example, actors within Islamic politics may seek political changes that affect women's lives, while feminists may seek reforms that some actors in Islamic politics consider problematic. The organizations in this study are located in these overlapping fields in different ways and they interact with and influence each other through their activism. From my fieldwork, I came to see how the different forms of agency exhibited by these activists emerge from their locations and experiences within these fields.

The women in Solidaritas Perempuan (SP) came from striving middle- and lower middle-class families. Growing up in the Suharto era of expansion, they had the opportunity to attend state universities. Many of these women were involved in student activism and social justice campaigns during and after the *reformasi* era, and their involvement made them passionate about equality, rights, and democracy. This network led them to jobs with SP, a central actor in the field of gender politics. Through their work, the activists of SP have developed a *feminist agency* that is internationalist, incorporates religious piety, and focuses on challenging the subordination of women in all spheres of life. Many SP women are pious Muslims, and they tend to see Islam and feminism as compatible, but they have chosen a more secular form of activism. Although Indonesia has a history of secular women's activism, in the current political context SP must tread carefully to avoid accusations of being anti-Islamic. The organization transforms and localizes global discourses of human rights and feminism by interweaving them with discourses on local culture. The concern for economic justice and critique of global neoliberalism is also central to SP's work and helps to bridge differences between women.

The rise of Islamic politics and the increasing intersections between the fields of Islamic and gender politics also provide new challenges for SP. Conforming to the norms of a more Islamic public sphere sometimes requires SP members to play up their pious Muslim identities and de-emphasize feminism while in the field. This dynamic risks affirming the status quo of a more religiously oriented public sphere. Nevertheless, SP's feminist agency, which aims at both social and economic inequality, represents an important and distinctive mode of mobilizing women. Moreover, opposition to Islamic extremism and religious intolerance has brought SP closer to Muslim women's rights activists like Fatayat and Rahima. This demonstrates that the rise of pious agency has not destabilized feminist agency. Quite to the contrary, SP women show how pious agency and feminist agency coexist and interact. Women in SP are constructing feminist subjectivities that are often informed by Islam, and this itself is significant in light of the frequent positioning of Islam and feminism as contradictory. In this sense, they are transforming the public sphere by making it more inclusive of women; by proposing that it is possible to be a pious Muslim and an outspoken feminist; and, perhaps more radical in this context, by quietly suggesting that religious devotion does not have to be a matter of public interest.

Activists of Rahima and Fatayat also came from striving lower middle-class families. However, in most cases, their families were part of the Nahdlatul Ulama milieu, and they attended Islamic schools, and many continued on to Islamic state universities. While at university, many of these women also became involved in student activism, especially through national Muslim student organizations. From their schooling, they were educated in a relatively flexible and contextual approach to Islamic texts, and through their activism, they were influenced by global discourses of equality and rights. Once they joined Rahima and Fatayat, they were further trained in a contextual and feminist approach to Islamic texts, which allows for flexibility in interpretation. They have developed a pious critical agency that engages critically with these religious texts. They seek to live up to Islamic norms, but in a way that can integrate new ideas. Thus, they draw on discourses of transnational feminism and Islamic reformism, and they refer to Indonesia's own Islamic heritage to make their arguments for women's rights and religious reform. As Islam becomes entrenched in the Indonesian public sphere, framing arguments for social change within Islam lends credibility to these activists and helps them in their efforts to mobilize women.

Fatayat and Rahima occupy an unusual location in the overlap between the fields of Islamic and gender politics. They draw on the cultural resources and norms of both fields. The activists of Rahima and Fatayat embody a *pious critical agency* that allows them to combine influences from Islam and feminism. This is a new form of agency for Muslim women, who have not been centrally involved in religious interpretation, and who are also new as actors in Islamic politics. The vitality of these groups demonstrates that religious texts and practices are subject to extensive debate and interpretation, and that Muslim women's political subjectivities are diverse. They mobilize the heterogenous Islamic tradition in unexpected and transformative ways. The case of Rahima and Fatayat also demonstrates that pious agency is not incompatible with rights and equality, and that it can overlap with feminist agency. Moreover, they are forging a new kind of egalitarian Muslim womanhood.

Women in the Prosperous Justice Party followed a third kind of pious trajectory. Like SP women, they came from diverse, lower middle-class and middle-class backgrounds and mostly attended state universities. Their experiences in the *Tarbiyah* movement in the 1980s and 1990s led them into the field of Islamic politics, helped to school them in a more textual approach to Islam that emphasizes formal practice over theological debate, and led them into the party in the post-*reformasi* era. The party itself has become a central actor in the field of Islamic politics. PKS women tend to reject feminism as Western and secular and argue that women's primary responsibilities are to be found in the domestic sphere. The party is adept at mobilizing women, many of whom share its espousal of Islamic values as a way to solve Indonesia's problems.

Women in the party are not passive, as stereotypes suggest, nor are they mere tools of the party. Their understanding of Islam permits women to have careers and be involved in politics, although they must have permission from their husbands. This reflects the party's textualist approach to Islam, which rejects contextual interpretations but is also pragmatic. In addition, their viewpoints reflect how pressure from women's rights activists has influenced Islamic politics (see Salime 2011 for a similar argument about Morocco).

Moreover, the textualist approach to Islam facilitates *pious activating agency*, in which women cadres mobilize the party's religious interpretations to argue for social and economic change. Certainly PKS women interpret Islam in a broad sense, but interpretive debates and discussions are not a priority for them, in contrast to Fatayat and Rahima. Pious activating agency differs from feminist agency and pious critical agency in that it does not readily facilitate challenges to the subordination of women. However, it does make possible a more active role for women in Islamic politics, and this greater involvement of women does constitute a change in the field of Islamic politics.

The party's emphasis on public piety and its goal of Islamizing Indonesia require the active participation of both men and women, and PKS women are enthusiastic about this project. PKS women can thus fulfill their ambitions to be politically active pious Muslims, as well as good wives and mothers. Women in the party are rarely in leadership or powerful positions. Nevertheless, their numbers may be compelling the party to take greater account of them.

Through their involvement in the party, PKS women construct modern middle-class selves based on public piety and a textual approach to Islam. Empowered and inspired by their participation, PKS women have helped to set a new standard for more conservative women as political actors. Nevertheless, space for women in PKS is narrower than for women in other Muslim organizations such as Nahdlatul Ulama, and the textualist approach leaves women with few tools if they disagree with the party leadership. Perhaps this is what accounts for the greater ideological uniformity of women in PKS.

THE IMPACT OF MUSLIM WOMEN'S ACTIVISM

How is this new generation of women activists changing Indonesia? And does their activism have an impact beyond Indonesia? First and foremost, they are democratizing the Indonesian public sphere to include a wider variety of women's voices in political and social debates. Although women have never been excluded from the public sphere, visibly pious women were certainly marginalized until quite recently. During the Suharto era, women whose voices were heard in national debates were usually from political or business elites. Women in Solidaritas Perempuan, for example, are addressing the gendered consequences of global inequality in ways that were not possible under Suharto. Similarly, the veiled women of Fatayat, Rahima, and PKS are not necessarily the masses, but they do represent something new in Indonesia and elsewhere—the rise of pious women as political subjects.

By providing women with conceptual tools to make credible arguments for reform, the changes brought by the Islamic revival, especially greater access to religious education, have helped to produce new forms of agency and collective action. For Solidaritas Perempuan, Fatayat, and Rahima, a contextual interpretive approach facilitates feminist and pious critical agency, which serve as a basis for seeking a more egalitarian and pluralist nation. Among women in PKS, a strict textualist approach to interpretation underlies a pious activating agency. This form of agency is evident in PKS women's work toward a society with stronger moral regulation and their attempts to bolster women's participation in that effort.

Feminists often assume that all women are or should be interested in women's rights. This assumption sits uneasily with the widespread perception that Islam is incompatible with gender inequality. Many Muslim women do not seek gender equality. But the case of Indonesia demonstrates that the Islamic revival coexists with and even complements some women's aims for egalitarian social transformation, including challenges to gender hierarchies. The Islamic revival also seems to encourage a broader desire for social and political inclusion on the part of women. This may be a significant factor in the recent Arab Spring upheavals in Tunisia, Egypt, Yemen, and beyond, in which women protestors have played a noteworthy role.

Much has been written in recent years about Muslim feminism (Badran 2009; Moghadam 2009). The emerging transnational Muslim feminist network Musawah, with its insistence on equality in the Muslim family, is an intriguing development. Musawah, however, remains a rather elite movement that may be too closely tied to Western funders such as the Ford Foundation to achieve much credibility within Muslim societies. Yet Rahima and Fatayat illustrate the promise of Muslim feminism with their creative ability to adapt and synthesize Islamic and feminist schemas and thereby forge new cultural repertoires. They have helped to promote a broader trend in Indonesia of advocating for women's rights in Islam. This can be seen as a more culturally legitimate way of pressing for social reforms, but it may also be changing Islam itself. Their activism, like that of Musawah, is a signal to both global and national audiences who see feminism and Islam as irreconcilable that religion is not necessarily patriarchal.

Yet we must remember that agency is not the same as equality. Agency is an ability to act or to choose, shaped by and within social structures, and it often works to reproduce those structures (Sewell 1992). Since Indonesia's democratization, there is not much evidence that the majority of women's lives have changed greatly or that gender equality has increased. Middle- and upper-class women have benefited from economic growth and greater freedom to express their opinions and views. However, there has been little major legislation arising from women's activism, with the notable exceptions of the bill criminalizing domestic violence in 2004, and the antipornography bill (2008), which many women activists opposed. In 2009, about 50% of Indonesia's population still lived on less than two dollars a day, which is down from 77% in 1996, but indicates that a majority of women are not sharing in many of the comforts afforded to the more-middle-class women in this study.[1]

Solidaritas Perempuan and Fatayat aim to mobilize and improve the lives of poor women. Like the efforts of most women's rights activists, their work is small scale, often reaching one village or *kampung* at a time. As activists acknowledge, it is difficult for poor women to take advantage of a more open public sphere because of structural issues like a lack of access to education and health care, lack of free time due to household work, and lack of transportation.

Agency must also be understood within its own context. PKS women in many ways are not strikingly different from the women in the other groups in this study when it comes to their moderately conservative views on gender. It is their political vision for Indonesia that is a contrast. They may in fact be innovative compared to women in societies where women's public participation is very limited. But Indonesia, as I have stressed, has a history of women's participation, particularly in reformist Muslim efforts. PKS women are indeed working for greater inclusion within their party, but they are doing so within fairly narrow limits, and they do not appear to be pushing the party in a substantially different ideological direction. More women's involvement does not necessarily mean equality. The greater visibility of women in the Indonesian public sphere does not always translate into power or liberation.

Nevertheless, it is clear that PKS women represent an increasing trend among pious women to be involved in public projects of moral and political reform. This may eventually result in unexpected social changes. As social scientists who have studied the Temperance Movement, an early American social movement that sought prohibitions on alcohol, have shown, women in that movement were also acting within the accepted definitions of femininity, in the sense that they were calling for moral reform within a Protestant framework. However, their efforts spurred large numbers of middle-class women to act on their own outside the home, taking on an unprecedented public role (Murdock 2001). Many of these women who protested against alcohol also began to demand the vote. Women's involvement in moral reform projects ended up shifting the boundaries of femininity in unforeseen ways. The same may be true for women in PKS.

Finally, it is important to stress that women's agency can be used in multiple ways and that the definition of empowering or liberatory action is highly subjective. The experience in India with Hindu nationalism suggests that some women feel empowered by their newfound ability to marginalize other women (Jeffery and Basu 1997). In multicultural Indonesia, this is also a real danger. Recent years have seen violent attacks on heterodox Muslim sects such as Ahmadiyah, increased harassment of Christian communities, and continuing assaults by self-styled Muslim thugs on businesses or activists they deem a threat to Islam. The growing hegemony of Islam in the Indonesian public sphere threatens to marginalize secular and non-Muslim citizens, but Muslim women activists have done little to openly confront this issue. So, the question must be asked, does advocating for women's rights solely within a Muslim framework ultimately solidify the boundaries between religious groups? And does it in fact limit who can participate in the public sphere by narrowing the voices and ideas deemed legitimate? For now, given that groups like Fatayat and Rahima pursue their work in ways that are deeply respectful of religious and cultural diversity, I think the answer is no. But the rights of minorities will continue to be an important challenge for progressive activists in a climate of escalating religious intolerance.

RELIGION, AGENCY, AND SOCIAL CHANGE

Through my fieldwork with these four organizations, I was repeatedly reminded that women activists' engagements with global discourses are not simply individual and not at all passive. Religion and feminism are cultural schemas that women activists mobilize, and because the interpretive possibilities of each are so varied they can be interwoven in diverse ways. These combinations, I learned, can underpin quite different moral visions for Indonesia's future. Given the state of global politics post-9/11, it is especially important to recognize that Islam is a heterogeneous tradition that women can and do interpret and practice differently. Islam provides resources for multiple types of agency and women activists' agency is shaped by their locations in the overlapping fields of Islamic and gender politics. They mobilize religion and feminism in different kinds of public interventions, producing not just new activist repertoires, but also new norms of middle-class womanhood.

This framework for thinking about religion and feminism as cultural schemas could be used to study other social or religious movements. Indeed, sociologists are increasingly taking a "cultural approach" to social movements, examining how culture shapes collective action. The cultural tool-kit approach (Swidler 1986) and its variants have been important for restoring attention to agency and recognizing that culture is more a matter of skills, habits, and dispositions than ideas. But this perspective doesn't adequately explain how and why similar actors use culture differently. Closer scrutiny of how actors interpret religion and other ethical frameworks can help to show how they are translated into both identities and actions. A focus on fields of action can help us to understand how locations, experiences, and trajectories influence how individuals understand themselves and how they act in the world. Moreover, this study makes clear that different fields give rise to different forms of agency and that the *overlap* between fields is an especially rich location for new forms of agency. Understanding the kinds of agency and subjectivity in an increasingly globalized society should be an agenda for sociology in the twenty-first century.

This study also reveals that an emphasis on the role of interpretation can also contribute to a more sociologically grounded approach to religion and politics. In the twenty-first century, religion is intertwined with politics the world over. Evangelical Christians are a force in American elections; European nations have struggles over the accommodation of religious minorities, especially Muslims; Islamists are increasingly influential in the democratizing states of the Middle East and North Africa; and South and Southeast Asia have lively religious movements and political parties.

Such global patterns often sound ominous to progressives, who fear the consequences of religious politics for women, sexual minorities, and others. Yet many social justice movements have origins in religious ideas and institutions. Distinguishing between social movements and political tendencies along the lines of religious versus secular seems naïve and perhaps even unproductive. A focus on interpretation can help us to understand how different approaches to religion (or other cultural discourses) underpin very different visions of a just society. How religion influences politics depends on how people interpret and practice religion. As this study has shown, interpretations are diverse and influenced by national histories, textual approaches, and locations in fields of action. There are indeed many who see Islam and feminism as irreconcilable opposites. But women activists in Indonesia demonstrate that global discourses are malleable and that they can be interwoven in unexpected ways. Indonesian women activists are transforming Islam and feminism in multifaceted ways, embodying new forms of agency and identity that are shaping Indonesia's future. These new forms of agency may well reverberate far beyond Indonesia, as other Muslim societies around the globe undergo their own transformations.

APPENDIX A
Methodology

This book is based on eighteen months of ethnographic fieldwork in Indonesia. I spent twelve months conducting research from 2002 to 2003, and an additional three months in the summer of 2005. I returned for three months of follow-up research in 2008 and 2010. Fieldwork was conducted entirely in Bahasa Indonesia, the national language of Indonesia. The study encompassed women activists in Solidaritas Perempuan, Rahima, and Fatayat and women in the Prosperous Justice Party (PKS). Research focused on the Jakarta headquarters of these organizations. In addition to participant observation, I collected demographic information from group members with a short survey. In 2002 and 2003, I conducted twenty-seven individual interviews. In 2005, I conducted nine follow-up interviews along with ten new interviews of women in PKS, all in Bahasa Indonesia. In 2008, I conducted nine additional follow-up interviews and ten new interviews. These interviews averaged 1.5 hours and included questions about respondents' backgrounds, information about their activities in the organizations, and their opinions on a variety of topics, especially Islam, feminism, and women's roles in society.

In 2008, I expanded the scope of my research by interviewing members of the groups in this study who were located in Malang, East Java, in order to understand how their concerns were similar and different from their organizations' headquarters. I also conducted interviews with several Catholic women activists who provided an important perspective on Islam in Indonesia. I used a research assistant in 2005, 2008, and 2010, primarily to schedule and transcribe interviews. All translations in this book are my own.

Much of my fieldwork took place at a time of intense polarization between the United States and the Muslim world. Not long after I arrived in Jakarta in 2002, a terrorist bombing in Bali killed two hundred people. Because of the security situation, as well as the timing of religious holidays, it took me several months to gain entry to my field sites. Moreover, just six months after I arrived, the United States launched the invasion of Iraq, leading to increased hostility toward Americans and massive demonstrations against the war. Despite the difficulties involved with doing research in Indonesia at such a time, my research benefited from the opportunities presented by such a dynamic and heightened political context.

At my field sites, I attempted to be more than just an observer. My hope was that I would be able to contribute something to the organizations I was studying. This turned out to be somewhat naïve, as they were very busy with their work, and sometimes it was hard to figure out what a foreign volunteer could do. I had the most success in this regard with Rahima. As a small and not very hierarchical organization, they put me to work translating some of their journal articles into English to post on their website. Similarly, with Fatayat, I translated a number of their pamphlets and booklets into English and occasionally helped with translating a grant application. Solidaritas Perempuan struggled to integrate me, a somewhat frustrating situation. Occasionally, they asked me to translate a document, but much of the time I wandered around their office trying to find people who weren't too busy to chat. Often I ended up reading materials in the library. Fortunately, a few staff members made an effort to integrate me into their activities, which resulted in some of my richer fieldwork.

My connections with Muslim women's nongovernmental organizations (NGOs) allowed me to become one of the few researchers at the time to study the strongly Islamic Prosperous Justice Party. However, my access to PKS women was more limited than with the other organizations. I could not just hang out at PKS offices, as party cadres came and went during the day. The women's division of the party gave me a list of women in the Jakarta area whom I could contact for interviews, which was helpful though hardly systematic. Because many PKS members at the time were suspicious of the United States and its foreign policy goals, it is likely that many of these women would not have spoken to me without having been asked to by a party leader. From what I could tell, the women were not given much information about my project or the subject matter of the interviews. Although my interactions with PKS were usually good and some women cadres went out of their way to be helpful with my research, I was disappointed that the party was closed to me in some respects. Meetings were not public, and I was only able to attend a few events. I don't know if this would have been the case with other political parties, but from my conversations with other researchers controlled access seems to be a hallmark of PKS.

I chose to conduct ethnography because I wanted to approach this study as a personal and intellectual dialogue with these activist women and because of my lifelong attraction to writing. My methodology is inspired by feminist research methods, such as those outlined by Dorothy Smith (1989), which emphasize the social location of the observer and the relationship between the observer and the observed., I also thought that ethnographic writing, with its emphasis on rich description and ability to incorporate long quotes and field note excerpts, would best allow me to present the voices of those I studied, to the extent that is possible.

During my fieldwork, I considered myself not a neutral observer but an involved participant whose background as a middle-class, white, feminist American informed my observations and analysis. I am aware that as a relatively privileged American researcher, I have the power to represent my informants to the broader public in a way they themselves could not. At a time of increased anti-Muslim sentiment in the West, this feels like a weighty responsibility. Nevertheless, the relationship between my informants and me was not as unbalanced as one might expect. Most of the women in this study were well educated, and in some cases the leaders of these organizations hold positions of greater influence and power in Indonesia than I do as an academic in the United States. While I do not want to underemphasize my position of privilege, I was quite aware in my fieldwork that I was not always "studying down." Although I am skeptical of claims of objectivity in research, I have endeavored to understand my informants' opinions and worldviews as much as possible. I shared drafts of my dissertation with my informants to give them the opportunity to make suggestions or correct any mistakes, and I have made my articles available to them. But the book is indeed my own sociological interpretation. As C. Geertz (1973) famously observed, social scientists interpret others' interpretations of the world, and that is what I have done here.

The other critical influence on my research and theoretical perspective has been Michael Burawoy's (2000) call for global ethnography. Burawoy argues that ethnographers should attempt to link the large-scale processes of globalization with the fine-grained observation of everyday life. Ethnography can allow us to see what is happening in particular settings while also showing how the local and the global are mutually constitutive. From the outset, my aim of understanding how activists engage with transnational discourses has been informed by the global ethnography framework. My intention is to illuminate the daily lives and actions of activists in Jakarta while also examining how they are connected to global transformations. I hope that in doing so, I have succeeded in the goal of using the sociological imagination to connect individual biographies to larger social structures.

Human Development and Gender Indicators in Indonesia

Table 1. LIFE EXPECTANCY AT BIRTH

Year	Life Expectancy
1980	57.6
1990	62.1
2000	65.7
2011	69.4

Source: United Nations Development Programme, Human Development Index 2011.

Table 2. GROSS DOMESTIC PRODUCT PER CAPITA (IN US$)

Year	GDP
1970	82
1980	526
1990	679
2000	773
2010	2,949

Source: UNData.org

Table 3. PERCENTAGE OF POPULATION LIVING ON LESS THAN US$1.25 PER DAY

Country	Percentage
Indonesia	18.7
Philippines	22. 6
China	15.9

Source: United Nations Development Programme, Human Development Index 2011.

Table 4. FEMALE LABOR FORCE PARTICIPATION RATE

Country	Rate
Indonesia	52.0
Philippines	49.2
China	67.4

Source: United Nations Development Programme, Human Development Index 2011.

Table 5. FEMALE SEATS IN PARLIAMENT (2011)

Country	Seats
Indonesia	18.0
Philippines	21.5
China	21.3

Source: United Nations Development Programme, Human Development Index 2011.

Table 6. PERCENTAGE OF POPULATION WITH AT LEAST A SECONDARY EDUCATION (2011)

Country	Female	Male
Indonesia	24.2	31.1
Philippines	65.9	63.7
China	54.8	70.4

Source: United Nations Development Programme, Human Development Index 2011.

Table 7. TOTAL FERTILITY RATE (AVERAGE NUMBER OF CHILDREN PER WOMAN)

Years	Rate
1960–1965	5.62
1970–1975	5.30
1980–1985	4.11
1990–1995	2.90
2000–2005	2.38
2010–2015	2.06

Source: World Population Prospects 2011.

NOTES

CHAPTER 1

1. I use Islamist to describe those who argue for a state that governs according to Islamic law.
2. It has also often been part of nationalist politics (Yuval-Davis 1997).
3. Such regulations were part of a political decentralization process initiated in 2002 that gave more power to local authorities. By 2010, 69 districts/municipalities had passed approximately 154 regulations, many of which were said to be inspired by Islamic law. The National Commission on Violence against Women reports that 63 of the regulations restrict women's right to freedom of expression, including 21 policies that regulate dress codes. Women's mobility is restricted by the 37 regulations that aim to curb prostitution. Eighty-two regulations also restrict religious freedoms (Komnas Perempuan 2010). Enforcement of these regulations is uneven.
4. *Keadilan* means justice, but it is also often used to mean equality, and the meanings are fairly interchangeable.
5. In this book, I distinguish between *conservative* and *liberal* political views, particularly when it comes to women's rights. I use these terms in the most conventional sense: conservatives are those who do not challenge the status quo, or who support gender practices considered to be traditional, while liberals are those who argue for greater liberty and equal rights. It is important to recognize that these terms sometimes have different meanings in Indonesian political discourse, with liberal sometimes being associated with economic neoliberalism.
6. I use the organizations' real names, as they asked me to do so and they are recognizable to those who know the Indonesian context. I do not use real names of individuals unless they are well-known public figures.
7. There are other organizations I could have selected, such as Aisyiyah, the women's group of Muhammadiyah, the other major Muslim organization in Indonesia. However, I felt Aisyiyah was too similar to Fatayat to make meaningful distinctions. I also did not study women in more extreme Muslim groups because I consider such organizations to be outside the Indonesian mainstream
8. At the time of my research, only Rahima had male staff. I interviewed some men, but my research focused on the women in these organizations. A detailed discussion of my methodology can be found in the methods appendix.
9. Muslim clothing is an alternative to "traditional" clothing, as well as Western styles (which remain popular). It usually consists of a long-sleeved tunic with an ankle-length skirt or wide pants. There are many variations, including fashionable

outfits pairing headscarves with narrow tunics and jeans. A minority of women have adopted conservative Persian Gulf styles, including the *niqab* (face-veil).

10. One difference is that Islamic revivalism seems to contain strands that are more strongly focused on gaining state power and using Islamic law to govern (Juergensmeyer 2003).

11. In Indonesia, such covering usually indicates that women are adherents of ultra-conservative forms of Islam such as Salafism. Salafism is a movement originating in Saudi Arabia that purportedly seeks to return to the pure Islam of the earliest Muslims. See Nisa (2012) for a study of Indonesian Salafist women.

12. See, for example, Mernissi (1987).

13. Some scholars argue against the idea that veiling demonstrates agency. Moghissi (1999) argues that agency must involve acting against domination, while Lazreg (2009) questions whether women really choose freely in contexts where there is strong state or social pressure to veil.

14. Mahmood's work has generated considerable debate, and Schielke provides an extended critique that is outside the scope of this book. For other discussions see Bangstad (2010) and Soares and Osella (2009).

15. Fligstein and McAdam (2012) similarly argue that fields are constituted by strategic actions of various kinds.

16. Many sociologists have productively used field approaches to analyze social movement activism. For example, Raka Ray (1998) explores how the Indian women's movement is different in Calcutta and Bombay because of differences in the local political field of each city. However, I am interested in how the activism I describe is part of subfields within a national public sphere.

17. For Saeed, contextualism and textualism are two of three major approaches to interpretation in Islam. Semitextualists, according to Saeed, are similar to textualists but attempt to frame the text in more contemporary terms. For my purposes semitextualists are considered textualists. These differences should be seen as more of a continuum than a binary. Finding appropriate terms to categorize different traditions of interpretation in Islam is difficult, and not all scholars agree on these categories. I recognize that these are crude categories that elide important differences, but I have found this to be a significant divide among Muslims in Indonesia.

CHAPTER 2

1. http://www.pbs.org/newshour/multimedia/indonesia/index.html.

2. http://data.worldbank.org/indicator/SI.POV.2DAY. See appendix B for other relevant statistics and indicators.

3. The Hadiths are the collected reports of statements or actions of Muhammad, which are considered to be vital for understanding the Quran and for Islamic jurisprudence.

4. This term was popularized by Egyptian Muslim modernists in the early twentieth century and signifies a more rationalistic approach to texts, as opposed to reliance on long-accepted interpretations.

5. In Indonesia and other non-Arabic-speaking contexts, students traditionally memorize long sections of the Quran and are told the meaning of those sections by the teacher.

6. Geertz used the term *abangan* to describe Indonesians who integrate local traditions with Islam, but in recent years the word has become a pejorative reference to nonpracticing Muslims. Some who emphasize their Javanese identity now use

the term *kejawen* (Javanist) instead, and this category often includes those who incorporate mysticism or local traditions into their Islamic practice (Beatty 1999; Hefner 2000; Fox 2004).

7. This school was probably inspired by Raden Ajeng Kartini, an aristocratic Javanese woman who became interested in women's rights. In 1903, she opened the first Indonesian primary school for native girls. Kartini was lionized by the Suharto regime as an ideal model of womanhood, and her legacy has been both rejected and reclaimed by women activists (Rutherford 1993).

8. Fatayat is now for women between the ages of twenty-five and forty-five, while Muslimat is for women over forty-five.

9. The other tenets of Pancasila are as follows: Just and civilized humanity; The unity of Indonesia; Democracy guided by inner wisdom in the unanimity arising out of deliberations amongst representatives; and Social justice for all of the people of Indonesia. Pancasila remains the governing philosophy of the Indonesian nation-state.

10. The Suharto regime quickly became one of the world's top recipients of US and International Monetary Fund (IMF) aid.

11. After October 1965, the PKI and its women's organization, Gerwani, were banned. The regime also purged the national women's federation Kowani, and its platform was revised to include only aims congruent with government policy. Independent women's organizations did not reappear until the 1980s. These groups existed under a new loophole permitting "Self-reliant social institutions," a category similar to NGOs (Blackburn 2004, 27).

12. Starting in the 1980s, NU also launched several NGOs. P3M focused on Islam, gender, and democracy and was influential in developing a more egalitarian Muslim discourse on women's rights.

13. The Ford Foundation has sponsored visits by scholars and activists to Indonesia.

14. This material was banned at the time. It circulated in photocopied form, often translated by students themselves.

15. Many Muslim students enroll in Christian schools because they are believed to provide rigorous education.

16. See the methods appendix for more detailed information.

17. Indonesia also has Protestant and Catholic women's rights groups, which work in these communities but for the most part do not use religious arguments. A small number of Catholic feminists have called for religious reforms.

18. Some of SP's communities are in areas with significant Christian populations and have more Christian members.

19. *Fiqh an-Nisa* refers to a Quranic verse that discusses marital relations in Islam and has been used to justify men's control over women. Feminist theologians argue that this verse talks about women's rights in relation to their husbands, and that it counsels men to treat wives equitably.

20. What constitutes membership is ambiguous. Most likely, the figure of 45 million is an estimate of those who are considered to be supporters.

21. The age limit for Fatayat was forty until recently. Fatayat's and Muslimat's activities are similar, but some consider Muslimat to be more conservative (Van Doorn-Harder 2006).

22. http://www.seasite.niu.edu/Indonesian/Indonesian_Elections/Election_text.htm.

23. http://en.wikipedia.org/wiki/Indonesian_legislative_election,_2009.

24. Commonly used Arabic phrase meaning to do what is right and oppose what is wrong.

25. "Visi and Misi" from PKS official website: http://pks.or.id/content/visi-dan-misi (accessed October 9, 2012).

26. PKS has been rumored to accept funding from foreign sources, particularly Saudi Arabia, which is illegal under Indonesian law. I have no information to deny or confirm such allegations. However, it is the case that PKS has branches overseas, some of which raise funds from Indonesian expatriates.

27. Jakarta city government Department of Population and Civil Registration: http://dki.kependudukancapil.go.id/?option=com_content&view=article&id=4&Itemid=63. This figure includes only the legally defined boundary of the city. In the last decade, Jakarta has largely engulfed surrounding towns, and so there is a strong argument for including such places in the Jakarta population count.

CHAPTER 3

1. Munir passed away in 2011.

2. Liberalism here is understood as an ideology that espouses individual liberties and equal rights.

3. Historically, feminism was also embraced by Marxists and left critics of liberalism. However, it has also been identified with imperialism because colonizers often used women's rights to justify domination (Ahmed 1993).

4. Both organizations often draw on more established (often male) Islamic scholars associated with NU for religious interpretations. This is because there are not yet many women with training in Islamic interpretation, although the number is growing. Rahima is unusual for having Islamic scholars on its staff, as well as on its board, who do much of the interpretive work for the organization.

5. Chapter 2 has background on Nahdlatul Ulama. Founded in 1926, its membership is estimated at forty-five million. NU comprises youth and women's wings, think tanks and NGOs, and a central board. It also funds schools and NGOs.

6. I am aware that there are important differences between the Jakarta headquarters of Fatayat and its smaller regional branches. However, because the Jakarta office houses the leadership of the organization, it sets the agenda and the tone for all others.

7. Later, Fatayat moved to a modest building of its own on a nearby street.

8. A narration of the sayings and deeds of the Prophet Mohammad. Hadiths are used for interpreting the Quran and for jurisprudence. One method for contesting interpretations is to challenge the authenticity or path of transmission of a Hadith

9. Sometimes considered synonymous with Hadith, Sunnah consists of what Muhammad believed or approved. It is the second source of Islamic jurisprudence, after the Quran.

10. In the Indonesian context, traditionalist is also used to mean Islam that incorporates local practices/beliefs.

11. The NU approach is different from the approach of Muslim "modernists" who advocate greater reliance on the Quran. Modernists also advocate a closer reading of the text without many additional sources or interpretations and reject many local practices as mystical or irrational. Middle Eastern Islam has been strongly influenced by modernism, which originated in Egypt in the late nineteenth century. Modernism also has a long heritage in Southeast Asia. See chapter 2 for more discussion of Islam in Indonesia.

12. Influential Islamic thinkers from outside the NU milieu, such as Nurcholish Madjid, also explored contextual approaches. However, NU circles seem to have embraced contextualism more so than the modernist milieu.

13. Muslimat is the NU organization for women over forty-five years of age.
14. PPP was the officially permitted Muslim political party during the Suharto regime.
15. In Indonesia, these guidelines are debated, and many Muslim women do not follow them. Some Rahima and Fatayat activists say that the headscarf is not an obligation for women, except during prayer. Some also argue that modest clothing is required for men.
16. Outside Jakarta, Fatayat members are less educated and affluent. However, I met several heads of Fatayat branches from smaller cities or semirural areas who also had university educations.
17. In the 1990s and early 2000s, a number of IAINs were transformed into more prestigious State Islamic Universities (UIN), which teach business, law, and education in addition to the traditional Islamic sciences. The UIN-IAIN system now admits an increasing number of public school graduates (Azra et al. 2007).
18. *Shariah* banks are banks whose practices are consistent with the principles of Islamic *Shariah* law, including prohibitions on charging interest for loans. This is a recent trend in Indonesia and many other countries.
19. Fatayat Mission and Vision: http://fatayat.or.id/VisiMisi.
20. Rahima Profile: http://www.rahima.or.id/index.php?option=com_content&view =article&id=23&Itemid=344.
21. The curriculum is also very similar to that used by Solidaritas Perempuan for its "feminist trainings."
22. In 2010, Ayu told me that most communities now had few problems with women's rights framed in Islamic terms. According to her, what is more controversial is cultural and religious pluralism, which Rahima also promotes.
23. Ika is referring to the typology of feminism (liberal, radical, socialist) that is taught in gender trainings. Socialist feminism is defined as a feminism that critiques women's economic oppression, as well as patriarchy.
24. Like Ika, Mei refers to the typology of feminisms. In this typology, liberal feminism is understood as a feminism that argues for equality (defined as sameness) in all spheres.
25. Words in italics were spoken in English by Ayu.
26. Words in italics were spoken in English.
27. I did not observe household tasks, so it is impossible to know if activists lived up to their ideals. Recent research by Tickamyer and Kusujiarti (2012) demonstrates that in Javanese villages, despite rhetoric about husbands helping, women do the vast majority of household tasks.
28. This is not necessarily the same as a marriage in which both partners see themselves as equal. However, companionate marriage differs from notions of marriage that prioritize reproduction above all else.
29. Among others, the city of Tangerang, West Java, has implemented such laws, resulting in the arrests of women using public transportation to return from work or shopping after dark. Activists have attempted to challenge such ordinances as unconstitutional. Such laws are sometimes framed by their advocates as a way to instill religious values but are also construed more broadly as ways to maintain social order and morality. The laws have in some cases been promoted by secular nationalist political parties who use them to prove their moral credentials. However, the ordinances are mostly aimed at women and they draw on conservative interpretations of Islamic law (such as requiring women to be accompanied by male relatives as guardians).

30. The verse translates as follows: "Men are in charge of women by [right of] what Allah has given one over the other and what they spend [for maintenance] from their wealth. So righteous women are devoutly obedient, guarding in [the husband's] absence what Allah would have them guard. But those [wives] from whom you fear arrogance - [first] advise them; [then if they persist], forsake them in bed; and [finally], strike them. But if they obey you [once more], seek no means against them. Indeed, Allah is ever Exalted and Grand." Translation from Quran. com. http://quran.com/4.

31. Contextualism comprises various methods. Many Indonesian reformists have been influenced by the work of Islamic scholars such as Fazlur Rahman, who taught at the University of Chicago and who helped to substantiate this approach.

32. Mir-Hosseini (2006) proposes that *fikh* is a useful tool for reformists because it is understood to be a human creation and therefore fungible. It is also the source of much of Islamic law and practice related to gender. However, not all Muslim feminists use *fikh* to produce alternative interpretations.

33. Faqihuddin Abdul Qodir, MA, "Women's *Aurat*, a Limit Without Borders?" *Swara Rahima*, February 21, 2011, http://www.rahima.or.id/index.php?option=com_content&view=article&id=633:womens-aurat-a-limit-without-borders&catid=63:hadith&Itemid=374.

34. *Itjihad* means the application of reason and reinterpretation to the message of the Quran. It is a term associated with Islamic reformism around the world, but especially with Muslim modernism.

35. *Modul Analisis Gender* (P. P. Fatayat Nahdlatul Ulama 1999, 50).

36. In the module, this saying is attributed to Imam an-Nawawi, who compiled a popular book of Hadiths consisting of the sayings of the Prophet Muhammad.

37. Also from the module, the first text is a verse of the Quran. The second is attributed to Muhammad Isma'il al-Buhkari, who also compiled an extensive collection of Hadiths.

38. English translation from http://www.rahima.or.id/index.php?option=com_content&view=article&id=646:giving-authority-to-women-tafsir-5th-edition&catid=62:tafsir&Itemid=375.

39. Many Indonesian Muslim intellectuals are familiar with Liberation Theology, and Wahid's work here may be a conscious attempt to contribute to a Muslim liberation theology.

40. The verse follows a verse discussing the treatment of orphans. Translation from USC Center for Muslim-Jewish engagement: http://www.usc.edu/org/cmje/religious-texts/quran/verses/004-qmt.php#004.003.

41. In Islamic law, human behaviors fall into a scale of five categories, ranging from obligatory through various forms of optional to prohibited (Saeed 2005).

42. Abortion is illegal in Indonesia except to save the mother's life or in cases of rape or incest.

43. *Aborsi Dalam Perspektif Fikh Kontemporer*, Fakultas Kedokteran Universitas Indonesia, 2002.

44. In 2003, Fatayat also signed on to an international letter to President Bush opposing the "global gag rule" in US-funded HIV prevention efforts. This policy specified that US family planning assistance will not be provided to foreign NGOs that use funding from any other source to perform abortions for any reason other than a threat to the woman's life, rape, or incest; provide counseling and referral for abortion; or lobby to make abortion legal or more available in their country. The rule was overturned by President Obama.

45. E-mail communication in 2006.
46. Margot Badran, "Islamic Feminism: What's in a Name?" *Al-Ahram Weekly Online*, January 17–23, 2002, http://weekly.ahram.org.eg/2002/569/cu1.htm.

CHAPTER 4

1. A *fatwa* is a religious opinion concerning matters of Islamic law. As a government-sponsored council of representatives from Islamic organizations, MUI has the authority to issue *fatwa*s, but like all *fatwa*s, they are not binding. However, they do influence public opinion.
2. *Haram* means forbidden under Islamic law.
3. *Dakwah* groups stress religious practice, especially prayer, and also discuss religious texts. They are heterogeneous. Some disdain politics, while others are politicized. Scholars have also noted the influence of *dakwah* groups in the Middle East and South Asia. *Tarbiyah* networks seem to be strongest in Indonesia's state universities (Brenner 2005; Smith-Hefner 2007; Machmudi 2008). See chapter 2 for more information.
4. As discussed in chapters 1 and 2, there are many methods of interpreting Islam. Following Saeed (2005), one of the most major differences is between more textual and more contextual approaches. These should be thought of as a spectrum rather than a strict dichotomy.
5. As mentioned in chapter 2, I use *feminism* to describe a set of ideas and institutions that seek to challenge women's subordination to men, that are informed by feminist theory, and that can be utilized by individuals and organizations in many different ways (Ferree and Tripp 2006). I am interested in feminism as a set of global discourses that women activists adapt and transform. It is important to note that PKS women often have in mind a stereotype of feminism as "Western" and "secular," both of which they reject.
6. Recent reports indicate tensions over attempts by some PKS leaders to be more inclusive and moderate (Woodward et al. 2011).
7. Many potential party members meet their partners at university or in study groups and marry before they join PKS.
8. Marriage is discussed later in the chapter. Some women I interviewed were reluctant to provide details about how they met their husbands. I was alerted to this by my research assistant, who had heard about arranged marriages in *dakwah* groups. Smith-Hefner (2005) argues that while many Indonesian women are delaying marriage until their midtwenties and seeking to find their own partners, a minority of pious women are seeking out quasi-arranged marriages through religious groups. Some of those in *dakwah* groups are opposed to conventional dating practices. Nevertheless, these women still emphasize companionship in their marriages.
9. Data from "Women in National Parliaments": http://www.ipu.org/wmn-e/classif.htm.
10. From 2004 to 2009, PKS had three women out of forty-five representatives (Sherlock 2007). Also see http://www.thejakartapost.com/news/2009/05/27/record-number-female-legislators-elected-house.html.
11. This may also be because PKS women did not want to appear to be questioning the party when they spoke to me.
12. PKS women are required to wear the white *jilbab* and a long skirt for public events.
13. While PKS has supported such regulations, the party has not usually initiated them.

14. Italicized words here indicate that Yulia used the English terms.
15. Indonesian translation of an Arabic phrase meaning to command or enjoin what is right and to forbid what is wrong. This phrase is used by PKS cadres, as well as other Muslims, to sum up the essence of Islam. It is sometimes interpreted as encouraging Muslims to respond to public ethical errors.
16. Sarah Pandji, "Bukan Sekedar Peran Tambahan," *Suara Keadilan* 1, no. 16 (2001): 14.
17. Another discrepancy between women in PKS and the other groups in this study is PKS women's larger number of children. The PKS women I met in 2005 had an average of 3.9 children, more than women in the other groups in this study, who were more in line with the Indonesian average of 2.2 children.
18. Abu-Lughod (1998) argues that in early twentieth-century Egypt, Islamism and feminism shared a common goal of modernizing the family.
19. See chapter 2 for more historical background on the polygamy controversy.
20. "Ini Pandangan Hidayat Nurwahid tentang Poligami," *Kompas*, April 25, 2012, http://megapolitan.kompas.com/read/2012/04/25/20173044/Ini.Pandangan. Hidayat.tentang.Poligami.
21. PKK was one of the keystones of the Suharto regime's development programs, a way for the state to mobilize women, especially in rural areas (Blackwood 1995). PKK still exists in diminished form.
22. See PKS website for more information. http://www.pks.or.id/content/ pks-launching-pos-wanita-keadilan-dan-rumah-keluarga-indonesia.
23. Pornography in the bill is defined as coital acts, foreplay, and sexual diversions pertaining to intercourse, sexual violence, masturbation or onanism, nudity or illusions/allusions to nudity, and genitalia.
24. Many women's rights activists opposed the bill because of concerns about censorship and gender equality. The bill was also opposed by many Balinese who argued that sensual expression is intrinsic to their culture.
25. DH. Al-Yusni, Anggota Komisi VII DPR FPKS, "Indonesia Negeri Full Pornografi," Originally posted on Fraksi PKS website, February 14, 2006, can be found at http://ruuappri.blogsome.com/2006/03/24/indonesia-negeri-full-pornografi/.
26. Jason Tedjasukmana, "Indonesia's New Anti-Porn Agenda," *Time Magazine*, November 6, 2008.
27. See http://www.indonesiamatters.com/2474/porn-laws/ for English text of the bill.
28. Australian Broadcasting Corporation, "Indonesia Pornography" broadcast transcript, http://www.abc.net.au/foreign/content/2006/s1693094.htm.
29. One celebrity was sentenced to three years in jail after his sex tapes were circulated, without his knowledge, on YouTube. Some local authorities have used the law to cancel concerts by entertainers deemed too risqué.

CHAPTER 5

1. Indonesians tend to use *secular* and *secularism* interchangeably. As discussed in chapter 1, I use *secular* here to categorize activism that does not usually frame arguments for social change in religious terms.
2. Feminism has long had been a global movement, but in recent years social scientists have turned attention to the emergence of transnational feminist networks (Moghadam 2005), whose activism usually aims to mobilize women across national borders. I use the term *transnational discourses* to describe ideas that circulate globally and *transnational feminism* to refer to global feminist networks/movements.

3. http://www.ilo.org/jakarta/info/public/pr/WCMS_164551/lang--en/index.htm.
4. SP also has 604 members across the country, many of whom are involved in the 10 regional SP offices.
5. This group was formed in the wake of the 1998 riots in which hundreds of women were abused and raped. It has official status as a quasi-governmental body and serves as an umbrella group for women's organizations.
6. *Jilbab* is the Indonesian term for the modern Islamic headscarf which can come in a variety of styles. Further discussion of the rise of veiling in Indonesia in the late 1980s and 1990s can be found in chapter 2.
7. Following other scholars, I use *liberal left* to characterize a diverse milieu of NGOs and civil society groups that are working toward social justice and more egalitarian democratization.
8. *Reformasi* is the name to describe the prodemocracy movement that began in the early 1990s, peaked with the resignation of Suharto in June 1998, and wound down by the 1999 elections.
9. Human rights, for example, claims that all humans should have certain basic rights.
10. With this combination of concern for equality, emphasis on daily life, interest in economic globalization and ecological issues, and reference to human rights, SP bears a strong resemblance to women's groups in India. Indian feminism displays a concern with domestic violence, advocacy for poor and marginalized women, attention to environmental issues, and opposition to neoliberal economic policies (Ray 1998).
11. Like the other activists in this study, and like many Indonesians, most SP women I met disapproved of sexuality outside heterosexual marriage.
12. *Santri* usually means a student at a Muslim school, but here Sari uses it to describe a Javanese Islamic teacher, normally called *kyai*.
13. In Indonesia, NGOs are considered to be part of the "social sector" as opposed to politics. As I discussed in chapter 2, NGOs became one of the few outlets for political activism in the 1980s and 1990s.
14. *Adat* means custom or tradition. This concept has legal status in Indonesia, as some *adat* laws are accepted by the government as legitimate. Such laws usually pertain to marriage, religious practice, artistic expression, and so forth. Each ethnic group is considered to have its own *adat*.
15. Although I dislike this term, I use it here because SP activists employ it (they Indonesianize it to *fundamentalisme*). It is important not to conflate socially conservative Islam with violent extremism.
16. Derogatory term meaning "unbelievers" (from Arabic).

CHAPTER 6
1. http://data.worldbank.org/indicator/SI.POV.2DAY?page=2.

REFERENCES

Abu-Lughod, Lila. 1998. "The Marriage of Feminism and Islamism in Egypt: Selective Repudiation as a Dynamic of Postcolonial Cultural Politics." Pp. 243–69 in *Remaking Women: Feminism and Modernity in the Middle East*. Princeton, NJ: Princeton University Press.

Abu-Lughod, Lila. 2002. "Do Muslim Women Really Need Saving? Anthropological Reflections on Cultural Relativism and Its Others." *American Anthropologist* 104(3):783–90.

Abu-Lughod, Lila. 2010. "The Active Social Life of 'Muslim Women's Rights': A Plea for Ethnography, Not Polemic, with Cases from Egypt and Palestine." *Journal of Middle East Women's Studies* 6(1):1–45.

Ahmed, Leila. 1993. *Women and Gender in Islam: Historical Roots of a Modern Debate*. New Haven, CT: Yale University Press.

Ali, Ayaan Hirsi. 2010. *Nomad: From Islam to America: A Personal Journey through the Clash of Civilizations*. New York: Free Press.

Almond, Gabriel A., R. Scott Appleby, and Emmanuel Sivan. 2003. *Strong Religion: The Rise of Fundamentalisms around the World*. Chicago: University of Chicago Press.

Amnesty International. 2011. *Indonesia: Briefing to the UN Committee on the Elimination of Discrimination against Women*. (http://www.amnestyusa.org/research/reports/indonesia-briefing-to-the-un-committee-on-the-elimination-of-discrimination-against-women-women-and?page=show).

Ansor, Maria Ulfah. 2002. "Poligami: Manifestasi Dominasi Suami terhadap Istri." *Kompas*, March 4, 35–36.

Anwar, Etin. 2004. "'Directed' Women's Movements in Indonesia: Social and Political Agency from Within." *Hawwa* 2(1):89–112.

Asad, Talal. 2003. *Formations of the Secular: Christianity, Islam, Modernity*. Palo Alto, CA: Stanford University Press.

Asad, Talal. 1986. *The Idea of an Anthropology of Islam*. Occasional Paper, Center for Contemporary Arab Studies, Georgetown University, Washington, DC.

Aspinall, Edward. 2005. *Opposing Suharto: Compromise, Resistance, and Regime Change in Indonesia*. Palo Alto, CA: Stanford University Press.

Avishai, Orit. 2008. "'Doing Religion' in a Secular World: Women in Conservative Religions and the Question of Agency." *Gender & Society* 22(4):409–33.

Azra, Azyumardi, Dina Afrianty, and Robert W. Hefner. 2007. "Pesantren and Madrasa: Muslim Schools and National Ideals in Indonesia." Pp. 172–98 in *Schooling Islam: The Culture and Politics of Modern Muslim Education*, edited by Robert W. Hefner and Muhammad Qasim Zaman. Princeton, NJ: Princeton University Press.

Badran, Margot. 2009. *Feminism in Islam: Secular and Religious Convergences.* Oxford: Oneworld Press.

Badran, Margot. 2002. *"Islamic Feminism: What's in a Name?"* Al-Ahram Weekly Online, Issue 569 (http://weekly.ahram.org.eg/2002/569/cu1.htm).

Bangstad, Sindre. 2010. "Book Review: Saba Mahmood, Politics of Piety: The Islamic Revival and the Feminist Subject." *Feminist Theory* 11(2):216–18.

Barlas, Asma. 2002. *'Believing Women' in Islam: Unreading Patriarchal Interpretations of the Qur'an.* Austin: University of Texas Press.

Bartkowski, John P., and Jen'nan Ghazal Read. 2003. "Veiled Submission: Gender, Power, and Identity among Evangelical and Muslim Women in the United States." *Qualitative Sociology* 26(1):71–92.

Barton, Greg, and Greg Fealy. 1996. *Nahdlatul Ulama, Traditional Islam, and Modernity in Indonesia.* Clayton, VIC, Australia: Monash Asia Institute.

Beatty, Andrew. 1999. *Varieties of Javanese Religion: An Anthropological Account.* Cambridge: Cambridge University Press.

Bidang Kewanitaan DPP PK Sejahtera. 2004. *Perempuan-Perempuan Pilihan: Profil Singkat 150 Caleg dan Politisi Perempuan PK Sejahtera [Chosen Women: Short Profiles of 150 Female PKS Candidates and Politicians].* Jakarta, Indonesia: Misykat Publication.

Blackburn, Susan. 2004. *Women and the State in Modern Indonesia.* Cambridge: Cambridge University Press.

Blackburn, Susan. 2008. *Indonesian Islam in a New Era: How Women Negotiate Their Muslim Identities.* Clayton, VIC, Australia: Monash Asia Institute.

Blackwood, Evelyn. 1995. "Senior Women, Model Mothers, and Dutiful Wives: Managing Gender Contradictions in a Minangkabau Village." Pp. 124–58 in *Bewitching Women, Pious Men: Gender and Body Politics in Southeast Asia,* edited by Aihwa Ong and Michael G. Peletz. Berkeley: University of California Press.

Blackwood, Evelyn. 2007. "Regulation of Sexuality in Indonesian Discourse: Normative Gender, Criminal Law and Shifting Strategies of Control." *Culture, Health & Sexuality* 9(3):293–307.

Boellstorff, Tom. 2005. *The Gay Archipelago: Sexuality and Nation in Indonesia.* Princeton, NJ: Princeton University Press.

Bourdieu, Pierre. 1987. *Distinction: A Social Critique of the Judgment of Taste.* Cambridge, MA: Harvard University Press.

Bourdieu, Pierre, and Loïc J. D. Wacquant. 1992. *An Invitation to Reflexive Sociology.* Chicago: University of Chicago Press.

Bowen, John. 2006. *Why the French Don't Like Headscarves: Islam, the State, and Public Space.* Princeton, NJ: Princeton University Press.

Braidotti, Rosi. 2008. "In Spite of the Times: The Postsecular Turn in Feminism." *Theory, Culture & Society* 25(6):1–24.

Brenner, Suzanne. 1996. "Reconstructing Self and Society: Javanese Muslim Women and 'the Veil'." *American Ethnologist* 23(4):673–97.

Brenner, Suzanne. 1998. *The Domestication of Desire: Women, Wealth, and Modernity in Java.* Princeton, NJ: Princeton University Press.

Brenner, Suzanne. 1999. "On the Public Intimacy of the New Order: Images of Women in the Popular Indonesian Print Media." *Indonesia* 67(April):13–37.

Brenner, Suzanne. 2005. "Islam and Gender Politics in Late New Order Indonesia." Pp. 93–118 in *Spirited Politics: Religion and Public Life in Contemporary Southeast Asia.* Ithaca, NY: Cornell University Press.

Brenner, Suzanne. 2006. "Democracy, Polygamy, and Women in Post-Reformasi Indonesia." *Social Analysis* 50(1):164–70.

Brown, Wendy. 1995. *States of Injury*. Princeton, NJ: Princeton University Press.

Bruinessen, Martin. 2011. "What Happened to the Smiling Face of Indonesian Islam?: Muslim Intellectualism and the Conservative Turn in Post-Suharto Indonesia." RSIS Working Papers *222*, 1–62. S. Rajaratnam School of International Studies, Singapore.

Bubalo, Anthony, Greg Fealy, and Whit Mason. 2008. *Zealous Democrats: Islamism and Democracy in Egypt, Indonesia and Turkey*. Paper 25, 1–147. Lowy Institute for International Policy, New South Wales, Australia.

Budiman, Manneke. 2008. "Treading the Path of the Shari'a: Indonesian Feminism at the Crossroads of Western Modernity and Islamism." *Journal of Indonesian Social Sciences and Humanities* 1:73–93.

Burawoy, Michael. 2000. "Introduction: Reaching for the Global." Pp. 1–40 in *Global Ethnography: Forces, Connections, and Imaginations in a Postmodern World*, edited by Michæl Burawoy et al. Berkeley: University of California Press.

Bush, Robin. 2008. "Regional Sharia Regulations in Indonesia: Anomaly or Symptom?" Pp. 174–91 in *Expressing Islam: Religious Life and Politics in Indonesia*, edited by Greg Fealy and Sally White. Singapore: Institute of Southeast Asian Studies.

Casanova, Jose. 1994. *Public Religions in the Modern World*. Chicago: University of Chicago Press.

Casanova, Jose. 2009. "A Debate on the Public Role of Religion and Its Social and Gender Implications." *UNRISD Gender and Development Programme Paper 5*, 1–59.

Charrad, Mounira M. 2011. "Gender in the Middle East: Islam, State, Agency." *Annual Review of Sociology* 37(1):417–37.

Chatterjee, Partha. 1993. *The Nation and Its Fragments: Colonial and Postcolonial Histories*. Princeton, NJ: Princeton University Press.

Chong, Kelly H. 2008. *Deliverance and Submission: Evangelical Women and the Negotiation of Patriarchy in South Korea*. Cambridge, MA: Harvard University Press.

Collins, Patricia Hill. 2008. *Black Feminist Thought: Knowledge, Consciousness, and the Politics of Empowerment*. New York: Routledge.

Connell, Raewyn. 2009. *Gender*. London: Polity.

Damanik, Ali Said. 2002. *Fenomena Partai Keadilan: Transformasi 20 Tahun Gerakan Tarbiyah di Indonesia*. Jakarta, Indonesia: Teraju.

Davidman, Lynn. 1993. *Tradition in a Rootless World: Women Turn to Orthodox Judaism*. Berkeley: University of California Press.

Davis, Kathy. 2007. *The Making of Our Bodies, Ourselves: How Feminism Travels across Borders*. Durham, NC: Duke University Press.

Deeb, Lara. 2006. *An Enchanted Modern: Gender and Public Piety in Shi'i Lebanon*. Princeton, NJ: Princeton University Press.

Eickelman, Dale F., and James P. Piscatori. 1996. *Muslim Politics*. Princeton, NJ: Princeton University Press.

Eliasoph, Nina. 1998. *Avoiding Politics: How Americans Produce Apathy in Everyday Life*. Cambridge: Cambridge University Press.

Errington, Shelly. 1990. "Recasting Sex, Gender and Power: A Theoretical Overview." Pp. 1–58 in *Power and Difference: Gender in Island Southeast Asia*, edited by J. Atkinson and S. Errington. Palo Alto, CA: Stanford University Press.

Esposito, John L., ed. 2004. *The Islamic World: Past and Present*. New York: Oxford University Press.

Feillard, Andree. 1997. "Traditionalist Islam and the State in Indonesia: The Road to Legitimacy and Renewal." Pp. 129–55 in *Islam in an Era of Nation-States. Politics and Religious Renewal in Muslim Southeast Asia*, edited by Robert W. Hefner and Patricia Horvatich. Honolulu: University of Hawaii Press.

Ferree, Myra Marx, and Aili Mari Tripp. 2006. *Global Feminism: Transnational Women's Activism, Organizing, and Human Rights*. New York: NYU Press.

Fligstein, Neil, and Doug McAdam. 2012. *A Theory of Fields*. New York: Oxford University Press.

Foley, Rebecca. 2004. "Muslim Women's Challenges to Islamic Law: The Case of Malaysia." *International Feminist Journal of Politics* 6(1):53–84.

Fox, James J. 2004. "Currents in Contemporary Islam in Indonesia." Working paper presented at *Harvard Asia Vision 21*:1–24. Australian National University Open Access Research (http://hdl.handle.net/1885/42039).

Fraser, Nancy. 1989. *Unruly Practices: Power, Discourse and Gender in Contemporary Social Theory*. Minneapolis: University of Minnesota Press.

Fraser, Nancy. 1990. "Rethinking the Public Sphere: A Contribution to the Critique of Actually Existing Democracy." *Social Text* (25/26):56–80.

Fuller, Graham E. 2002. "The Future of Political Islam." *Foreign Affairs* 81(2):48–60.

Gade, Anna. 2004. *Perfection Makes Practice: Learning, Emotion, and the Recited Qur'an in Indonesia*. Honolulu: University of Hawaii Press.

Gallagher, Sally K. 2003. *Evangelical Identity and Gendered Family Life*. New Brunswick, NJ: Rutgers University Press.

Gallagher, Sally K. 2004. "Where Are the Antifeminist Evangelicals?: Evangelical Identity, Subcultural Location, and Attitudes toward Feminism." *Gender & Society* 18(4):451–72.

Geertz, Clifford. 1960. *The Religion of Java*. New York: Free Press.

Geertz, Clifford. 1973. *The Interpretation of Cultures: Selected Essays*. New York: Basic Books.

Geertz, Hildred. 1961. *The Javanese Family: A Study of Kinship and Socialization*. New York: Free Press.

Giddens, Anthony. 1991. *Modernity and Self-Identity: Self and Society in the Late Modern Age*. Palo Alto, CA: Stanford University Press.

Goldberg, Jonah. 2011. "Taking Feminism Overseas." *National Review Online*. (http://www.nationalreview.com/articles/263350/taking-feminism-overseas-jonah-goldberg).

Goldstone, Jack A. 2010. "From Structure to Agency to Process: The Evolution of Charles Tilly's Theories of Social Action as Reflected in His Analyses of Contentious Politics." *The American Sociologist* 41(4):358–67.

Göle, Nilufer. 1996. *The Forbidden Modern: Civilization and Veiling*. Ann Arbor: University of Michigan Press.

Göle, Nilufer. 2002. "Islam in Public: New Visibilities and New Imaginaries." *Public Culture* 14:173–90.

Göle, Nilüfer, and Julie Billaud. 2011. "Islamic Difference and the Return of Feminist Universalism." Pp. 116–41 in *European Multiculturalisms: Cultural, Religious and Ethnic Challenges*, edited by Anna Triandafyllidou. Edinburgh, UK: Edinburgh University Press.

Gorski, Philip. 2003. "Historicizing the Secularization Debate: An Agenda for Research." Pp. 110–122 in *Handbook of the Sociology of Religion,* edited by Michelle Dillon. Cambridge: Cambridge University Press.

Hafez, Sherine. 2011. *An Islam of Her Own: Reconsidering Religion and Secularism in Women's Islamic Movements*. New York: NYU Press.

Hasan, Noorhaidi. 2009. "Islamist Party, Electoral Politics and Da'wa Mobilization Among Youth: The Prosperous Justice Party (PKS) in Indonesia." *RSIS Working Papers* 184, 1–27. S. Rajaratnam School of International Studies, Singapore.

Hefner, Robert. 2000. *Civil Islam: Muslims and Democratization in Indonesia*. Princeton, NJ: Princeton University Press.

Hochschild, Arlie. 1989. *The Second Shift: Working Parents and the Revolution at Home*. New York: Viking.

Hoesterey, James. 2008. "Marketing Morality: The Rise, Fall and Rebranding of Aa Gym." Pp. 95–112 in *Expressing Islam: Religious Life and Politics in Indonesia*, edited by G. Fealy and S. White. Pasir Panjang, Singapore: Institute of Southeast Asian Studies.

Howell, Julia Day. 2005. "Muslims, the New Age and Marginal Religions in Indonesia: Changing Meanings of Religious Pluralism." *Social Compass* 52(4):473–93.

Huntington, Samuel P. 1993. "The Clash of Civilizations?" *Foreign Affairs* 72:22–49.

Hwang, Julie Chernov. 2010. "When Parties Swing: Islamist Parties and Institutional Moderation in Malaysia and Indonesia." *South East Asia Research* 18(4):635–74.

Inglehart, Ronald, and Pippa Norris. 2003. *Rising Tide: Gender Equality and Cultural Change around the World*. Cambridge: Cambridge University Press.

IRIN. 2010. "Indonesia: Female Genital Mutilation Persists despite Ban." *IRIN News* (http://www.irinnews.org/Report/90366/INDONESIA-Female-genital-mutilation-persists-despite-ban).

Jasper, James M. 1999. *The Art of Moral Protest: Culture, Biography, and Creativity in Social Movements*. Chicago: University of Chicago Press.

Jayawardena, Kumari. 1986. *Feminism and Nationalism in the Third World*. London: Zed Books.

Jeffery, Patricia, and Amrita Basu, eds. 1997. *Appropriating Gender: Women's Activism and Politicized Religion in South Asia*. New York and London: Routledge.

Jones, Gavin W. 2005. "The 'Flight from Marriage' in South-East and East Asia." *Journal of Comparative Family Studies* 36(1):92–103.

Joppke, Christian. 2009. *Veil: Mirror of Identity*. London: Polity Press.

Juergensmeyer, Mark, ed. 2003. *Terror in the Mind of God: The Global Rise of Religious Violence*. Berkeley: University of California.

Kahin, George McTurnan. 1952. *Nationalism and Revolution in Indonesia*. Ithaca, NY: Cornell University Press.

Kandiyoti, Deniz. 1988. "Bargaining with Patriarchy." *Gender & Society* 2(3):274–90.

Karam, Azza. 1998. *Women, Islamisms, and the State: Contemporary Feminisms in Egypt*. New York and London: Palgrave Macmillan.

Kepel, Gilles. 1994. *The Revenge of God: The Resurgence of Islam, Christianity and Judaism in the Modern World*. University Park: Pennsylvania State University Press.

Kepel, Gilles. 2002. *Jihad: The Trail of Political Islam*. Cambridge: Belknap Press.

Komnas Perempuan. 2010. *In the Name of Regional Autonomy: The Institutionalisation of Discrimination in Indonesia. A Monitoring Report by Komnas Perempuan*. Jakarta: Komnas Perempuan.

Lazreg, Marnia. 2009. *Questioning the Veil: Open Letters to Muslim Women*. Princeton, NJ: Princeton University Press.

Lewis, Bernard. 2001. *What Went Wrong?: Western Impact and Middle Eastern Response*. New York: Oxford University Press.

Locher-Scholten, Elsbeth. 2000. *Women and the Colonial State: Essays on Gender and Modernity in the Netherlands Indies, 1900–1942*. Amsterdam: Amsterdam University Press.

Machmudi, Yon. 2008. *Islamizing Indonesia: The Rise of Jemaah Tarbiyah and the Prosperous Justice Party (PKS)*. Canberra: Australian National University E-Press.

MacKinnon, Catharine A. 1991. *Toward a Feminist Theory of the State*. Cambridge, MA: Harvard University Press.

Macleod, Arlene Elowe. 1992. "Hegemonic Relations and Gender Resistance: The New Veiling as Accommodating Protest in Cairo." *Signs* 17(3):533–57.

Madrid, Robin. 1999. "Islamic Students in the Indonesian Student Movement, 1998–1999: Forces for Moderation." *Critical Asian Studies* 31(3):17–32.

Mahmood, Saba. 2005. *The Politics of Piety: The Islamic Revival and the Feminist Subject*. Princeton, NJ: Princeton University Press.

Martin, David L. 2003. *Pentecostalism: The World Their Parish*. Oxford: Wiley-Blackwell.

Martin, John Levi. 2011. *The Explanation of Social Action*. New York: Oxford University Press.

Martyn, Elizabeth. 2005. *The Women's Movement in Post-Colonial Indonesia: Gender and Nation in a New Democracy*. London: Routledge.

Mernissi, Fatima. 1987. *Beyond the Veil: Male-Female Dynamics in Modern Muslim Society*. Bloomington: Indiana University Press.

Mernissi, Fatima. 1992. *The Veil and the Male Elite: A Feminist Interpretation of Women's Rights in Islam*. New York: Perseus Books.

Merry, Sally Engle. 2006. *Human Rights and Gender Violence: Translating International Law into Local Justice*. Chicago: University of Chicago Press.

Meuleman, Johan. 2002. "The Institut Agama Islam Negeri at the Crossroads." Pp. 205–17 in *Islam in the Era of Globalization: Muslim Attitudes toward Modernity and Identity*, edited by Johan Meuleman. London: Routledge.

Mir-Hosseini, Ziba. 2006. "Muslim Women's Quest for Equality: Between Islamic Law and Feminism." *Critical Inquiry* 32(Summer):629–45.

Mitchell, Richard Paul. 1993. *The Society of the Muslim Brothers*. New York: Oxford University Press.

Moghadam, Valentine. 2005. *Globalizing Women: Transnational Feminist Networks*. Baltimore: Johns Hopkins University Press.

Moghadam, Valentine. 2009. *Globalization and Social Movements: Islamism, Feminism, and the Global Justice Movement*. Lanham, MD: Rowman and Littlefield.

Moghadam, Valentine M. 1994. *Identity Politics and Women: Cultural Reassertions and Feminisms in International Perspective*. Boulder, CO: Westview Press.

Moghissi, Haideh. 1999. *Feminism and Islamic Fundamentalism: The Limits of Postmodern Analysis*. London: Zed Books.

Mohanty, Chandra Talpade. 1988. "Under Western Eyes: Feminist Scholarship and Colonial Discourses." *Feminist Review* 30: 61–88.

Moustafa, Tamir, and Asifa Quraishi-Landes. 2012. "Paradoxes of 'Religious Freedom' in Egypt." *The Immanent Frame*. Retrieved December 12, 2012 (http://blogs.ssrc.org/tif/2012/04/16/paradoxes-of-religious-freedom-in-egypt/).

Murdock, Catherine Gilbert. 2001. *Domesticating Drink: Women, Men, and Alcohol in America, 1870–1940*. Baltimore: Johns Hopkins University Press.

Narayan, Uma. 1997. *Dislocating Cultures: Identities, Traditions, and Third World Feminism*. New York: Routledge.

Nef, Claudia. 2011. "Standing Up for Morals." *Inside Indonesia*, March. Retrieved December 12, 2012 (http://www.insideindonesia.org/content/standing-up-for-morals).

Nisa, Eva F. 2012. "Embodied Faith: Agency and Obedience among Face-veiled University Students in Indonesia." *Asia Pacific Journal of Anthropology* 13(4):366–81.

Noor, Farish A. 2011. "The Partai Keadilan Sejahtera (PKS) in the Landscape of Indonesian Islamist Politics: Cadre-Training as Mode of Preventive Radicalisation?" *RSIS Working Papers 231*:1–37. S. Rajaratnam School of International Studies, Singapore.

Nurmila, Nina. 2009. *Women, Islam and Everyday Life: Renegotiating Polygamy in Indonesia*. London: Routledge.

Ong, Aihwa. 1995. "State versus Islam: Malay Families, Women's Bodies, and the Body Politic in Malaysia." Pp. 159–94 in *Bewitching Women, Pious Men: Gender and Body Politics in Southeast Asia*, edited by Aihwa Ong and Michael G. Peletz. Berkeley: University of California Press.

P. P. Fatayat Nahdlatul Ulama. 1999. *Modul Analisis Gender*. Jakarta, Indonesia: P. P. Fatayat Nahdlatul Ulama and the Asia Foundation.

Pambudy, Ninuk Mardiana. 2009. "Poligami dan Menteri Perempuan." *Kompas*, October 23.

Pandji, Sarah. 2001. "Bukan Sekedar Peran Tambahan." *Suara Keadilan* 1(16):14.

Peletz, Michael G. 2009. *Gender Pluralism: Southeast Asia since Early Modern Times*. New York: Taylor & Francis.

PKS, Dewan Syariah DPP. 2006. *Fatwa-Fatwa Dewan Syariah Partai Keadilan Sejahtera*. Jakarta, Indonesia: Harakatuna Publishing.

Qodir, Faqihuddin Abdul. 2011. "*Women's Aurat, a Limit Without Borders?—Hadith* 2nd Edition." *Swara Rahima*. (http://rahima.or.id/index.php?option=com_content&view=article&id=633:womens-aurat-a-limit-without-borders&catid=63:hadith&Itemid=374).

Ray, Raka. 1998. *Fields of Protest: Women's Movements in India*. Minneapolis: University of Minnesota Press.

Ricklefs, M. C. 2008. *A History of Modern Indonesia since c. 1200*, 4th ed. Palo Alto, CA: Stanford University Press.

Rinaldo, Rachel. 2002. "Ironic Legacy: The New Order and Indonesian Women's Groups." *Outskirts Online Journal: Feminisms Along the Edge 10* (http://www.outskirts.arts.uwa.edu.au/volumes/volume-10/rinaldo).

Rinaldo, Rachel. 2007. "Mobilizing Piety: Women, Islam, and the Public Sphere in Indonesia." PhD dissertation, Department of Sociology, University of Chicago.

Rinaldo, Rachel. 2008. "Envisioning the Nation: Women Activists, Religion and the Public Sphere in Indonesia." *Social Forces* 86(4):1781–1804.

Rinaldo, Rachel. 2010a. "The Islamic Revival and Women's Political Subjectivity in Indonesia." *Women's Studies International Forum* 33(4):422–31.

Rinaldo, Rachel. 2010b. "Women and Piety Movements." Pp. 584–605 in *The New Blackwell Companion to the Sociology of Religion*, edited by Bryan S. Turner. Oxford: Wiley-Blackwell.

Rinaldo, Rachel. 2011. "Muslim Women, Moral Visions: Globalization and Gender Controversies in Indonesia." *Qualitative Sociology* 34(4):539–60.

Robinson, Kathryn. 2009. *Gender, Islam, and Democracy in Indonesia*. London: Routledge.

Roy, Olivier. 2006. *Globalized Islam: The Search for a New Ummah*. New York: Columbia University Press.

Rutherford, Danilyn. 1993. "Unpacking a National Heroine: Two Kartinis and Their People." *Indonesia* 55(April):23–40.

Sadiqi, Fatima, and Moha Ennaji. 2006. "The Feminization of Public Space: Women's Activism, the Family Law, and Social Change in Morocco." *Journal of Middle East Women's Studies* 2(2):86–114.

Saeed, Abdullah. 2005. *Interpreting the Qur'an: Towards a Contemporary Approach.* New York and London: Routledge.

Salime, Zakia. 2011. *Between Feminism and Islam: Human Rights and Sharia Law in Morocco.* Minneapolis: University of Minnesota.

Salvatore, Armando, and Mark LeVine. 2005. *Religion, Social Practice, and Contested Hegemonies: Reconstructing the Public Sphere in Muslim Majority Societies.* New York: Palgrave Macmillan.

Schielke, Samuli. 2010. "Second Thoughts about the Anthropology of Islam, or How to Make Sense of Grand Schemes in Everyday Life." *Zentrum Moderner Orient Working Papers* 2:1–16.

Scott, Joan W. 1999. *Gender and the Politics of History.* New York: Columbia University Press.

Scott, Joan Wallach. 2007. *The Politics of the Veil.* Princeton, NJ: Princeton University Press.

Sewell, William H. 1992. "A Theory of Structure: Duality, Agency, and Transformation." *American Journal of Sociology* 98(1):1–29.

Sewell, William H. 2005. *Logics of History: Social Theory and Social Transformation.* Chicago: University of Chicago Press.

Sheikh, Mayy El, and David Kirkpatrick. 2013. "Rise in Sexual Assaults in Egypt Sets Off Clash over Blame." *New York Times*, March 26, A1.

Sherlock, Stephen. 2007. "The Indonesian Parliament after Two Elections: What Has Really Changed?" Working Paper from the Centre for Democratic Institutions, Australian National University, Canberra, Australia.

Shiraishi, Takashi. 1990. *An Age in Motion: Popular Radicalism in Java, 1912–1926.* Ithaca, NY: Cornell University Press.

Sidel, John T. 2001. "It Takes a Madrasah: Habermas Meets Bourdieu in Indonesia." *South East Asia Research* 9(1):109–22.

Sidel, John Thayer. 2006. *Riots, Pogroms, Jihad: Religious Violence in Indonesia.* Ithaca, NY: Cornell University Press.

Smilde, David. 2009. *Reason to Believe: Cultural Agency in Latin American Evangelicalism.* Berkeley: University of California Press.

Smith, Dorothy E. 1989. *The Everyday World as Problematic: A Feminist Sociology.* Boston: Northeastern University Press.

Smith-Hefner, Nancy J. 2005. "The New Muslim Romance: Changing Patterns of Courtship and Marriage among Educated Javanese Youth." *Journal of Southeast Asian Studies* 36(3):441–59.

Smith-Hefner, Nancy J. 2007. "Javanese Women and the Veil in Post-Soeharto Indonesia." *Journal of Asian Studies* 66(2):389–420.

Soares, Benjamin, and Filippo Osella. 2009. "Islam, Politics, Anthropology." *Journal of the Royal Anthropological Institute* 15:S1–S23.

Staggenborg, Suzanne. 1988. "The Consequences of Professionalization and Formalization in the Pro-Choice Movement." *American Sociological Review* 53(4):585–605.

Stoler, Ann. 1977. "Class Structure and Female Autonomy in Rural Java." *Signs* 3(1):74–89.

Sullivan, Norma. 1994. *Masters and Managers: The Study of Gender Relations in Urban Java.* Sydney, Australia: Allen & Unwin.

Suryakusuma, Julia I. 1996. "The State and Sexuality in New Order Indonesia." Pp. 92–119 in *Fantasizing the Feminine in Indonesia*, edited by L. J. Sears. Durham, NC: Duke University Press.

Swidler, Ann. 1986. "Culture in Action: Symbols and Strategies." *American Sociological Review* 51(2):273–86.

Tadros, Mariz. 2011. "The Muslim Brotherhood's Gender Agenda: Reformed or Reframed?" *Institute for Development Studies Bulletin* 42(1):88–98.

Tickamyer, Ann, and Siti Kusujiarti. 2012. *Power, Change, and Gender Relations in Rural Java: A Tale of Two Villages*. Athens: Ohio University Press.

Trotter, Lydia. 2006. "Islam, Women and Indonesian Politics: The PKS Challenge to Substantive Theories of Democracy." Undergraduate thesis, Department of Indonesian Studies, University of Sydney.

Turner, Bryan S. 2007. "Religious Authority and the New Media." *Theory, Culture & Society* 24(2):117–34.

Uddin, Yurnalis. 2010. *Female Circumcision: Social, Cultural, Health, and Religious Perspectives*. Jakarta: YARSI University Press.

UNdata (http://data.un.org).

United Nations Development Programme. 2011. *Human Development Report 2011*. New York: UNDP.

United Nations, Department of Economic and Social Affairs, Population Division. 2011. *World Population Prospects: The 2010 Revision*. New York: United Nations.

UNFPA Technical Services Team for East and Southeast Asia. 2006. *Maternal and Neonatal Health in East and South-East Asia*. Bangkok, Thailand: UNFPA (http://www.unfpa.org/public/home/publications/pid/1276).

Van Doorn-Harder, Pieternella. 2006. *Women Shaping Islam: Reading the Qur'an in Indonesia*. Chicago: University of Illinois Press.

Van Doorn-Harder, Pieternella. 2008. "Controlling the Body: Muslim Feminists Debating Women's Rights in Indonesia." *Religion Compass* 2(6):1021–43.

Van Wichelen, S. 2009. "Polygamy Talk and the Politics of Feminism: Contestations over Masculinity in a New Muslim Indonesia." *Journal of International Women's Studies* 11(1):173–88.

Wahid, Marzuki. 2011. "Giving Authority to Women—Tafsir 5th Edition." *Swara Rahima*. (http://www.rahima.or.id/index.php?option=com_content&view=article&id=646:giving-authority-to-women-tafsir-5th-edition&catid=62:tafsir&itemid=375).

Weber, Max. 1949. *The Methodology of the Social Sciences*. New York: Free Press.

Weber, Max. 2001. *The Protestant Ethic and the Spirit of Capitalism*. New York and London: Routledge.

Wickham, Carrie Rosefsky. 2011. "The Muslim Brotherhood after Mubarak." *ForeignAffairs.com* (http://www.foreignaffairs.com/articles/67348/carrie-rosefsky-wickham/the-muslim-brotherhood-after-mubarak).

Winter, Bronwyn. 2008. *Hijab & the Republic: Uncovering the French Headscarf Debate*. Syracuse, NY: Syracuse University Press.

Woodward, Mark, Ali Amin, Inaya Rohmaniyah, and Chris Lundry. 2011. *A New Cultural Path for Indonesia's Islamist PKS?* Tempe, AZ: Consortium for Strategic Communication, Arizona State University.

World Health Organization. 2012. *Trends in Maternal Mortality: 1990 to 2010 WHO, UNICEF, UNFPA and the World Bank Estimates*. Geneva: World Health Organization.

Yuval-Davis, Nira. 1997. *Gender and Nation*. London: Sage.

INDEX

Note: Page numbers followed by *f* and *t* indicate figures and tables, respectively.

Budiman, Manneke, 155
Budi Utomo, 35
Buillaud, Julie, 18
Burawoy, Michael, 205
Burqa, 3
Bush, George W., 216n44
Bush, Robin, 183

Cahyawati, Jenny, 51*f*
Calvinism, 88–89
Capitalism, 88–89. *See also* Global
    capitalism
  and gender and class inequality,
    Solidaritas Perempuan stance
    on, 169
  neoliberal, 158, 164
Career(s), of Indonesian women, 14,
    51, 66, 70, 74, 82, 86, 137,
    139–140, 142, 196
  husbands' support for, 137–138
Casanova, Jose, 15, 95
Catholic women activists, 203
Catholic women's rights groups,
    Indonesian, 213n17
Censorship, anti-pornography effort
    and, 146–147, 218n24
Center for Reproductive Health
    Information. *See* PIKER
    (Pusat Informasi Kesehatan
    Reproduksi)
Charrad, Mounira M., 4, 19
Chatterjee, Partha, 114
Children. *See also* Family
  average number of, in Indonesia,
    218n17
  number of, of PKS women, 218n17
Chong, Kelly H., 16, 151
Christians/Christianity, 32, 41. *See also*
    Evangelical Christianity
  harassment of, in Indonesia, 200
  and Solidaritas Perempuan, 171
Cigarettes, Islam's taboo on, 126
Circumcision. *See also* Female
    circumcision
  for men, 101
Class. *See also* Lower class; Middle class
  in Indonesia, 61–62
  and Indonesian women's agency,
    198–199
  and religious practice, 28, 127–128

Clothing. *See also* Muslim clothing
  men's, 13, 215n15
  of PKS women, 125–126, 128–130
  politicization of, in Indonesia, 73
  religious, and liberalism, 18
  of Solidaritas Perempuan staff, 6
  styles, in Indonesia, 72–73
  symbolism and, 92
  traditional, 211n9
  Western style, 211n9
  women's
    in New Order Indonesia, 46
    as pious practice, 128–130
    restrictions on, 13
Collins, Patricia Hill, 19
Communism, 35, 38–40, 77, 155
Communist Party (PKI), 38, 40–41, 69,
    213n11
Communists, Indonesian purge of,
    1965–1967, 40–41
Companionate marriage, 83, 136,
    215n28
Confucianism, 32
Connell, Raewyn, 135
Conservative religion. *See also* Islam,
    conservative
  and anxieties about gender,
    113–114, 151
  global resurgence of, 2, 8
  and women's agency, 114
  and women's rights, 8
Conservatives, 211n5
Contextualism, 9, 23–25, 29, 53,
    57, 65–68, 84, 86, 90–100,
    105–106, 109–110, 158, 174,
    195, 198, 212n17, 214n12,
    216n31, 217n4
  and women's rights, 92–96
Contraception, 104
Convention on the Elimination of
    All Forms of Discrimination
    against Women, 46
Counter Legal Draft, 99
Criminal punishment, Islamic law and,
    115, 183
Cultural approach, to social movements,
    200–201
Cultural Islam, 42
Cultural schemas, 9, 20
  used in new contexts, 158

Culture, 201
    and agency, 20
    and biology, distinction between, 77
    definition of, 9, 20
    local, Solidaritas Perempuan and, 181
    sociological perspective on, 9
Curfews, for women. *See* Women's
        freedom

Dahlan, Ahmad, 36
Dakwah, 42, 59–60, 114, 118, 120–121,
        127, 132, 136–137
Dakwah groups, 114, 130, 152, 217n3
    and marriages, 122, 217n8
Dakwah party, 59
Damanik, Ali Said, 59
Dance-in, 12
Danita (Solidaritas Perempuan woman),
        159–161, 164, 170, 172–175,
        181, 186, 188
Daratista, Inul, 146–147
Davidman, Lynn, 16
Davis, Kathy, 100, 165
Deeb, Lara, 4, 14–15, 87
Democracy, 44
Democracy movement
    in New Order Indonesia, 48
    in 1990s, 47
Democratization, Indonesian, 13, 28,
        31, 33, 62, 64, 70, 109, 126,
        197–198
    and conservative turn in Islam, 5
    and controversies about gender and
        morality, 114
    and economic equality, Solidaritas
        Perempuan stance on,
        168–169
    and modes of agency, 3
    women's participation in, 1
Demonstrations, 12
    against ban on *jilbab,* 46
    against pornography, 113
    pro- and anti-polygamy, 98–99
    for *reformasi,* 49
    spatial segregation of PKS women
        in, 125
    in support of Inul Daratista,
        146–147, 147f
Deployment of religious texts, 23

Desa Siaga dan PHBS (Prepared Villages
        and Healthy and Clean
        Lifestyles), 58
Dewan Dakwah Islamiyah Indonesia
        (DDII), 41
Dewi (Rahima staff member), 80, 85, 92
Dharma Wanita, 44–46
    Five Duties for Women, 45
Dian (Solidaritas Perempuan woman),
        173
Difference feminism, 133
Discursive tradition, Islamic, 24, 27
Dita (Fatayat staff member), 75
Divorce, civil service employees and, 45,
        96
Docile agent, 17, 19
The Domestication of Desire (Brenner), 44
Domestic help. *See also* Domestic
        workers
    for middle-class women, 82, 137, 139
Domestic sphere
    equality in, 81
    feminism and, 134
    gendered division of labor in, 82, 139,
        143, 215n27
    inequities in, and inequality in public
        sphere, 164–165
    as women's priority, 23, 29, 35,
        82–83, 114, 125, 196
        in New Order Indonesia, 48
    as women's traditional place, 4, 44–45
Domestic violence, 54, 58, 77, 86, 107,
        161, 165
    criminalization of, 199
Domestic workers, Indonesian, 159
    poor women and girls as, 82
    women migrants as, advocacy for,
        30, 54
Double standard, gendered, 100
Dukuns (traditional healers), abortions
        by, 104
Dutch East India Company, 33

Economic equality, democratization and,
        Solidaritas Perempuan stance
        on, 168–169
Economics, and women's oppression,
        Solidaritas Perempuan's stance
        on, 164–165, 187

as lived experience, 166–168,
170, 176
and Marxists/leftists, 214n3
militant, Solidaritas Perempuan
women and, 155
Muslim, 47, 63, 78, 88, 167, 198
negative connotations of, in
Indonesia, 6, 8, 14, 77,
106, 108, 155, 166, 175,
192–193, 196
PKS women and, 132–141
politicization of, Solidaritas
Perempuan and, 169–170
in postcolonial contexts, 156
Rahima and, 6, 74–83
rejection by PKS women, 115, 217n5
and religion, 79
religion and, 16–19, 26, 63
secular, 18, 63–64, 110, 175
as secular, 217n5
socialist, 78–79, 215n23
Solidaritas Perempuan women and,
155, 161–171
transnational, 14, 23, 29, 33, 65,
76, 110, 156–158, 162, 168,
195–196, 218n2
typology of, 215n23–215n24
as Western, 132–133, 217n5
and Western imperialism, 4, 8, 214n3
and women's agency, 2–3
Feminist agency, 10, 23, 26, 30, 67
and fundamentalism, 182–188
and pious agency, 18–19, 26, 66,
110, 195
and pious critical agency, 99–100
of Solidaritas Perempuan women,
23, 156, 162–171, 189–191,
194–195
Feminist research methods, 205
Feminists
Iranian, 63
Middle Eastern, 47, 72, 91
radical, 80
third world, 78
and women activists, differentiation
of, 134
Feminist training, for Solidaritas
Perempuan staff, 165–166
Ferree, Myra Marx, 8, 217n5
Fetus, viability of, 104

Field(s), 21, 212n15
Field theory, 20–22, 201, 212n16
Fikh, 33–34, 57, 68, 89–91, 104–105,
107, 109, 130, 216n32
discriminatory concepts in, 91
Films, Islamic, 98
Filsafat perempuan, 180
Fiqh an-Nisa, 55, 213n19
Fligstein, Neil, 21, 212n15
Foley, Rebecca, 133
Food sovereignty, 164
conference on, 180
Ford Foundation, 46–47, 77–78, 198,
213n13
Foreign aid, to Indonesia, in Suharto
era, 213n10
Formalist approach, to religious
practice, 92
Fox, James J., 213n6
Fraser, Nancy, 170
Fromm, Erich, 47
Fuller, Graham E., 33
Fundamentalism, 182, 219n15
in Indonesia, 159, 182–188, 195
religious, 182, 219n15
Funding, for women's rights activists,
77–78

Gade, Anna, 25
Gadjah Mada University, 55, 71–72, 161
Gallagher, Sally K., 16, 140
Geertz, Clifford, 13, 20, 205
Geertz, Hildred, 34
Gender, 10, 77
anxieties about, social change and,
113–114, 151
Islam and, 134
PKS women's views on, 122,
134–136, 139
religion and, 17
social construction of, 76–78,
110, 136
Gender activists, 77
Gender discourses, in New Order
Indonesia, 48–49
Gender equality, 3, 10, 27, 29, 46, 56–57,
77, 88, 93, 95–96, 108–109,
198, 211n4
Fatayat and Rahima and, 75–76
Islam and, 85, 175